Faulkner and Modernism

Faulkner and Modernism

Rereading and Rewriting

Richard C. Moreland

THE UNIVERSITY OF WISCONSIN PRESS

The University of Wisconsin Press
114 North Murray Street
Madison, Wisconsin 53715

The University of Wisconsin Press, Ltd.
3 Henrietta Street
London WC2E 8LU, England

5   4   3   2   1

Printed in the United States of America

An earlier version of "Introduction: Compulsive and Revisionary Repetition in 'Barn Burning' "
appeared as "Compulsive and Revisionary Repetition: Faulkner's 'Barn Burning' and the Craft
of Writing Difference" in *Faulkner and the Craft of Fiction,* ed. Doreen Fowler and Ann
J. Abadie, 48–70. Faulkner and Yoknapatawpha 1987. Jackson: University Press of Mississippi, 1989. Copyright ©1989 The University Press of Mississippi.

An earlier version of "From Irony to Humor and Rage in *The Hamlet*" appeared as
"Antisemitism, Humor and Rage in Faulkner's *The Hamlet*" in *The Faulkner Journal* 3.1
(Fall 1987) 52–70. *The Faulkner Journal* is published at Ohio Northern University, Ada, Ohio.

To Susan, Gavin, and Luke

Contents

Acknowledgments

ONE theme of this book, along with that of revision, is debts and gifts. I have a number of people to thank for making what might be a heavy accumulation of debts feel more like gifts—harder to pay off conclusively, but much more gladly acknowledged. For helping me to resee some version or part of this work and variously encouraging me along the way, I am happy to thank Mitchell Breitwieser, Bainard Cowan, Jacques Daignault, George C. Freeman, Robert Harvey, Ralph Hurwitz, Edward Hutchinson, Prabhakara Jha, Debbie Lichtman, Ojars Kratins, John T. Matthews, James Mellard, David Minter, Allison Moreland, Carolyn Porter, Michael Rogin, Neil Schmitz, Lewis P. Simpson, Eric Sundquist, Rick Swartz, Wallace Warren, Steven Wartofsky, and the LSU Council on Research. I had the benefit of Mitchell Breitwieser's, Barbara Hanrahan's, John T. Matthews', David Minter's, Carolyn Porter's, and Susan Tarcov's larger or more generous appetites for this material. And I want to offer particular thanks to Mitchell Breitwieser for the hearty gifts of his teaching, his writing, his many readings of my writing, his friendship, and his humor. For what they have taught me about another theme here, that of mourning, though of course not only for this, I thank my parents, Joyce and Joe Moreland. And for teaching me much of what I know of love, another theme throughout these pages, I thank Luke, Gavin, and Susan, to whom this work is dedicated.

Faulkner and Modernism

Introduction:
Compulsive and
Revisionary Repetition
in "Barn Burning"

WHILE reading the typescript of *The Mansion,* Faulkner's Random House editor, Albert Erskine, kept finding "discrepancies and contradictions" between the earlier, already published novels of Faulkner's *Snopes Trilogy* and this typescript of the last, in which Faulkner retold some of the same stories about some of the same events and characters, but retold them differently. As Erskine reported these discrepancies and contradictions, Faulkner became somewhat impatient with his editor's worrying so much about what Faulkner thought would pose problems only for readers he tended to call "academical gumshoes." He agreed to correct some such discrepancies, but eventually decided to let many more stand uncorrected, and decided to steal our gumshoe thunder by writing a prefatory note to the novel asserting his awareness of many of these discrepancies and explaining his reason for letting them show. Erskine had already offered what would have been a New Critical line of defense in suggesting that these three novels might not be a trilogy after all (Blotner 1720–35), implying that Faulkner could fall back safely on the idea that each of his novels was an autonomous new creation by a peculiarly literary genius, who would therefore speak the language of poetry and religion, identified at the time as a language of oracular paradox.[1] But this was not the explana-

1. Michael Millgate, for example, whose focus is the discrete, finished artifact and the original "conception" it completes in a "wholly organic structure" (186), is surprised that Faulkner could ever have considered including a version of Wash Jones's story near the beginning of *The Hamlet,* taking Faulkner's hindsighted word for it that the story had no place in the book at all: "It seems remarkable that Faulkner should ever have thought that 'Wash,' much of which he had already incorporated into *Absalom, Absalom!,* might find a place in the 'Snopes Saga' " (184–85). I will suggest instead that much of Ab's story as Faulkner used it near the beginning of *The Hamlet* had already been told as Sutpen's (and Wash's) story in *Absalom,* and that this is a typical and even crucial kind of connection between

3

tion Faulkner gave. Instead, perhaps more candidly, he says in his prefatory note that over his life's work of writing he has continued to *learn* more than he knew before about the human heart and about his characters. If readers notice differences, then, in Faulkner's repetitions or rewritings of previous work, perhaps we should not gloat so thunderously that Homer nods, but neither should we pass over such discrepancies silently, apologetically, or sentimentally as part of this Mississippi native's woodsy wildness, something only a "better craftsman" like Pound or Hemingway would have bothered to prune and tame. These repetitions and especially the differences they emphasize might represent, instead, importantly critical, published revisions of Faulkner's ongoing thinking and writing, revisions not just of minor details but of whole plots and structures of thought, revisions, even, of (modernist and structuralist) assumptions about how thought is structured and how it changes. In the course of Faulkner's career, he constantly recycled and refit plots, episodes, characters, and phrases from poems to stories to filmscripts to novels to other stories and other novels: not only were such repetitions and differences unusually prolific and undisguised, they amounted to an ongoing critical project, as he repeated certain dominant structures of thought in the post–Civil War American South and the post–World War I United States and Europe, first to explore and understand their motivations and consequences, then critically to revise certain structural contradictions and impasses that were shared by both these postwar cultures, and that were elaborated in Faulkner's own and others' literary modernism.

Faulkner's revisions of his modernism involved an important shift in the function of repetition, both in his own work and also in its historical and literary contexts as he understood them. In order to understand this shift, the notion of repetition with a significant, critical difference, which I will call *revisionary repetition,* should be distinguished from repetition of another kind which I will call, after Freud, *compulsive repetition.* Revisionary repetition repeats some structured event, in order somehow to alter that structure and its continuing power, especially by opening a critical space for what the subject might *learn* about that structure in the different context of a changing present or a more distant or different past. As Sartre says, "a life develops in spirals; it passes again and again by the same points but at different levels of integration and complexity" (106). This is the kind of repetition I have attributed to Faulkner's revisions of his modernism. But in compulsive repetition, it is precisely this unpredictable

---

works that are rarely such distinct performances as Millgate often assumes, but repetitions and revisions of previous works, repetitions to be considered not as unoriginality but sometimes as critique.

possibility of critically altering a familiar structure in the light of changing or different circumstances which repetition attempts to avoid. It attempts to expunge or ward off all such changes and variations as insignificant departures from an abstractly unchanged, unaffected original. Even the most unpleasant, restrictively habitual repetitions may seem in this way preferable to the unpredictability and impurity of change and difference. Inasmuch as every repetition, then, involves both an identity of the same content or structure and also a difference and change at least in time and context, compulsive repetition attempts to exclude that difference and change; revisionary repetition attempts to alter the structures of identity. This is of course a functional—not an absolute—distinction. Even compulsive repetition is never static, try as it may. Given a linguistic, social, or psychological structure of such continuing power that it cannot be simply ignored, forgotten, or denied, but must be more or less acknowledged as a repetition, either compulsively or in a spirit of critical revision, revisionary repetition works to inscribe marks of change, specificity, and difference within and around that structure. Whereas compulsive repetition tends to repeat the familiar and familial, revisionary repetition places these familiarities (with critical effect) in the midst of irrepressibly ambivalent, fearful, but strong desires for other voices.

The issue of these two kinds of repetition arises in Faulkner's work in two ways, as method and then as topic—topic for a critique that led in turn to a shift in method. In his novels before *Absalom, Absalom!* Faulkner's method shared a tendency with that of other modernists (as described especially by Michael O'Brien 138–45) toward repeated juxtapositions of various "unified sensibilities" from the past—Eliot's Elizabethans, Joyce's Greeks, Yeats's Byzantines and Celts, the Southern Agrarians' Agrarian South—and the supposedly meaningless disarray and banality of everyday modern life, typically represented from an ironic distance as a "heap of broken images."[2] As Faulkner extended his treatment of such broken

2. My somewhat reductive characterization here of modernism addresses a set of oppositions actually quite important in modernist literature and society, but they are also a select group of oppositions that have been actively promoted and canonized by modernist writers themselves, notably Eliot, and by Southern Agrarians later turned founding fathers of the New Criticism, such as Tate and Warren. Less critical of these oppositions than Faulkner was, the New Criticism has largely obscured the social and historical context of modernist strategies of irony, ambiguity, and unresolved tension in juxtaposition, for example, by making them into general criteria for aesthetic merit. The most influential Faulkner critic in this tradition is of course Cleanth Brooks, who tends to measure change and difference in Faulkner's work against a vast backdrop of "true community" (found in the agrarian societies and in the pastoral tradition of literature), a backdrop against which Flem Snopes, for example, takes his measure as a "sinister deformation of universal human nature and a terrifying vision of appetitive man, modern style" (*Yoknapatawpha Country* 368, *Toward Yoknapatawpha* xii).

images in *Light in August* and especially *Absalom, Absalom!* from the realm of the personal and familial toward the racial and historical,[3] and from metaphysical themes of destruction and loss toward social, historical themes of change and difference, he explored and analyzed certain compulsive habits of memory, narration, and (in)action on the parts of his characters—in their protomodernist vacillation between a more or less explicit nostalgia for a diseased social structure and the ironic contemplation of scenes of its inevitable and total collapse—that were in many ways similar to modernist methods of his own. After interrupting his work on *Absalom* for a parodic treatment of cosmopolitan literary modernism in *Pylon,* Faulkner continued to examine in these characters of the postwar South the social and historical motivations and consequences of their now more culturally dominant vacillation between forced nostalgia and bitter irony. In *Absalom* Faulkner traces the motivations of such a vacillation not to the deeper metaphysical nature of time and loss[4] but to the social and historical climate of disillusionment, defeat, and depression that was already decades old, somewhat threadbare, and all too familiar in the South in 1909–10 as his characters remembered it—and that was even more familiar by the time Faulkner was writing this novel in the 1930s, when World War I and the Great Depression had pulled the rest of the United States and Europe into a similar but much wider cultural climate of disillusionment.[5] Turning his own relatively longer and more intense regional,

---

3. Richard H. Brodhead (among many others) also sees the source of Faulkner's achievement in these two novels in his exploration of larger social and historical contexts. I disagree, however, that Faulkner reaches a "final knowledge" about certain "essential realities," especially "a past lost to memory but still so potent that it dooms the present to repeat it" (9). This is precisely the kind of ironic repetition Faulkner subjects in *Light in August* and especially *Absalom* to social, historical, and critical scrutiny. The historical context provides not just variants of an essential myth (though characters try to think so), but challenges to that myth by other myths and by other excluded voices. The "logic of remaking" so well described by Brodhead in Faulkner's career up to *Absalom* also continues beyond *Absalom,* not merely in efforts at consolidation and completion (Brodhead, Stonum), but in a radical revision of his earlier work, looking progressively farther back into increasingly difficult issues, first of class (in *The Hamlet,* 1940, looking back at *Absalom,* 1936), then race (in *Go Down, Moses,* 1942, looking back at *Light in August,* 1932), then gender and sexuality (in *Requiem for a Nun,* 1951, and *The Reivers,* 1962, both looking back at *Sanctuary,* 1931).

4. This is one significant difference between my reading of *Absalom* and that of John T. Irwin, with its emphasis on an inexorable process of repetition and revenge in the artist's and the son's futile struggles with the immutable structures of time, originality, and secondariness as such. I would agree more, though, with his reading of *The Sound and the Fury* were he to differentiate more between the two novels.

5. David Minter has suggested to me that this familiarity with defeat and poverty may account for some of Faulkner's influence in Europe and in other, "always already poverty-stricken parts of the world."

historical, and personal familiarity with such a climate to critical advantage, Faulkner began to discover and demonstrate in *Absalom* how this repetitive vacillation between nostalgia and irony in reaction to such disillusionment works—by attempting retroactively to ward off and soften the impact of a once unexpected blow, forestalling the implications of historical change and difference by insisting on the unchanging drama of fated destruction and loss. While Faulkner thus comes to understand the motivations of such a vacillation between nostalgia and irony, he also comes to understand its consequences when it becomes a compulsive impasse attempting indefinitely to exclude change and difference, often with an increasingly frustrated violence. Faulkner's critical explorations of this repetitive impasse as a historical topic in *Absalom* led him to seek a way out in "Barn Burning" and *The Hamlet,* by revising a scene that in *Absalom* is said to have started a series of compulsive repetitions (from which neither Sutpen nor his various biological and cultural descendants could escape). In finding a way out of those repetitions for Ab Snopes, Faulkner also discovered his own way out of certain widespread, compulsive modernist methods, finding in this new process of revisionary repetition both a strikingly different fictional method and also openings for several new, formerly marginalized topics, notably the makeshift economy and precarious humor of the Old Southwest; mourning as a way of working through the relentless and hollow repetitions of melancholia; and blacks' and women's critically different voices.

In this introduction I will only point to certain promising openings for such new topics, focusing instead on "Barn Burning" as a pivotal moment in Faulkner's career, poised between one method of repetition and the other, turning from the compulsive toward the revisionary for a change in method that made such changes in topics possible. In later chapters I will return in greater detail to the crises in one mode of repetition (in *Absalom*) that led Faulkner toward the other mode, then study the different projects and results of Faulkner's ongoing revisionary repetitions in *The Hamlet, Go Down, Moses,* and *Requiem for a Nun.*

An exemplary site for Faulkner's discovery of his way out of his native culture's and his artistic peers' compulsive repetitions is a series of repetitions and revisions of one particular structured social event in *Absalom, Absalom!* It is the scene where the ragged young Thomas Sutpen comes with a message from his tenant-farming father to the majestic front door of the planter for whom his father works. The liveried black slave who opens and bars the door tells Sutpen "even before he had had time to say what he came for, never to come to that front door again but to go around to the back." Stunned and shattered here by his own social silencing and exclusion, Sutpen idealizes and internalizes the image of a planter perfectly purified, invulnerable, and invisible somewhere inside the house. Years later Sutpen represents this scene to General Compson as the determining incident — a primal scene, as it were — at the very origin of his life's design to found his own family dynasty inside the same unviolated, unbroken Southern plantation tradition. He represents it as a primal scene, that is, in the sense of his being henceforth powerlessly compelled only to re-present and to repeat what he thinks he has learned here once and for all about the structure of his society and even of life in general. The rest of *Absalom* traces Sutpen's and his adopted culture's variously relentless, compulsive repetitions of this same structured social event, this apparently inescapable primal scene of purifying exclusion.

In "Barn Burning," published three years later, in 1939, Faulkner returns to this scene again, not compulsively, however, but in order to make significant revisions, and to open a critical space for reconceiving this oppressive primal scene. Again a poor-white boy inclined to idealize the planter's house sees his own way into the front door of that house barred by a liveried and insulting black servant; however, this time the boy, Sarty Snopes, is accompanied by his less impressionable father, Ab Snopes, who is not awestruck by the insult but has clearly expected and provoked it, and who responds by pushing his way inside to deliver his message anyway by smearing horse manure on the blond rug inside the door. After some ambivalence about his father's peculiar writing style (what Kristeva might call a minor revolution in poetic language), Sarty eventually repeats his society's tendency to refuse to read such gestures at writing difference, and repeats its violent condemnation and exclusion of Ab's social difference as only so much social filth. At least from Sarty's frightened and therefore humorless perspective, Ab's potentially critical difference seems here a failed and fatal alternative.

However, Faulkner himself would enlarge prolifically on this same critical and creative potential for revising the plantation society's primal scene, as he rewrites it once again as an opening episode of *The Hamlet,* published another year later in 1940.[6] He now replaces Sarty's frightened, humorless perspective on Ab's "bad attitude" at the planter's door with V. K. Ratliff's humorous appreciation of Ab's singular history and his singularly unsettling provocations. Whereas in "Barn Burning" Sarty thinks Ab's attitude at the planter's door leads toward his inevitable, tragic (actually uncertain) death at the end of the story, in *The Hamlet*'s version Ratliff enjoys telling of Ab's repeated escape from that expected tragedy

6. "Barn Burning" at first began Faulkner's manuscript of *The Hamlet,* then during the writing of the novel he detached this version (soon publishing it as a short story), and replaced it in chapter 1 of the novel with Ratliff's substantially rewritten version of the story as told to Jody Varner. See Millgate 185.

and of his surviving to outrage the planter's categories again and move on to Frenchman's Bend. By placing the scene at the opening of volume 1 of *The Snopes Trilogy,* the longest, most sustained work of his career, Faulkner makes this episode a primal scene now of a different kind. It is the occasion not for compulsive repetition but for humorous appreciation and elaboration as an exemplary scene of critical escape from reductive and oppressive social categories and oppositions, a scene that points a way out for others without pretending to point the one new way.

I have mentioned humor, mourning, and different voices as three openings for critical escape from *Absalom*'s compulsive primal scene, openings which Faulkner discovered in his revisionary repetition of that scene in "Barn Burning" and which he explored farther in his continuing revisions of that scene in *The Hamlet.* But in order to explain better Faulkner's discovery in his fiction of these openings for critical and revisionary escape, I should first explain briefly here the nature of those compulsive categories and oppositions in *Absalom* which Faulkner felt an increasing need to revise as he examined their social and historical implications. For in *Absalom,* while he does not yet open a way out of those compulsions, Faulkner does already discover and demonstrate the profoundly ambivalent motivations and extremely violent consequences of both the "innocent" and the "ironic" forms they tend to take in *Absalom,* as in much other modernist literature.

Thomas Sutpen's so-called innocence consists in his imitating and repeating, apparently without self-consciousness, apology, or extenuation, his society's essential gesture of self-purifying exclusion, that gesture he thinks he learned once and for all in his primal scene. In his internalization of his society's idealized image of the planter, Sutpen has erased from his own late memory the ambivalence of having been once, himself along with his closest family and friends, on the outside of that planter's door, wanting to get inside but all too closely tied emotionally and socially to those people and memories he would leave outside. It is this suddenly frightened and confusing ambivalence which motivates the violent imposition of the culturally dominant, idealized image of the planter on his consciousness. The emotional violence of this reductive, willful solution to his ambivalence has the social consequence that Sutpen (like others before him) repeatedly defends that same compulsively purified image of the planter and himself by violent social exclusions throughout his life. On the model of this first class exclusion, he later excludes his first wife, Eulalia, and his first son, Charles Bon, because of their race, and his second daughter (by Millicent Jones) because of her gender.

Faulkner makes both the emotional violence and the social violence of these repeated exclusions clear already in *his* representation of Sutpen's primal scene. It was "like an explosion," Sutpen said (192). His sudden internalization of the planter's monumental image with no remainder of "ashes" or "refuse" from his formerly groping ambivalence takes the form in the novel of a primal scene—not in the early Freudian sense of an original, determining encounter with an unalterable knowledge, but in the later Freudian sense of a "theoretical fiction" of such an origin, a fictional origin that is always already a simplifying, focusing repetition of more confusing earlier and later memories.[7] In Faulkner's novel Sutpen's primal scene imposes itself at the origin of his life's design as a violently reductive, purifying solution to his emotional confusion about two previous repetitions of this same socially structured event. In those two previous scenes, however, there had seemed to be more room for Sutpen's awareness of his own and others' ambivalence with regard to the violence of the event, whereas in the third that potentially critical awareness of ambivalence and violence is silently excluded from what has become a socially structured, ideologically naturalized event. Faulkner thus analyzes both Sutpen's emotional readiness as an outsider to adopt a neatly reductive, already culturally dominant ideology, and also Sutpen's representative Southern and American attraction to this particular ideology, as he will also analyze others' attractions to other particular ideologies and positions.

In the first of these three scenes, Sutpen is traveling with his father from the frontier society of the West Virginia mountains into the plantation society of Tidewater Virginia. While they are still on the margin of that plantation society Sutpen sees his first slave in the act of carrying and throwing Sutpen's drunken father out the door of a doggery; the slave's mouth is "loud with laughing and full of teeth like tombstones" (182): by comparison with Sutpen's later primal scene, here both the emotional ambivalence and the violence of this temporary, tenuous social exclusion are unmistakable. These become less clear, however, in the second scene, set farther into plantation country, as Sutpen watches his father being "not even allowed to come in by the front door" of taverns and then being ejected, but with "no laughter and jeers to the ejecting now, even if the laughter and jeers had been harsh and without much gentleness in them" (183). Sutpen still misses here the harsh laughter of the doggeries' frontier humor for what it did acknowledge of his and others' ambivalence toward, and mutual vulnerability to, such acts of physical and social violence. Sutpen can still notice here the absence of such laughter as a sign of this society's ideological naturalization of this still palpably unnatural event. In the scene I have called Sutpen's primal scene, however, this potentially

7. On this alternation in Freud's treatments of the primal scene, see Lukacher 136–67.

critical but confusing perspective is eliminated from his henceforth compulsive repetitions of the scene, as if from the very start: Sutpen accepts and teaches himself once and for all (though the lesson must be learned and taught with repeated, increasing violence) this naturalization of a social act as a simple, even an unobjectionable fact, a fact or presence which other re-presentations can only repeat, without significantly reinscribing or altering what they re-present.

These compulsive repetitions tend to take one other main form in their vacillations in *Absalom* and in Faulkner's earlier modernist work. Quentin Compson, in his self-conscious irony toward Sutpen's innocence, seems aware, as Sutpen was not, of what is repressed and excluded in these compulsive, repetitive acts of purificatory exclusion. However, Quentin's postwar Southern, postwar modernist irony offers only a mirror image of those same compulsions, an attempt to resolve at a higher level—but in the same terms—those oppositions made uncomfortably clear by Sutpen's innocent imitations of this society's defining structure. Irony here re-presents what has been repressed and excluded in innocence, but re-presents it only as the still repressed and excluded, without giving any articulate voices of their own to those repressed emotions or those excluded other subjects. That is, irony here preemptively, cautiously represents what innocence has repressed and excluded, but represents it only in the safely generalized, still repressive terms of the same opposition, in some version of what Conrad and Eliot called "the horror" and what Joyce called the "nightmare" of history. It is what Faulkner in *Absalom* represents as the repeatedly repressed and excluded voice of human suffering, desire, and grief heard only in the safely inarticulate, undifferentiated sound of the black idiot Jim Bond's howl.

The particular version of his society's compulsively repeated primal scene on which Quentin himself gets stuck is the scene when Thomas Sutpen's son Henry bursts into his sister's room to announce he has just murdered her fiancé, Charles Bon, at the front gate of the Sutpen plantation. Having been ambivalently attached to Bon as a friend, Henry has just repeated his father's act of purifying exclusion at the plantation gate in a gesture of protecting his sister's and his family's honor from the "spot" of black blood which he has discovered in Bon. Having thereby secured his own place, as it were, in the *father's* place on the inside of the plantation threshold, he enters now into his sister's room as if "into his own," as if to claim now the father's oedipal prize. But he discovers he is now again on the outside bursting in, coming face to face in his sister's room with Judith half naked and sewing her wedding dress: he is coming face to face, that is, with his own incestuous erotic desire and the violence he has done to Judith by seeing her as an oedipal prize rather than as another subject, capable of speaking from her *own* erotic desire, if he could have listened. Quentin's ironic fixation on this scene does represent some such discovery, on Henry's part, of the violent repression of his ambivalence toward both Bon and Judith, as well as the violent exclusion of Judith's and Bon's own (i.e., different, specific) subjectivities, in his compulsive repetition of his father's primal scene. Presumably Quentin also recognizes in this scene his own ambivalence toward his own sister Caddy and the violence his fixation on her virginity does to her as another subject, capable of her own erotic future. But if Quentin and Henry here do somehow confront ironically that other subjectivity which in their innocence they have previously repressed, it is not now to let that other subject speak in a different voice, but only to fixate on the scene of their own ironic discovery of the exclusion, represented here as a discovery not of particular other subjects but of their own mirror image in the form of the inescapable Other — the Other escapable only in Henry's death as in Quentin's impending suicide. As long as that other is only *the* Other, one can only be inside or outside the door, either father or son, either in possession or not in possession of the contested object of desire. Only when the contested object speaks as another recognizable subject, speaking thus outside the terms of this opposition — only then can the compulsive repetition of this opposition be broken. Here that other voice might have been that of the liveried slave whom Sutpen meets on the threshold of the plantation. Or it might have been the voice of the sister whom Henry finds in two places at once, both inside the plantation ideal, purified and protected from Bon but also outside that same ideal, excluded and silenced as subject with Bon. Such voices are almost everywhere silent in *Absalom,* even though Faulkner's irony like Quentin's almost everywhere here represents their silence and the doors that repeatedly close them out.

In "Barn Burning" the critically different voice at the threshold of the plantation, though hard to read, is that of the poor-white Ab Snopes. Standing alongside Ab on that precarious margin, Ab's son Sarty is tempted in his ambivalence and fright, as Thomas and Henry Sutpen were, to accept his society's compulsive resolutions of that fearful ambivalence. For the sake of such resolutions, Sarty is prepared to accept certain implicit oppositional terms for what he feels in his ambivalence, even though (or perhaps because) those oppositional terms violently bar the door to his father Ab and translate Sarty himself inside the house, in another compulsive insistence on self-purifying exclusion. Ab, however, here at the door and throughout the story, repeatedly provokes, frustrates, and escapes all such attempts by his society to account for him in terms of its usual mediations and resolutions: Ab provokes those resolutions to the point of exposing the violence of those oppositions they usually disguise in order to preserve and repeat them compulsively. Ab also speaks and writes here and inter-mittently throughout the story in his own critically different voice and style, effectively setting these dominant oppositions *and* their dialectical resolu-tions off to one side of what they cannot account for—not by oversight but by design—what those oppositions and resolutions are constructed in order to leave out of account. Thus Sarty cannot or will not listen to the singular impertinence of Ab's own history and potential humor, a voice the narrator here urges readers to read better than Sarty does. It is an impertinence which Faulkner himself would return to read much more elaborately and appreciatively in his next rewrite of this scene one year later in *The Hamlet*.

In the version of the scene at the planter's door in "Barn Burning," set thirty years after the war, Sarty attempts two different currently avail-able cultural means to resolve the ambivalence he feels. His first, more innocent attempt is in terms of a plantation myth which has become in many ways stronger after the war than before. It is the now nostalgically idealized myth of the plantation as trickle-down source of moral and even economic blessings to all its humble dependents. Sarty has felt with dis-turbing ambivalence the stark contrast between the apparently invulner-able "peace and dignity" of the planter's house, and his own father's world of frightening social and economic violence and indignity. Sarty seeks a sentimental resolution to that ambivalence in the hope for a moral change in his father's character under the influence of "the spell of the house": "*Maybe he will feel it too. Maybe it will even change him now from what maybe he couldn't help but be.*" But instead of this baptism and redemp-tion of Ab in the planter's image, Faulkner's revision here of the scene at the planter's door represents Ab's muddying of the water. Instead of dissolving Ab's difference into its mythically purifying solution, the spell of the house is broken by Ab's indelible signature on the blond rug placed just inside the door. Ab tests this false welcome by wiping the horse manure on his boot on the expensive, imported rug, provoking another of his perennial exclusions in terms of those same compulsive social and economic oppositions which are only disguised and not revised by such mythic attempts to resolve the social division. Thus even Ab himself repeats the myth of the magical plantation house to Sarty, but in order to suggest a revision of what he knows is Sarty's awestruck view of that mythic house: " 'Pretty and white, ain't it?' he said. 'That's sweat. Nigger sweat. Maybe it ain't white enough yet to suit him. Maybe he wants to mix some white sweat with it' " (12). As in his markings on the rug, Ab revises by smudging here Sarty's and their society's mythic image of the plantation as radiant and redeeming source of beauty, cleanliness, and moral improvement, to stress instead its relation to its dependents (and labor pool) in the under-lying, oppositional terms of exploitation and purificatory exclusion. Its cleanliness functions not to redeem blacks and poor whites "from what maybe they couldn't help but be"; its cleanliness rather functions and exists at the direct expense of those blacks' and poor whites' excluded and degraded toil. Thus too when the planter brings the rug for Ab to wash the tracks out, Ab has his daughters wash the rug (and ruin it) with their own "harsh homemade lye" and a handy fragment of field stone: Ab here again rejects this ritual gesture at settling and resolving his differences with the planter, by instead exaggerating the compulsive violence of this com- pelled erasure of his signature, the planter's attempt to erase Ab's singular, ineradicable mark of his difference on the rug.

Let me point out, however, that Ab's apparent irony here, in his smudging of Sarty's innocence, and in associating himself with manure, with slavery, and with blackness, is in fact not irony but a potential humor, not a compulsive self-exclusion but a revisionary repetition of such exclu- sions. It represents a potential for speaking and writing humorously aside from those same compulsive oppositions. Quentin's irony in *Absalom* only represents and confronts, even if within himself, a blackness that he still finds, for all his irony, no less horrifying than Thomas or Henry Sutpen did. Quentin's irony is a cold comfort in private surrender and disillu- sionment — ultimately a suicidal disillusionment enforcing the same horror upon himself. Ab's potential humor similarly repeats those violent opposi- tions usually smoothed over but still compulsively repeated in his society's dominant gestures at resolution (including the gesture of irony). But Ab's potential humor is a much more active strategy than Quentin's irony, repeating and provoking those same inadequate oppositions, but only in order then to escape them, setting them critically to one side of what they cannot account for in his own singular history and peculiarly critical, potentially humorous stance and agency. Even Sarty recognizes that Ab's character is captured and framed adequately by neither the spell of the plantation house nor their tenant house's squalor, where "His father appeared at the door, framed against that shabbiness, as he had been against that other bland perfection, impervious to either" (13). In other such overtly inadequate descriptions of Ab in terms of ready oppositions — as, for example, "at once formal and burlesque" in his dress or as "shabby and ceremonial" in his actions (20) — we can perhaps understand better now the function of Faulkner's often-noted stylistic tendency (I would say the subtly changing tendency) to oxymorons. These "uncorrected" stylistic discrepancies and contradictions are not a sign of Faulkner's bad habit of thinking in obscurantist paradoxes, as Walter Slatoff and others have charged, nor are they a sign of his achieving resolutions of such paradoxes in his art, as some have no doubt defended him on New Critical grounds. They are rather instances in miniature of his increasingly revisionary repetitions of such inadequate ready oppositions, and of his rejection of those stylistic resolutions that would often only disguise those same inadequate oppositions.

Sarty's other attempt at a peaceable resolution of his emotional and social ambivalence is in terms of the law, another attempt at resolution which Ab sets aside as one more compulsive repetition only raised to a higher ground. When Sarty first sees the apparently magical plantation, he thinks *"Hit's big as a courthouse"* (10), and this immediate association with the law suggests the force of this other main cultural alternative for resolution of social differences when the old plantation magic fails. Thirty years after the war, the planter's feudal privilege over his tenants still largely exists, but it is subject to question on supposedly higher moral and legal grounds, as even Sarty knows. Like irony in *Absalom,* here the law will recognize Ab's existence, but in implicitly repressive terms.

The background for the court trial is that Ab's ruining the rug again in washing it has provoked the planter to an angry, indiscreet assertion of absolute legal sovereignty over his tenant as he declares he will write into Ab's contract unilaterally a charge of twenty bushels of corn. He says this figure is meant not to cover the damages to the rug, but to "teach" Ab to wipe his feet before he enters the planter's wife's house. The planter insists, that is, not on his own economic or legal rights, but on requiring from Ab a gesture of feudal obeisance to the lady of the manor (16). At these signs of an oppositional, arrogantly despotic relationship between planter and tenant, Sarty all too eagerly restores his allegiance to his father on now higher moral and legal grounds that offer him new hope for his father's moral and legal recognition and redemption, as well as his own emotional resolution: "'You done the best you could!' he cried. 'If he wanted hit done different why didn't he wait and tell you how?'" (16). This rather desperate moral claim for Ab's good intentions, however, completely misses the point—or avoids the point—of Ab's violent way of washing the rug. In pretending that Ab would have washed the rug in the way the planter wanted, if only the planter had made his instructions clear, Sarty is hoping again that his father did want to settle his differences with the planter, and wanted to settle them in the planter's way. Ab, however, harshly rejects any such moral whitewash of his contrary behavior, knowing that any such moral resolutions in this society will implicitly favor the planter, by leaving the deeper structural oppositions in place. He does not want to erase and be forgiven for his mark on the planter's rug; he wants a more adequate reading of that mark.

Ab's legal claim in his suit is only superficially the same as Sarty's moral claim. Ab, too, repeats the planter's instructions and claims he followed the letter if not the spirit of what the planter told him to do.

However, the motivations and consequences of Sarty's and Ab's two repetitions of these instructions are altogether different (in ways that you may have guessed). Each one's kind of repetition reflects a radically different conception of law and language. Sarty hopes, compulsively, that in repeating and following only the letter of those instructions, their spirit should somehow follow. Their letter should have been an embodying *symbol* of the planter's intention, which Ab would have done his innocent best to read. The consequence of this conception of law and language when a difference exists in interpretation, as in Ab's suit, is that one meaning is judged more reasonable than another, one as the spirit or tenor and one as merely the letter or vehicle of the disputed language or symbol. Thus Ab loses his suit, for the social hierarchy in the trial matches this hierarchy of representation, with meaning conceived of as an interior presence at the privileged center of all its different but always secondary re-presentations in language, representations that are either faithful to that true meaning or only literal-minded, poor imitations. On the other hand, Ab's own repetition of the planter's instructions in the trial is revisionary, repeating the letter of those instructions not as symbol but as *sign* or *trace,* not as an embodiment of only the planter's intention, but as a negotiable social *contract* or temporary, local *pact*[8] between them both, open to certain legitimate social differences of interpretation. Ab insists on his own contrary interpretation of the planter's instructions by refusing the vast, unspoken social axiomatic of reasonableness and "mere" respect for the expectations of people like the planter and the planter's wife. When the justice rephrases and reinterprets the planter's instructions in line with this socially reasonable interpretation, Ab's long silence emphasizes the legal partisanship and privilege of the justice's decision against Ab, exposing it in its function as not an impartial resolution but another forcible exclusion of Ab's meaning in favor of the planter's that makes of Ab not another speaker of this society's language, but one of its socially illiterate victims. Likewise Ab's suit focuses critical attention on the supposed fairness of the justice's "settlement" when that settlement has to be imposed in a

---

8. The "trace" and the temporary, local "pact" would represent further stages (than "sign" or "contract") in Ab's effective deconstruction of his society's assumptions about language and law. Gregory S. Jay usefully differentiates and historicizes Saussure's stress on the (diachronically) "arbitrary" but still (synchronically) systemic quality of the *sign,* and then Derrida's stress (in his reading of Saussure in *Of Grammatology*) on the asystemic, historical, political qualities of the sign, as represented by the terms "trace" or "gramma" (Jay 187). In terms of the law, Derrida does appreciate, however, Saussure's greater suspicion of such systemic qualities in his demystification of a "social contract" theory of language, with the result that he presumes "that a law accepted by a community is a thing that is tolerated and not a rule to which all freely consent" (Saussure 71, quoted by Jay 162). On the notion of consent to social "pacts" see also Lyotard, *Postmodern Condition* 66.

context of such extreme social and economic inequality that the planter's ninety-five-dollar cash loss on the rug has to be figured as equal with Ab's five-dollar loss in uncertain future earnings.

This same extreme inequality is one reason barn burning was such a favorite form of violent protest for Ab as for many others in the postwar South, as Albert C. Smith has recently documented.[9] Those blacks and poor whites who owned virtually no property had in that lack of property both a simmering motivation for arson and also a strong protection against a like revenge, either by the property owner or by the law, since their own property had always already been taken from them, and since their labor was often a source of profit to their landlords. Ab can repeatedly set planters' barns on fire and move to the side as the planter appears to battle his own shadow in a rage. In battling the fire and then in trying to prosecute the arsonist, the planter here rather more clearly than usual is battling not against Ab himself but against a consequence of the planter's own over-extended monopoly on property and wealth. The planter's repeated exclusion of the poor white from his property reaches here its economic crisis, in an enraged attempt to repeat the exclusion even when there is no one left there to exclude.

Ab thus dangerously brings to a head his society's dominant oppositions by provoking the planter to repeated fits of rage. Sarty, in his mounting fright and confusion, is unable to read Ab's critical, potentially humorous way out of those oppositions, and Sarty's own emotional ambivalence with regard to those oppositions reaches a crisis as well. Sarty finally cannot appreciate Ab's unaccountable difference from his society's dominant dialectics of master and slave, planter and tenant, white and black, clean and filthy, legal and criminal; unable to read Ab's difference as a potential criticism of the exclusive terms of those dialectics, Sarty reads it more simply as a condemnation of Ab and perhaps of Sarty himself. Sarty feels forced to choose, and, in the terms most ready to hand, his choices are always already made, there merely for him to repeat. Earlier, Ab tried to describe their family "blood" to Sarty in terms of a shared kinship and loyalty. But when Sarty realizes that Ab is preparing to burn another barn, he violently recoils from that blood—recoils as Thomas and Henry Sutpen did in similar moments of nauseated horror—from a "blood" that seems now hereditarily, almost inescapably tainted and cursed. Sarty therefore bursts out of his family's tenant house and bursts in through the front door of the planter's house. He thinks he can force an apparently final, apocalyptic resolution to all these frightening oppositions by enabling the planter to catch Ab in the act, Sarty effectively calling down on Ab

9. This intriguing history of barn burning was brought to my attention by Wallace Warren.

both the planter's mythic power and the legitimating force of the law. When
he later hears the planter's shots from the direction of the fire, Sarty turns
away from the scene to light out for the territories, but the narrator
comments that his terror seems resolved now, once and for all. His sudden
grief when he thinks his father is dead threatens momentarily to upset this
resolution again as Sarty calls out, "Pap! Pap!" but he is unprepared at
this point for the more attentively specific work of mourning, resorting
for now to what Freud describes as the compulsive, stalled idealizations
and repetitions of melancholia, idealizing the more personal, more
ambivalent term "Pap! Pap!" into "Father! Father!" and introjecting his
father's memory in his society's crudest terms of heroic idealization: "He
was brave! . . . He was! He was in the war! He was in Colonel Sartoris'
cav'ry!" As the narrator intercedes to object, this idealization of Ab completely ignores and excludes Ab's own singular history as not a soldier
of either army but a professional horse trader throughout the war. Sarty
excludes that singular history to translate (and traduce) Ab's memory
instead to the inside of his society's most unambivalently nostalgic, heroic
myth. Ab's violence is redeemed by his supposed service to the one Cause,
a cause that was defeated but that was supposedly without internal division, a cause whose despotism has supposedly been focused only on
another race and its violence focused supposedly only on an "alien" army.
Ab has provoked here that myth's determined ignorance of his situation
before, during, and after the war as also in his apparent murder now.[10]

Ab does suggest (to Faulkner, as it were) an alternative to this apparently
final, compulsive repetition of this society's self-purifying exclusion of its
own bad blood and the history of that bloodline. If we return to the afternoon in town between the trial and the barn burning, we find Ab talking
and listening at a horse-lot fence and in the blacksmith shop, where Sarty
hears his father tell "a long and unhurried story out of the time . . . when

10. Mitchell Breitwieser suggests that Freud's and more recently Abraham and Torok's
and Derrida's accounts of the stalling effect of melancholia ignore "the pre-emptive intrusion
of ideology into the course of mourning": "In his introduction to the work of Nicolas Abraham
and Maria Torok, Derrida claims that for Freud mourning accomplishes an *introjection*
whereas melancholia is stalled by having *incorporated* the dead: introjection brings the image
of the dead into full assimilation with the self, but incorporation assimilates the dead as
an alien presence, a *crypt* in the midst of the self with which the self does not communicate.
This distinction is useful, but does not seem to me complete: in the case of the sort of prolonged
and intimate contact that exists between family members, the dead does not need to be intro-
jected into the self because that self is in large measure already determined by the history
of the relation—the task is not to bring the dead in, but to convert the dead from being
an element of life *taken for granted* to being an object of representation, to being an inner
image with which the self can communicate to the limit of all the messages that memory
proposes" ("Early American Antigone" n. 8).

he had been a professional horse trader" (19–20). This is as much as we hear in "Barn Burning" of such long and unhurried horse-trading stories, but this is stuff of the same tradition of Old Southwestern and frontier humor on which Faulkner would draw for a different fictional method and different fictional topics from those of his earlier, more modernist writing.[11] Instead of representing his society's compulsively repeated exclusions of what it repeatedly cannot exclude, and instead of repeating the intensities and the inescapable ironies of this apparently unalterable socially structured or metaphysical event, Faulkner would begin increasingly himself to tell such long and unhurried stories. He would continue to repeat such powerful, restrictive oppositions and resolutions, but he would also rewrite them; he would critically and humorously reshape and reconceive those dominant oppositions in the presence of other unaccountably different voices. Thus his novels would take the form of proliferating series of sketches, or collections of short stories that repeatedly overflow their traditional generic boundaries as stories of revealing, essential single events.

Not only as method but also as topic, the Old Southwestern and frontier tradition of horse-trading stories would become in Faulkner's work what Walter Benjamin discusses as an endangered and dangerous memory (253–64)—a precapitalist or marginally capitalist social and economic tradition on which Faulkner would draw in *The Hamlet* and steadily thereafter for his own critical alternative to both the property-based capitalism of the Old South and the money-based capitalism of the New. In stories of trading in *The Hamlet*, for example, when unexpected differences arise about a verbal or written agreement, there is no appeal to what the more powerful or respectable or wealthy party really meant, as in the case of the planter's instructions for cleaning the rug. The accepted challenge and the intersubjective appeal of trading for both parties is to read each other carefully and probingly for signs of differences, to try to account for or to accept the risk of those always unpredictable differences, and then to accept that a deal is a deal. To trade with Ab would mean to know you are risking trading at least partly on Ab's singular terms. In Ratliff's retelling of the "Barn Burning" story in *The Hamlet*, he stresses and appreciates both the potential humor and the potential for economic criticism and change in Ab's acute understanding of his own social and economic relationships with the planter. After ruining the planter's rug, bringing him to court, and burning his barn, Ab enters the planter's house on his way out of town the next morning to say, "It looks like me and you aint going

11. On the critical potential of humor in the history of American literature, and for useful distinctions between irony and humor, see especially Neil Schmitz, *Of Huck and Alice: Humorous Writing in American Literature.*

to get along together, . . . so I reckon we better quit trying before we have a misunderstanding over something" (17). Of course they *have* had a misunderstanding, but the misunderstanding has been the planter's, who has consistently refused to read the signs of Ab's singular difference from the usual categories of planters and their humble tenants. The planter has been particularly unprepared for the unsettling possibility that Ab would repeatedly find more effective ways to take advantage of his lack of social dignity and property, particularly in daring to burn the barn. It is precisely this possibility that Ab's next landlord learns about in hearing Ratliff retell this story in *The Hamlet,* and this possibility becomes, for Ab's son Flem, a silent bargaining partner used to get himself some property.[12]

To conclude this introduction, this humorous possibility of an unexpected economic leverage is by no means the only topical opening out of "Barn Burning" and into *The Hamlet* and Faulkner's later work. In *The Hamlet* Ratliff will expand on the "Barn Burning" story to remember Ab from a time before he was "soured," a time when his humor and love for his wife enabled him to escape not only the terms of the Old South's plantation myth and economy, but also the terms of the New South's money-based economy, those differently restrictive terms in which his son Flem would get so skillfully entangled. (These issues will be the subject of Chapter 3 below.) Ratliff's own ambivalent and affectionate memories of Ab's singular history and character will also provide an example of that same long and unhurried work of mourning which will become a more central topic in *Go Down, Moses.* In Faulkner's ongoing revisions of the primal scene I have discussed, as well as of other such socially structured events, he will listen more closely and specifically not only for the singular voices of white trash males such as Ab and Flem, but also for other critically different voices that have been similarly concealed, such as those of

12. Again, I am reading Ab's signature and his escape as one way out of one particular set of confining (mostly class-related) cultural alternatives, and not as the one new way out of all such cultural oppositions (assuming any such perfect escape from culture were either possible or desirable). His method of reinscription and escape serves here as a model for other, more difficult escapes from other, more stubbornly naturalized oppositions, to be examined more critically later in Faulkner's career. Ab's violence toward blacks, toward women, and toward his son Sarty is obvious throughout the story. It is not in defense of this violence but in an effort to understand it—the "savage blows . . . but without heat" (6)—that I might add that Ab seems here to be passing on, in a more explicitly despotic, violent form, the naturalized, axiomatic social and economic violence he feels directed against himself. That is, Ab savagely, bitterly exaggerates, while still repeating, the racism and patriarchal sexism of his society and class, a repetition that is in these cases unrevisionary and uncritical unless perhaps in the otherwise unaccountable, unarticulated *force* of his smoldering rage.

blacks and women (as in *Go Down, Moses* and *Requiem for a Nun*, treated in Chapters 4 and 5 below). These voices will suggest new topics; they will also throw into relief the fact that modernism's supposedly universal consciousness was a consciousness predominantly middle class, white, and male. This was a fact about modernism as about the postwar South's dominant culture which becomes most clear in Faulkner's most demanding elaboration and test of that modernism in the social and historical context of the postwar South, as he examined modernist attitudes and habits first as cultural symptoms and habits, then as willful, often violent social exclusions (the subjects of my Chapters 1 and 2).

Perhaps I should add a note on one peculiarity of my method here. While I will often criticize New Critical readings of Faulkner, I have honored the same New Criticism's injunction to close reading of Faulkner's texts. Paul de Man has recognized the particular "insight" such close reading has provided in tracing informing oppositions down to minute details and nuances of literary expression, even if such insight has usually come only at the expense of a certain "blindness" to historical and social circumstances deemed to be outside the text (20–35). Faulkner has had more than his share of such New Critical close readings, notably by Cleanth Brooks. With the benefit of more recent structuralist, Marxist, and deconstructive readings like those of Wesley Morris, Carolyn Porter, John Irwin, and John T. Matthews, I hope to push this method of proof in close reading somewhat farther to show that the oppositions isolated by Faulkner's New Critical readers may in this phase of Faulkner's work be charged with a blindness not only to the history and society "outside" the text, but also to odd details, nuances, discrepancies, and contradictions "within" the text, if that text is reread closely enough—as Faulkner was himself rereading it in his own ongoing revisions of previous work. My own close readings will show, I hope, how those informing literary and historical oppositions repeatedly (and productively) fail to exclude, or to contain, certain other competing voices both outside and inside the text.

To put this another way, I want to acknowledge the methodological debt that American deconstructive criticism owes to the New Criticism's tradition of close reading, but at the same time I also want to insist on the possibility that deconstructive and other poststructuralist criticism might acknowledge the ethical and political implications of the questions posed in literary and other social texts more candidly than the New Criticism has, and more candidly than structuralism and even poststructuralism itself always has. Faulkner's modernism does not just self-destruct, caving in on a vacuum within itself. It sees ghosts and hears voices, both within its own "Dark House" and without, ghosts that begin to materialize and voices that grow haltingly but increasingly articulate and specific.[13] Whereas Hemingway buries such ghosts and voices in ominous allusions to the bulk of the iceberg hidden beneath the controlling surface, even the surface of Faulkner's writing is everywhere disturbed by and drawn toward other voices in the (always social) text.

13. "Dark House" was Faulkner's working title for the manuscript of the novel eventually titled *Absalom, Absalom!*

Nausea and Irony's Failing Distances in *Absalom, Absalom!*

Rosa Coldfield begins *Absalom, Absalom!* as a modernist muse addressing the artist as a young man of the American South, Quentin Compson, who "maybe . . . will enter the literary profession as so many Southern gentlemen and gentlewomen too are doing now and maybe some day you will remember this and write about it." Otherwise, she tells him, "there is little left in the South for a young man" (5). Faulkner had recently written as much elsewhere:

> the South . . . is dead, killed by the Civil War. There is a thing known whimsically as the New South to be sure, but it is not the south. It is a land of Immigrants who are rebuilding the towns and cities into replicas of towns and cities in Kansas and Iowa and Illinois. ("An Introduction to *The Sound and the Fury*" 24)

Faulkner is speaking in 1933 here of a Southern legacy from the Civil War—a sense of alienation from a landscape and culture of which the original is destroyed and which seems now rebuilt or Reconstructed by strangers not on the original plan but on the more easily reproduced but meaningless model of the general equivalent. This specifically Southern alienation, however, is an older, more local version of a much wider alienation which, at the time he writes in the decades after World War I, Faulkner shares with many other "literary professionals" well beyond the American South, for example, T. S. Eliot who, in his influential and representative *Waste Land* vision of the "Unreal City," "had not thought death had undone so many." This postwar sense of Western culture's general death and of disillusionment with its surviving unreality is amply articulated and documented in the cosmopolitan literary modernism in which Faulkner played a studious, prominent, but also a significantly exceptional, critical part.

Several other of those Southern men and women who entered the literary profession at about the time Faulkner did were in fact attempting in their alienation from the increasingly modernized, industrialized New South to remember another, living South and "write about it" in ways that paralleled the work of their more famous colleagues on the international literary modernist scene. Michael O'Brien's *The Idea of the American South, 1920–1941* traces the history of these Southern Agrarians as a special case of literary modernism's invocation of the romantic myth of the organic *volk* as a standard from which to view with irony the modern decline and disillusionment. While T. S. Eliot measured the modern dissociation of sensibility ironically against a more unified Elizabethan sensibility and tradition, and saw Joyce making similar juxtapositions of modern bourgeois life and that of classical Greece, the Agrarians were looking closer to home and much closer to the historical present for their version of a culture before the fall (O'Brien 138–45). This apparent proximity to their ideal offered both a nostalgic promise and also a rigorously revealing test, as they attempted to construct from their own region's recent history an agrarian social theory to match their blanket rejection of the industrializing, commercialized New South.

The story of the Agrarians' social theory parallels the story of Southern narrative and memory Faulkner tells in *Absalom*. As a result of putting their largely literary nostalgia to the test of social theory (the test of social policy was unattained and unnecessary), their alternative idea of an agrarian South was soon just as fragmented and contradictory as the idea of the New South which it had hoped to counter but with which it began to seem increasingly continuous and complicit. A nostalgic agrarian ideal (for example, Allen Tate's and Rosa Compson's) based on an aristocracy of landed, leisured planters was contradicted by competing Jeffersonian idealizations of the small yeoman farmer (for example, Frank Owsley's and Thomas Sutpen's as a boy in the "cave"). These ideals could be reconciled (for example by Howard Odum and Mr. Compson) by conceiving of the aristocratic planter as having democratic, yeoman farmer roots in a society permitting mobility to the deserving few. But this reconciliation resembled all too closely the New South boosterism which argued the continuity of the commercialized New South with the Old. Furthermore, this reconciliation of the aristocratic and Jeffersonian poles of agrarianism could be accomplished only by revealingly, absolutely excluding from the myth of continuing social mobility both the slavery before the war and the increasing segregation after the war and Reconstruction. In short, the test of social theory undergone by agrarianism revealed (as it also would in *Absalom*) both the exploitative capitalism often denied in nostalgic portraits of the Old South and the continuing racism and inflexible social hierarchy often denied even in ironic portraits of the New South.

C. Vann Woodward, among others, has appreciated the literary and historiographic results of such attentions in the South to nineteenth- and twentieth-century United States history; he has appreciated especially the irrepressible, well-learned sense, uncommon in the United States, of poverty, defeat, guilt, and place (16–25). This was not, however, the redeeming social vision of the South that the Agrarians had promised, and O'Brien maps their gradual retreat from social into aesthetic theory, from their (now apparently sentimental) vision of unified sensibility as an anti-industrial agrarian life-style and society in the South, toward the more restricted model of unified sensibility as the (only ironically sentimental) aesthetic experience of a poem (221–24). As described and institutionalized by that American New Criticism largely founded by former Agrarians, and later exemplified by Frank Kermode's "fictionalism," this aesthetic experience is characterized especially by an antiromantic, ironic assurance that fiction's varied attempts at, or intimations of, personal, social, or historical alternatives to modern alienation are all doomed to remain precisely that — fictions.[1] Thus Wallace Stevens: "The exquisite truth is to know that it is a fiction . . . that you believe in."[2] This purely negative, ironic assurance about human fictions becomes an alibi and a consolation, allowing in the midst of disillusionment ironically assured, secretly senti-mental representations of the landscape and culture as uniformly dead, dehumanized, by its very nature either antagonistic or inhumanly indiffer-ent to human fictions of whatever kind. Hence the critical warnings against the romantic poets' now superseded tendency toward "pathetic fallacy." This New Critical and modernist construction of a metaphysical opposition between reality and fiction appears hard enough on sentiment to seem the unsentimental truth, and not actually sentimentality's self-defense, a way to avoid questions about the particular origins and consequences of particular fictions and about their possible complicity in that cruel or indifferent reality they seem to oppose, a way to avoid, that is, the discomfiting results of tests like those the Agrarians' social fictions failed.

Faulkner did share much of his Lost Generation's post–World War I disposition to disillusionment and irony at those lost illusions, often over-estimating (and mystifying) such disillusionment as an unflinching confron-tation with the supposedly now demystified real; he also had, however, the *critical* advantage in the South of having inherited the experience and example of several generations of the "lost," an inheritance he accepted more critically than the Agrarians did. Perhaps because he had tested it more rigorously in his writing, he kept questioning their eventual,

---

1. The description of American New Criticism in this paragraph is largely indebted to Frank Lentricchia's *After the New Criticism* 28–60.

2. *Necessary Angel* 36, quoted by Lentricchia 28.

exemplary retreat into literature. In the same 1933 introduction to *The Sound and the Fury* in which he writes of a land killed by the war, he claims that the reason the typical Southern artist chooses an art "which has no place in southern life" is "not so much that it is forced back upon him or that he is forced bodily into it by the circumstance; forced to choose, lady and tiger fashion, between being an artist and being a man." This sense of art and life as an either-or does seem to be Yeats's view in "The Choice" (1933), and a common one among modernist artists, who often regarded art as an imaginary refuge for the sensitive few from an intolerable reality of degradation, poverty, vanity, and remorse: "The intellect of man is forced to choose / Perfection of the life, or of the work" (242). But Faulkner here rejects this idea that the Southern artist is forced to choose by a hard circumstance; rather, "He does it deliberately; he wishes it so" (24). Faulkner recognizes, that is, the partisanship and sentimentality of both the apparently opposite courses he sees Southern artists taking, either nostalgia for the past or bitterly ironic indictments of the present, attempts either

> to draw a savage indictment of the contemporary scene or to escape from it into a makebelieve region of swords and magnolias and mockingbirds which perhaps never existed anywhere. Both of the courses are rooted in sentiment; perhaps the ones who write savagely and bitterly of the incest in clay-floored cabins are the most sentimental. Anyway, each course is a matter of violent partizanship, in which the writer unconsciously writes into every line and phrase his violent despairs and rages and frustrations or his violent prophesies of still more violent hopes. (25)

David Minter suggests that in writing this introduction Faulkner "had finally discovered a way of telling the story of Thomas Sutpen, with whom he had been conjuring for several months" (143). He would counter the idealized nostalgia for the past with the savage indictment of the present, as he and many other modernists (notably T. S. Eliot) had often done before (and as the New Critics would later appreciate and recommend), but he would draw on these two typical "courses" of Southern narrative not in order to privilege irony over nostalgia, but to render his increasingly keen, critical sense of the motivations and consequences of that indictment's savagery. He would use Quentin Compson "because it is just before he is to commit suicide because of his sister, and I use his bitterness which he has projected on the South in the form of hatred of it and its people to get more out of the story itself than a historical novel would be" (*Selected Letters* 79). He intends to write neither idealization nor indictment, nor just a history either, but rather a book *using* that indictment's bitterness to tell more than only Sutpen's story—to tell, as well, the story of Quentin's and the Southern modernist artist's (Faulkner's own) ironic bitterness as grounded in just such a history as the one which Rosa urges him to remember and write about.

Having considerable trouble himself writing about that history, Faulkner interrupted his work on *Absalom* to write *Pylon,* as he said later, "just to get away from a book that wasn't going too well, till I could get back to it" (*Faulkner in the University* 36). It is worth speculating, at least, that in writing *Pylon* Faulkner attempted to exorcise the relatively unfocused ironic bitterness of cosmopolitan literary modernism in order to turn back to *Absalom* with a more acutely concentrated critical attention to those cosmopolitan ironies' more specifically Southern cousins. *Pylon* is a litany of explicit allusions to and parodies of Joyce and especially Eliot: one chapter is titled "Lovesong of J. A. Prufrock"; the airport is "Created out of the Waste Land at the Bottom of Lake Rambaud at a Cost of One Million Dollars" (11); and much of the rest of the novel occurs in a drunken haze in an unreal city, a graveyard, a junk heap, and a watery grave. In a later statement Faulkner dehumanizes and trivializes the book's airmen as a "fantastic and bizarre phenomenon on the face of a contemporary scene" (*Faulkner in the University* 36), and the book's organizing consciousness is a nameless Reporter unable either to understand this scene or to hide the violent sentimentality of his ultimate disillusionment.

After *Pylon* Faulkner returned to write the first four chapters of *Absalom* "with great intensity" (Minter 150), chapters which in a way reflect critically on Faulkner's own difficulty writing Sutpen's story. In these four chapters Faulkner has Quentin listen with increasing involvement in the story and with growing impatience at the inadequate narrative voices first of Rosa and then of Mr. Compson, representing between them the two "courses" of Southern narrative. It becomes clear that Compson's irony, with its pretended realism and cosmopolitan uninvolvement, can reveal no more about the characters he discusses than Rosa's nostalgia could, and that neither reveals so much about those characters they discuss as about their own violent despairs, hopes, and obfuscations. As the motivating, expressive "grain" of Compson's voice becomes more audible in his narration, he cannot suppress any longer the other quoted voices of Judith, Bon, Henry, and Wash Jones, voices that begin to speak not as merely fictitious, ghostly objects of irony but as other recognizable subjects. Quentin will turn his attention in later chapters of *Absalom* to these other repressed voices to learn more about the emotional, social, historical origins and consequences of Rosa's and Compson's narrative exclusions.

Absalom is usually considered Faulkner's most "historical" novel, yet it is also first a (historiographic) study in, and study of, this modernist irony which nearly overrules the book's interest in Southern (and American) history, in favor of ahistorical, metaphysical confrontations with the inhuman deadness of the real. Faulkner indirectly suggests one way of approaching this problem: if both nostalgia and irony say that the South is "dead," one potentially useful question to ask is whether the South's survivors in this novel have undertaken the work of mourning and understanding that death, or whether they are melancholically stuck repeating the traumatic scene of loss. Here I would largely agree with Richard H. King that "what Freud did in and for European culture [analytically, not therapeutically], Faulkner (and to a lesser extent Cash and Lillian Smith) did in and for the modern Southern cultural tradition" (9). I have suggested in the Introduction and will suggest later that one dimension of Freud's notion of mourning as the coming to terms with an objective reality was eventually taken farther by Faulkner. Faulkner's more critical, "revisionary" notion of repetition and narrative (like those of Gilles Deleuze in *Différence et répétition* and Jean-François Lyotard in *Just Gaming*) entails the continual rethinking of traditional and existing representations of reality with an eye toward what those representations tend to omit or obscure. But for now, for the purposes of understanding the two available "courses" of Southern narrative tested in *Absalom*'s first four chapters, it will be useful to draw on Freud's analyses of the repetition compulsion (in *Beyond the Pleasure Principle*), anxiety (in *Inhibitions, Symptoms and Anxiety*), and mourning and melancholia (in "Mourning and Melancholia").

Freud's melancholiac compulsively repeats a scene of trauma or loss in order to gain at least a degree of control over what, for the unprepared ego in the event, seems to have been an experience of overwhelming "fright," or (schematically) the intrusion by the ego's normally excluded "outside" past its normal defenses into its "inside." Repetitive attempts to repair that unpreparedness may place blame too exclusively on one particular source or event of danger, or too generally on danger as the nature of things. That is, representations of such a trauma may take the phobic form of a narrowed focus on an external threat to a (correspondingly reductive) internal or prior purity or utopia. Alternatively, representations of the trauma or loss may be repeated in a much less focused, more generalized "anxiety" about the external and now also internalized danger of object loss itself: the internal danger, for example, of constant unpreparedness for, or emotional vulnerability to, surprise, trauma, or loss. However, in either their overly restricted, obsessive form (as "fright"), or their overgeneralized form (as "anxiety"), representations and repetitions of fear and loss work in melancholy to procrastinate and prevent the more specific "reality-testing" work of mourning, the gradual sifting through one's ambivalent memories of the lost object or lost innocence toward a critical understanding of such oversimplifications of memory and toward an understanding and articulation of one's loss that is more adequate to the rest of one's ongoing experience.[3] Such an analysis would point toward a better understanding, for instance, of whether that loss can be success-fully focused and blamed on one demon or one war, as often in Rosa's nostalgia and fright, whether, alternatively, that loss teaches a generalized cosmopolitan anxiety and expectation of certain loss from all experience, as often in Compson's irony, or whether both such strategies are in fact understandable but misguided attempts to simplify both the continuing ambivalence toward past losses and also the continuing, unavoidable risks of further losses (also attractive gains) in emotional, social, and historical reinvolvements.

Thus Rosa in her "eternal black" seems to Quentin one more example of a widespread, melancholic nostalgia for an idealized prewar South, a nostalgia which he dismisses as narrow, outdated, irrelevant make-believe, with no real connection to the present: "the deep South dead since 1865 and peopled with garrulous outraged baffled ghosts, [Quentin] listening, having to listen, to one of the ghosts which had refused to lie still even longer than most had, telling him about old ghost-times" (3, 4). He can dismiss their defensive fixation on an old slaveholding society and its fatal war as a fixation on a now long-dead past, but he does admit and chafe at the fact that he is not yet free of such voices in himself:

> He was not a being, an entity, he was a commonwealth. He was a barracks filled with stubborn back-looking ghosts still recovering, even forty-three years afterward, from the fever which had cured the disease, waking from the fever without even knowing that it had been the fever itself which they had fought against and not the sickness, looking with stubborn recalcitrance backward beyond the fever and into the disease with actual regret, weak from the fever yet free of the disease and not even aware that the freedom was that of impotence. (7)

---

3. I am borrowing Freud's useful distinctions between fright, fear, and anxiety, but alter-ing his hierarchy among the three. Freud treats fright as the original emotion in association with the trauma that starts the entire process (rather like the primal scene, in its simplest formulations), and treats fear and anxiety as two reductions of that essential indeterminacy, whereas I suspect fright and anxiety as Freud describes them are both reductions of a more complex, ambivalent, and differentiated fear (at least in Faulkner's analyses, and perhaps in any representation of trauma, for example in memory). I will return to this question in Chapter 4, in relation to Faulkner's frequent distinctions between fright and fear in *Go Down, Moses*.

However much these ghosts' nostalgia may idealize a diseased time in opposition to its destroying war, or fever, Quentin recognizes the impotence
of such nostalgia to recreate now an idealization so thoroughly defined
(even largely motivated) by its death. He does not yet recognize, however, the similar impotence of his own ironic position, himself representing and repeating not a dead time and its destruction, but the generalized
(dead) lesson of loss such ghostly voices might seem to teach. Whereas
Rosa focuses her fear on a demon and war which she can attempt to
exclude from her nostalgic utopia or personal purity, Quentin effectively
focuses his anxiety (at a different level of generality) on the danger of object
loss itself, a danger incurred by Rosa perhaps in her innocence, but which
Quentin thinks to exclude from his higher stronghold and vantage point
in irony. That is, he too is focused on the fever and not the disease, on
the danger of innocence and loss in general and not on that particular innocence of Rosa's and the South's which by emotional and social exclusions
dialectically invited its own trauma and loss. Nor is Quentin focused,
either, on the impotence of his own position of ironic uninvolvement,
defined as it is by similarly constructed (and fated) exclusions of only more
general dangers of loss. He can enjoy only the retroactive comfort of irony,
attempting not just to reject but to preempt any particular fright or surprise by always having known all along: "What is it to me that the land
or the earth or whatever it was got tired of him at last and turned and
destroyed him? What if it did destroy her family too? It's going to turn
and destroy us all some day, whether our name happens to be Sutpen or
Coldfield or not" (7).

   In short, Quentin understands better at this point the self-protective
motives and self-destructive consequences of such repetitions of loss in
Rosa's case than in his own, realizing about Rosa's "implacable unforgiv-
ing" of Sutpen that

> when you have hated somebody for forty-three years you will know
> them awful well so maybe it's better then . . . because after forty-
> three years they cant any longer surprise you. . . . And maybe it (the
> voice, the talking, the incredulous and unbearable amazement) had
> even been a cry aloud once, . . . of indictment of blind circumstance
> and savage event; but not now: now only the lonely thwarted old
> female flesh embattled for forty-three years in the old insult. . . . (9)

Thus Rosa tries to reduce the various vicissitudes of history to a repetitive, even a single outrage, even as Quentin also tries here to reduce her
embattled history to that of an unrecognizable, ghostly old female flesh.
He wants to exclude from his position of irony her vulnerable, past inno-

cence (along with his own continuing vulnerability recognizable in hers), in much the same way as she wants to exclude Sutpen's outrage from that prior innocence. Much the same process of nonrecognition and exclusion has made of Rosa an impotent ghost and of Quentin an impotent cynic.

Rosa's plans to revisit the Sutpen mansion, also Quentin's plans to accompany her, will suggest, however, that neither her outraged nostalgia nor Quentin's detached irony has satisfactorily, finally laid the South's and Sutpen's history to rest, though Rosa and Quentin will both (ambivalently) continue trying to do so throughout the novel. This process often gives this novel the feel of a history somewhat self-consciously and preemptively reduced to a self-contained ironic lesson, but it becomes a more "moving" lesson than that insofar as various nostalgic and ironic repetitions fail to attain their ends and fail to contain their objects, fail to master, that is, the complexities of their live subjects, allowing other, less repetitive external and internal voices to speak alongside and within their own. The result (described in the metafictional passage excerpted below) is that the "yet-elapsing time" of history and social and emotional interaction, the duration in which we actually experience fright, pleasure, and amazement, often threatens to be reduced, but fails increasingly in *Absalom* to be reduced, to a merely formal, fictional, repetitive device. Thus Quentin resists but also begins in spite of himself to be moved by Rosa's tale, which seems

> to partake of that logic- and reason-flouting quality of a dream which the sleeper knows must have occurred, stillborn and complete, in a second, yet the very quality upon which it must depend to move the dreamer (verisimilitude) to credulity—horror or pleasure or amazement—depends as completely upon a formal recognition of and acceptance of elapsed and yet-elapsing time as music or a printed tale. (15)

This is a challenge to readers and listeners (including Quentin and Faulkner himself) that to appreciate Rosa's story (and Quentin's) requires an understanding of often stillborn and repetitive forms as reactions to and reductive condensations and displacements of events that are experienced nevertheless in "elapsed and yet-elapsing time."

Hugh Kenner has suggested that Faulkner's fiction differs radically from that of most cosmopolitan literary modernism particularly inasmuch as his "printed tales" do point emphatically toward the duration of "elapsed and yet-elapsing time." This makes Faulkner's tales in certain ways less written than oral: whereas the painstakingly pruned, ironically self-consuming, deconstructing artifacts of modernism (what Michel de Certeau calls modernism's "celibatory writing machines") kept "yet-elapsing time" under strict control as a merely formal, internal principle, and whereas such artifacts often ironically self-consume to enact their limit or death at the threshold not of an absent real or heterogeneous other but of a nothingness outside the celibatory text (de Certeau 156–57), Faulkner's fiction, on the other hand, draws as well on oral traditions in which, as A. B. Lord has shown, each retelling or singing of a tale is a repetition with difference, not just a compulsively mechanical, managerial restaging of the original but a new and living original of the "same" tale. Jean-François Lyotard has suggested that in such retellings, the tale is always an experimental and critical rethinking of the tradition, told always in a particular, changing circumstance and always addressed to a different, changing audience (*Just Gaming* 32–36; see also Deleuze, *Différence et répétition* 128–67).

This less compulsive, more differential, critical style of repetition and writing will become most obvious in the longer range of Faulkner's literary life, in the way that his life, as Sartre says of Flaubert's, "develops in spirals; it passes again and again by the same points but at different levels of integration and complexity" (106). This long-range critical repetition and revision is already legible too, however, in *Absalom,* in the variously revealing, increasing failures of this book's characteristically more melancholic, compulsively ironic repetitions. What repeats itself here, as for Constantin in Kierkegaard's *Repetition,* is the somewhat disturbing but also ambiguously promising failure to repeat—not yet repeated openings toward heterogeneous others but repeated confrontations with the barred doors blocking such openings. These failures and barred doors are usually hypostatized as the unspeakable real, like Conrad's "the horror," but always also here with suggestions of the violent motivations and consequences of such exclusions and hypostatizations, motivations in ambivalent fear and desire, and consequences in celibatory distortions of that ongoing ambivalence.

But before looking at *Absalom* in more detail, I want to be careful here to distinguish these suggestions about the failure of modernist irony in Faulkner from a set of related readings of Faulkner's modernist work as somehow ironically triumphant in its deliberate quest for failure (Slatoff), or in the collapse of Apollonian form before the reality of Dionysian change (Kartiganer), or in the artist's doomed internal struggle against the irreversible authority of time, an authority only ironically reconfirmed by the artist's struggle (Irwin). I think such readings tend to privilege ironies as truths, mistaking the experience of disillusionment for knowledge without illusion. Thus Paul de Man speaks of romantic irony as the pulling of a thread which proceeds unstoppably toward the thoroughly demystified position of Baudelaire's *comique absolu* (208–28). I do not think this brand (or simplification) of deconstruction is either Faulkner's goal or his unwitting achievement or endpoint. Rather Faulkner will show "absolute" irony, with its crossed-out invocation of the unnameable "it" of such aporiae, as still one more supposedly demystified but actually remystified position, with its own conditions of possibility, its own motivations and consequences, and its own social and historical context, attempting but always failing to exclude its own motivations and consequences, along with those other voices which threaten to reveal them. The failure of irony I want to study here should not be taken, then, as yet one more supremely or triumphantly ironic failure. I will suggest instead that the failure of irony in modernist works like *Absalom,* irony's largely barred confrontations with its human costs, victims, and remainders, prepares a stage for Faulkner's continuing exploration beyond the modernist "horror" and fright to that horror's more particular, more recognizable historical, social, and psychological motivations and consequences. This possibility of *recognizing* both the act of exclusion and the excluded comes to characterize particularly those works by Faulkner dominated less by modernist irony than by what I will be calling a mode of humor, mourning, and love, works like *The Hamlet, Go Down, Moses,* and *Requiem for a Nun.*

Rosa's tale in *Absalom*'s opening chapter forms a series of attempts to plead the South's and especially her own family's prewar, pre-Sutpen innocence by representing that innocence repeatedly in an absolute opposition to its apparent defeat and corruption by the war and by the demonic Thomas Sutpen, "the evil's source and head which had outlasted all its victims" (12). She tries to exonerate and purify the South's past by restricting its narrative continuity with Sutpen and the war to the form of an unaccountable but unrelenting "fatality and curse on the South and on our family" (14). Thus she repairs the indeterminacy of her long, ambivalent involvement with Sutpen, through certain strategies of representation and repetition, and offers a more focused and determined, phobic version of fear as fright. Repeating these scenes of innocence unaccountably, tragically overwhelmed from without, she tries to project onto this demon from beyond the pale all responsibility for her own family's vulnerability to Sutpen, involvement with Sutpen, and especially Ellen's and her own fascination, attraction, even love for Sutpen. As her attempted absolute oppositions between the idealized Old South and everything Sutpen suggests about the underside of that ideal continually fail to persuade either Quentin or herself, she resorts to the more recognizably ironic strategy of at least distancing herself from her own formerly naive innocence, from Ellen, from Henry, and from Judith. She represents these as the irrecoverably, naively lost, as opposed to the loss she is prepared to expect now more generally, her relative loss of innocence rationalized and compensated for by this supposed gain in disillusioned vigilance. This will be the pattern for a continuing dialectic or spiraling from nostalgic, "innocent" idealizations of the victimized as against their demon or curse, toward an apparently neutral, disinterested, realistic, dialectically synthetic transcendence of both the victims and their fates. This same dialectic, however, will go on to reveal this disinterested ironic position as still an injured, quite interested anxiety over the generalized danger of object loss "itself," an anxiety which is no less a function of the repetition compulsion than the nostalgic phobia it mocks, that phobia which only focuses on a danger of loss more particular and more obviously externalized than what irony hypostatizes and internalizes as the danger of loss itself.

For example, in Rosa's more nostalgic, demonizing mode, her sister Ellen is seen as having provided "respectability, the shield of a virtuous woman," for Sutpen, that "fiend blackguard and devil," whose wanting such a shield "was proof enough . . . that what he fled from must have been some opposite of respectability too dark to talk about" (9, 10, 11). This illogical, insistent projection of any suggestion of differences *within* respectability as an absolute (class) difference *between* the real gentleman and his plagiarizing opposite will change in the context of the war into a subtler difference between the South's "cause" and its temporarily necessary but still impure defenders. Rosa saves her own purity in her ironic awareness of that impurity, an impurity within the cause, perhaps, but an impurity, after all, not yet within her own class, or (later) still not within her family, or within herself, or within her own undistorted perspective: "But that our cause, our very life and future hopes and past pride, should have been thrown into the balance with men like that to buttress it—men with valor and strength but without pity or honor. Is it any wonder that Heaven saw fit to let us lose?" (213). That is, if she cannot quite maintain the purity of the South, perhaps she can at least in retrospect be unsurprised by, and even (narrowly) diagnose and isolate the cause of, its defeat, representing that defeat as a still more or less external problem after all. Her irony here is a more "realistic" account of the danger both without and now admittedly within, but an account given from a now safer, more circumspect position still within. Such moves from innocence and nostalgia toward "realizations" and negations of that innocence begin the dialectical mediation between innocence and its corruption which Compson and others want to think of as ending with the sublation and synthesis of these (prototypically Faulknerian) contraries in irony.

Rosa's first sight of the Sutpen family, a primal scene which sticks in Rosa's memory and narrative, is another such scene of innocence overwhelmed by a frightful fate and horrified realization, a scene which she

will repeat through the remainder of this chapter with an increasingly circumscribed innocence and (as each such representation of pure innocence
fails) an increasingly circumspect, compensatory irony. She remembers
waiting before the church with her father and aunt for the Sutpen children's
"one chance" to "approach the vicinity of salvation," but this was to be
the day when not just Rosa but the whole "town finally realized that
[Sutpen] had turned that road from Sutpen's Hundred in to the church
into a race track" (16, 15). The road to the church, the white sister, the
two children, the entire scene of imminent salvation is taken over as though
by storm, by wild Negroes, beasts, and dust, in a cataclysm that is unfocusable or focused only as an unfocusable fright:

> though I must have seen Ellen and the children before this, this is the
> vision of my first sight of them which I shall carry to my grave: a
> glimpse like the forefront of a tornado, of the carriage and Ellen's
> high white face within it and the two replicas of his face in miniature
> flanking her, and on the front seat the face and teeth of the wild
> negro who was driving, and he, his face exactly like the negro's save
> for the teeth (this because of his beard, doubtless)—all in a thunder
> and a fury of wildeyed horses and of galloping and dust. (16)

When the minister objects to this outrageous, meaningless sound and fury
"in the name of the women of Jefferson and Yoknapatawpha County" (17),
Sutpen himself quits accompanying his family, but the threat becomes
merely more insidious, less easily seen as the fault of a man now staying
home twelve miles away: "with [Sutpen's] face absent, it was only the wild
negro's perfectly inscrutable one with the teeth glinting a little, so that
now we could never know if it were a race or a runaway" (17). Then when
the "wild negro's" face is removed from the scene's next near-repetition,
the threat is nearly inextricable from its supposedly purest victim; they
can isolate the corruption only as Sutpen's face recognizable in his daughter's face, realizing "that his face had been in that carriage all the time;
that it had been Judith, a girl of six, who had instigated and authorized
that negro to make the team run away. Not Henry, mind; not the boy,
which would have been outrageous enough; but Judith, the girl" (18).

What makes this corruption of even this inner sanctum of the cult
of White Southern Girlhood especially unsettling for Rosa both in the event
and at this point in her narration is her final sense in this chapter of losing
even her compensatory ability (if unable to project blame onto an external
danger like Sutpen) at least to frame and interpret these outrages successfully herself. Whereas she pretended earlier to be able to understand
heaven's judgment against the South, Rosa comes to admit in the chapter's

climactic scene of Judith's "corruption" that she is herself now unsure whether it is "God or the devil" who has apparently supplied the "witnesses to the discharge of our curse not only from among gentlefolks, our own kind, but from the very scum and riffraff who could not have approached the house itself under any other circumstances, not even from the rear" (20). That is, if she cannot focus her blame in the infinite metaphysical distance on a "demon" like Sutpen, or on a natural calamity like a tornado, or on an inscrutable subservient race, or on Sutpen's lower-class, wild, bad blood in Judith's face, now she cannot even be sure it will be her own prerogative to be the autonomous author and not one heteronomous subject or character of her tale of vaguely wild, violent passions. Her vaguest theory, that of the unaccountable curse on her kind, now seems vulnerable to the unpredictable, potentially disrespectful (false) witness of this social riffraff whom she is otherwise accustomed to exclude absolutely from her consideration, even from her physical presence, a class which she will acknowledge here as one part of her Southern society (its inessential, insubstantial "scum"), but certainly not as a voice (like hers) authorized to speak of that society. As differences between the idealized society of the South and its outsiders come to seem like racial, class, and gender (social) differences among its insiders, or even like psychological ambivalences within the (real) insiders, and as the South's inside thus becomes defined ever more narrowly and exclusively as an ironic knowledge of those differences within, with even that epistemologically privileged position of ironic knowledge now feeling threatened, the gesture of exclusion on which such definitions of the South depend becomes increasingly obvious, as in the implied image above of the barred door to the house, an image to be repeated throughout the novel as the extreme limit of irony's spectral privilege in its (here cornered) retreat from its outside.

Rosa stages this public discharge of the curse in the scene when Judith's mother finds her watching one of Sutpen's "raree shows" in the stable. Rosa imagines Ellen Sutpen's having tried to accept her husband's unseemly involvement in these spectacles of "wild" black men "fighting not like white men fight, with rules and weapons, but as negroes fight to hurt one another quick and bad"; she can accept Sutpen's involvement in that savagery, in other words, to the extent of his being its white director and host to its spectators. She can rationalize and accept this much, "as though there is a breathing-point in outrage where you can accept it almost with gratitude since you can say to yourself, *Thank God this is all; at least I now know all of it*" (20). But this simple projection by Ellen of Sutpen's and other white men's violence onto black men, together with the ironic reassurance that Sutpen is only limitedly involved, is being represented here by the more ironic Rosa as another innocence that is bound to be overwhelmed when Ellen enters the barn to discover "not the two black beasts she had expected to see but instead a white one and a black one, both naked to the waist and gouging at one another's eyes as if their skins should not only have been the same color, but should have been covered with fur too," and especially when she recognizes this shockingly bestial white man as not just any riffraff but "her husband and the father of her children" (20–21). Apparently Rosa, if not Ellen, can even accept with a measure of irony this compromising of white and of human dignity, as she has accepted the South's dishonorable defenders and as she can understand these white spectators' view of this spectacle: as the evening's "grand finale . . . toward the retention of supremacy, domination" (21). The fight risks but effectively thereby naturalizes white supremacy in the carefully circumscribed arena of lower-class sport and spectacle, as though the genteel whites' now (mythically) refined social and economic domination of blacks were shown here to be founded on a natural, physical white superiority.

But if Rosa can excuse such behavior from "trash" like Sutpen, this class distinction is less reassuring for Henry, Sutpen's son, who "plunge[s] out from among the negroes who had been holding him, screaming and vomiting" (21). Though Henry is attempting one more "innocent" projection of absolute difference between himself and all this lower-class violence and strictly forbidden, here vaguely eroticized contact with blacks, his convulsive violence suggests he feels the difference all too deeply (if still vaguely) within himself (even physically within himself). Ellen tells Sutpen she will make herself try to understand Sutpen's bringing Henry to see this—since Henry as a man might be expected to resort to unseemly violence when forced by violent external necessities and outsiders—but Ellen draws the line at her (fourteen-year-old) "baby girl," as Sutpen apparently does too, both reserving to the last this sacred calf of female purity. When Rosa's tale and the chapter break off at the sight of "two Sutpen faces this time—once on Judith and once on the negro girl beside her—looking down through the square entrance to the loft" (22), the break in the text suggests a kind of unspeakable horror. This is Rosa's irony's last attempt here, if it cannot clearly distinguish corruption from its victim, at least to *manage* or control its least focused, blankest representation—the thorough corruption (by Sutpen) of even the mythically most pure—by representing Judith's purity as inextricably, hopelessly, unspeakably lost, compromised here by Sutpen's face as traced not only in Judith's own face but also in the face of "the negro girl beside her," with the implication of miscegenation and hopelessly impure, mixed "blood."

The hint of Rosa's irony's failure, however, is to be found here in the lack of horror on Judith's own face. Here as in the other, preceding scenes of her "corruption," that lack of horror is an ambiguous sign of either her being thoroughly corrupted (as Rosa and Ellen think with a horror on her behalf) or, more likely, of her feeling and acknowledging — without violence, rather with an ambivalence of fear and attraction — that she and her black half sister Clytie share already impurities, ambivalences, connections, even loves in their society, in their families, and in themselves, impurities and loves (in Judith especially) which Henry will still much later be trying violently (and revealingly) to expel. Pushed to its limit, the dialectic of irony's rationalizations and repetitions reverts to the violent exclusions of innocence; the ironic "synthesis" of purity with a mediating but still subordinate impurity still requires a strenuous hierarchy. This supposed solution, in other words, is an unstable compound; it takes account of the other not as different and differing, but rather as its own hypostatized opposite. Irony's supposedly most realistic, demystified, nonideological, noninnocent confrontation with the reality of loss ends by rejecting that reality as an indigestible horror; it projects its own emotional reaction (named only as "vomit") onto whatever or whoever it is that this violent repression and projection of difference serves to exclude.[4]

With the repeated failures of Rosa's more nostalgic projections of absolute, Manichean difference between the demon and his once innocent victims, she has resorted increasingly to more ironic disentanglements of herself and her perspective from the compromising differences appearing within the South, even within her family now, though not yet (at this point in her story) within herself or her irony. More directly involved in the event than Rosa at this point and less successful at keeping an ironic spectator's or narrator's distance, Henry has reacted with a convulsive, nauseated violence that will reflect increasingly on an irony which tries to distance itself from its own motivation in overwhelming, indigestible surprise. Most cautiously, transcendently ironic in the novel's second chapter are the hind-sighted narrative voices of Quentin's barracks full of ghosts (the remembered voice of local legend) and then of Mr. Compson (Quentin's father), narrators who are even less directly involved than Rosa in the events they describe, yet whose ironic repetitions of these events follow a similar dialectic of irony's serial failures and retreats to higher ground. Ellen figures here again as the naively innocent victim to offset other voices of irony, Ellen's aunt and father are Ellen's nearest allies (more cautiously removed from the event than she but not so safely removed as others), and the onlooking town attempts repeatedly, convulsively, to regurgitate some-

4. See Derrida's "Economimesis" on vomit as the "irrepresentable and unnameable, the absolute other of the system" (22), which is "interested in determining the other as *its* other, that is, as literally disgusting" (25).

thing they repeatedly find too late they have swallowed, something they attempt to focus and identify as Thomas Sutpen.

Rosa's supposedly primal scene of Sutpen's whirlwind approach to the church in chapter 1 appears now in chapter 2 to be itself a repetition in a legendary series extending back at least as far as the scene remembered here of Sutpen's first arrival in Jefferson, a scene constructed again, like Rosa's, as a kind of antidote or alibi, focusing and managing through representation and repetition the town's more thorough subsequent and perhaps prior involvement with everything Sutpen is made here to represent. Sutpen is presented in sharp contrast with another idyllic Sunday morning churchgoing scene of mostly ladies, children, and a few men who are all innocent, unprepared, and somewhat melodramatically surprised at his interruption:

> when the other men sitting with their feet on the railing of the
> Holston House gallery looked up, . . . there the stranger was. He
> was already halfway across the Square when they saw him . . . man
> and beast looking as though they had been created out of thin air
> and set down in the bright summer sabbath sunrise . . . face and
> horse that none of them had ever seen before, name that none of
> them had ever heard, and origin and purpose which some of them
> were never to learn. (23–24)

Unable to place him morally, socially, or even to see him physically approach before he is already among them, for the next few weeks they can only repeat the stranger's name "in steady strophe and antistrophe: *Sutpen. Sutpen. Sutpen. Sutpen*" (24). In the same way that the description above chafes at the limits of their ability to fix his place securely in their social system, this repetition rather oddly suggests that within their system of knowing and naming is a more general insecurity which they are already trying to recall and focus in this scene of Sutpen's first arrival, though even the moment of his intrusion seems elusive: when he arrived, he was already there. They later learn of his land acquisition with a similarly exonerating but also increasingly disturbing unreadiness: "even that knowledge came too late." He has already left again by the time they hear of the deal, to return again, "again without warning," bringing his soon legendary "wild negroes" with their reassuringly different and relatively uncivilized but also menacingly unplaced and unknown "dark and fatal tongue" (26, 27). However, as the men of the town gradually go out to watch Sutpen and his slaves work and later to hunt with them, these exaggeratedly frightful, obviously ambivalent legends of advancing demonic surprises from without change to less immediately threatening notions of Sutpen's life as a marginalized "masculine solitude" (30). Thus he is fixed more securely within the society now but at a certain (subordinate) social distance, until eventually in almost five years "the town now believed that it knew him" (31). The town's women, more protected but also less flattered by such a marginalization, supposedly know better than the men that he will eventually want a wife (for respectability), but they are no less imprudently sure than the men of his subordinate social place and of the more respectable women's invulnerability to his advances.

At this point, then, the ironic scenario of surprise almost compulsively repeats itself: "again on Sunday morning and again without warning, the town saw him cross the square . . . and enter the Methodist church" (31). When they realize his sights are set on Mr. Coldfield, "the assurance of the women became one with the men's surprise, and then even more than that: amazement." The women are surprised not by his courtship but by his choice of families:

> they watched in shocked amazement while he laid deliberate siege to the one man in the town with whom [they would have thought] he could have had nothing in common, . . . a man with a name for absolute and undeviating and even Puritan uprightness in a country and time of lawless opportunity, who neither drank nor gambled nor even hunted. (32)

This opposition between Coldfield's private moral virtues and the "lawless opportunity" of the country and time as represented by Sutpen's unknown past and his position as host to the town's drinking, gambling, and hunting on the town's outskirts is precisely the social distinction Sutpen threatens to blur, that between the wealth and power of a class legitimated by the private moral virtues of someone like Coldfield, and the wealth and power illegitimated by the private "immorality" of someone like Sutpen. This opposition is precisely the surest means the town has found for distancing and excluding someone like Sutpen and his violent, lawless opportunism from their Sunday-best image of their own uprightness and respectability, a class exclusion otherwise challenged especially by Sutpen's wealth. So they insist he can have "nothing in common, *least of all* money," with a man like Coldfield, "a man who obviously could do nothing under the sun for him save give him credit at a little crossroads store or cast a vote in his favor if he should ever seek ordination as a Methodist minister" (32, my emphasis). When Sutpen turns this Coldfield "credit" of supposedly some moral but no material benefit into four wagonloads of lavish furnishings for his plantation, he shows that moral credit to be not wealth and power's transcendence but its reproductive power and another of its legitimating ideological alibis, disguises, and effective supports. Thus Sutpen seems again to have uncannily returned to threaten the town as "in a sense a public enemy," as the more ironic Mr. Compson now explains, because of "the town's realization that he was getting it involved with himself" (33).

Exactly what the town somewhat anxiously "realizes" (or is frightened) that it is getting involved in is left quite unclear, except as something they know nothing about, a formulation serving both their innocence and Compson's irony. Mr. Compson ironically rules out as an objection (as the town has) Sutpen's previous cargo, "the *simple* wagonload of wild niggers," and also the land deal: "Heretofore, until that Sunday when he came to church, if he had misused or injured anybody, it was *only* old Ikkemotubbe, from whom he got his land—a matter between his conscience and Uncle Sam and God," not a matter, that is, between him and Ikkemotubbe (33, my emphases). But this *lawful* opportunism toward blacks and Native Americans, on which the entire American capitalist economy depends for its initial productive forces in labor and land (Rogin 166–69, cited by Porter, *Seeing* 233), has now needed to be more or less conspicuously acknowledged, rationalized, and legalized by the white townspeople and Compson in order to distinguish it from what the town wants to imagine as the altogether different, presumably "lawless opportunity," the "felony," in which Sutpen is now involving Coldfield and the town. In the vocabulary of deconstruction, their self-image, their self-possession, their authorization for their "property" here reveals within itself traces of their self-constituting act of deriving and differentiating their own lawful opportunity from lawless opportunism, traces which they have attempted repeatedly to oppose absolutely as an outside—or dialectically to appropriate, marginalize, or subordinate as an (outer or lower) inside.

Repeating that act of differentiation more luridly than before, some of the townspeople imagine Sutpen getting his wealth by means of "something performed in the lurking dark of a muddy [steamboat] landing and with a knife from behind" (33). This scenario focuses his illegitimacy in one frightful felony as opposed to their own blind innocence; it exonerates them but also suggests a growing anxiety about their inability to focus their fear. The danger seems now not out there before them in the Sunday morning light (as in a carriage approaching the town church or a man riding into the square) but lurking behind them somewhere in the dark, as for example in the blind spots of their own opportunism which they have here repressed from their own consciousness by condensing and projecting it onto Sutpen.

In short, they continue to fail to understand Sutpen because of this very sense of their own surprise which their stories and Compson's repetitions of those stories here continue to dwell upon, theirs mostly for the

sake of exonerating them and focusing their fright, Compson's mostly for
the sake of showing up their innocence as relatively naive and unprepared
for surprise next to his irony and anxiety about a more generalized
unknown. In both cases, dwelling upon the surprise avoids, either by con-
densation or by generalizing displacement, what it is these townspeople
see in Sutpen that they do not want to see among or within themselves,
and Compson's irony at his forebears' surprise is less a critical rethinking
than a repetition of their tradition of social exclusion. Thus their attending to their surprise, their fever, prevents their understanding Sutpen, but
also prevents their understanding their own disease, even when, or rather
especially when, someone like Sutpen shows them the disease in action,
both in his treatment (like theirs) of other races and in his potentially similar
treatment of the town's respectable class. The disease consists in their denying their own emotional, social, and economic ambivalence toward and
involvement with others by representing those others either as immoral
intruders as opposed to the subjects' moral innocence and social purity,
or as innocent (ignorant) dupes as opposed to the subject's coolly distant
irony. The other in either case is the object of a self-purifying exclusion,
by either a moralizing or a "knowing" insider, the other here representing
only differences between and not yet revealing (potentially shared) differences within insiders and outsiders.

Thus when "civic virtue" (34) issues forth in a committee to stand
in seamless front against Sutpen, they meet him almost immediately already
behind them on his way into town, just as Sutpen has already demonstrated the permeability of their other virtuous front in Goodhue Coldfield.
Compson can be ironic about their being taken aback, their civic virtue
"not knowing what to do exactly" (34) in the face of Sutpen's unashamed
insubordination to their invocation of moral difference and exclusion, but
Compson's irony, if pressed, also shows its own denied complicity with
their (cognitive) innocence just as their (moral) innocence shows here and
has shown before its denied complicity with Sutpen's guilt (or actually his
more thorough, willful innocence). Compson is not rethinking the conditions of their surprise, the internal reasons for the fall of their society,
but only restaging that surprise (the better to manage its threat) from the
greater distance of his jaded cosmopolitan hindsight. In the process of repetition, his irony shows its own secret alliance with what he narrates of the
townspeople's more sluggish efforts in the thick of events to maintain their
innocence by projecting the deeply compromising opportunism of their
economy onto Sutpen.

Compson stages the clumsiness and the failure of their moral and class
distinctions even while he reserves a higher and subtler social distinction
for himself and the Compson family: Rosa has already insisted, protested,

to Quentin in chapter 1 that Sutpen "wasn't a gentleman. He wasn't even a gentleman" (9). Compson here interprets Sutpen's imitations of respectability and good breeding not as "some opposite of respectability too dark to talk about" (11, there is supposedly nothing irony is unprepared to discuss), nor in terms of any embarrassing resemblance in Sutpen's imitation, but in terms of that imitation's crucially significant imperfections, describing and dismissing Sutpen's "florid, swaggering gesture to the hat" in a parenthetical, ironic, unflorid aside to Quentin: "(yes, he was underbred. It showed like this always, your Grandfather said, in all his formal contacts with people . . .)" (34). Compson's superior, insider's irony, then, at the tardy ineptitude of the town's attempts at innocence is only his own less threatened, more carefully guarded and stabilized, but still uncritical, repetition of these former townspeople's "public opinion in an acute state of indigestion" (35): he is ironic toward their innocence always already overcome or upset, but he thereby maintains and protects (interrupts the disinterested attitude of his history to turn to Quentin to insist upon) his own investment in a more restricted, vaguely aestheticized Southern composure and decorum. Like the Southern Agrarians turned New Critics with whom he shares his taste for irony, Compson is willing to sacrifice a full-blown feudal social ideal if he can maintain its defining gestures of purity and exclusion in an ironically restricted aesthetic sphere that is also effectively (if narrowly) social. Sutpen may know when and how to dance, that is, much to the townspeople's naive surprise, as Compson explains, but do be sure to notice carefully how Sutpen really doesn't follow the beat.

Having been repeatedly preempted from preventing Sutpen's reentry into the town, the committee is forced toward a more convulsive regurgitation to regain its imagined purity, now having to wait for Sutpen *outside* Coldfield's house, Sutpen himself already insinuated *inside* this community stronghold of rectitude. In a further unsettling of their self-possession, they must discover too late as usual, after they have arrested him, that he has been inside the Coldfield house getting engaged there to Coldfield's daughter, as Compson points out to Quentin with his characteristically retrospective sense of dramatic irony. They discover this engagement only when Mr. Coldfield and General Compson follow them to the jail to sign Sutpen's bond, as Compson imagines Sutpen himself remembering with his own irony at "civic virtue's" surprise:

> public opinion which at some moment during the past five preceding years had swallowed him even though he never had quite ever lain quiet on its stomach, had performed one of mankind's natural and violent and inexplicable voltefaces and regurgitated him. And . . .
> two of the citizens who should have made two of the teeth in the

outraged jaw served instead as props to hold the jaw open and
impotent while he walked out of it unharmed. (39–40)

This figure represents both public opinion's absolute rejection of Sutpen
out of its stomach (a violent rejection but authorized as natural) and also
its attempt then to recontain and redigest this elusive threat through the
more rationalized violence of exercising its legal teeth, that is, by incar-
cerating Sutpen in the simplifying representation of him as lawless criminal.
Thus Rosa in chapter 1 has also attempted an absolute opposition and
distance between the South and Sutpen, then she and Compson have
variously rationalized that failing distance as a difference perhaps within
the South, but a still hierarchical, stabilized difference not within her own,
Compson's own, or the South's own, essential self.
   While Compson is mildly ironic toward the townspeople's squeamish
but ineffectual attempts to keep Sutpen at a safe distance from their best
images of themselves, his own distress at Sutpen's insinuation into this
society's moral, domestic, and now sexual purity is expressed in the cynicism and violence of his irony toward Ellen Coldfield, whom he and the
town also finally abandon here to save themselves, much as Rosa has
before. Compson introduces Ellen's wedding scene as a foregone repetition
of a now familiar scene of intrusion and surprise, set at virtually the same
time and place as others in this series—"almost five years to the day from
that Sunday morning when he rode into town on the roan horse" and "in
the same Methodist church where he saw Ellen for the first time" (37).
Like a man feeling betrayed by his "own" wife, Compson reacts to the
apparent impurity and defection of one of his society's young ladies with
a bitter misogyny toward brides, the unmarried, and married women alike
(a misogyny familiar from *The Sound and the Fury* but here more critically represented by Faulkner). Compson sets Ellen up for her particularly
cruel surprise by imagining her in her prenuptial hopes as the duped fool
of her spinster aunt's and other women's idealizing and falsifying nostalgia.
She resembles women who married without ceremony and later wanted
a divorce, who perhaps

> still have in their minds even yet the image of themselves walking to
> music and turning heads, in all the symbolical trappings and circum-
> stances of ceremonial surrender of that which they no longer possess?
> and why not, since to them the actual and authentic surrender can
> only be (and have been) a ceremony like the breaking of a banknote
> to buy a ticket for the train. (37)

Projecting his own bitterness onto these married women, Compson regards
Ellen's coming "surrender" to Sutpen as a loss of a possession. There is no

question here of possible love, relation, or desire, except of the most impersonal, sordid kind; her personal "surrender" is reduced and generalized,
in the banknote analogy, to a kind of "general equivalent" of loss. Just
as the town has looked to the likes of Ellen's family for an image of moral
purity with which to identify and redeem themselves in their uneasily
growing sense of involvement with Sutpen, Ellen supposedly looks here
to the social ritual of a well-attended wedding to redeem her personal compromise and loss, presumably by elevating that loss to the universal, eternal
(repetitive) order of ceremonial ritual, in which her personal loss would
be magically and utterly subsumed. The invocation of myth and ritual
in modernist literature, however, is a private, literary nostalgia almost
always accompanied, as it is here, by an irony at its absence or impotence
in more public spheres. Ellen will need her society's participation to make
this ceremony work, and she is allowed to believe she has that social sanction for only a brief scene of cruel irony. Compson invites Quentin to share
the joke as he imagines Ellen, her aunt, her father, and Sutpen approaching
the church expecting first no guests but seeing after all that "the street before
the church was lined with carriages and buggies, though only Sutpen and
possibly Mr. Coldfield remarked that instead of being drawn up before
the door and empty, they were halted across the street and still occupied"
(43). That is, the townspeople, in irony's specular relation toward her
surprise, attempt to resolve their ambivalence about Sutpen's entry into
the bosom of their society by assuming the role of detached, invisible spectators on the entire scene, their internal divisions mirrored, unified, and
flattened out there in the scene before them.

Next in a series of attitudes toward the wedding which lead toward
Compson's own is that of Ellen's aunt, the other butt of Compson's ironic
joke, who is also imagined as counting on the town's ceremonial blessings
on the marriage, even though she is less directly involved herself. Compson
can suppose more easily in her case than in Ellen's that she feels acutely
this marriage's particular need for social sanction, since the aunt has been
herself one of many Jefferson women who have never forgiven Sutpen for
having no known past. She supposedly sees in the idea of a big wedding her
"one chance . . . to justify the action of her brother in getting him out of jail
and her own position as having apparently sanctioned and permitted the
wedding which in reality she could not have prevented" (40). Her later
elopement with a mule trader (another man without a known past) will cast
complicating doubts on this notion that she only apparently sanctioned this
marriage which she would have prevented if she could, that she was wholly
without even an ambivalent attraction to Sutpen. But whether it is a case of
her stoic defeat and forced acceptance, as Compson maintains, or actually
of her safely vicarious indulgence in ambivalence and desire, Compson can
well imagine her repairing that defeat (or imaginative indulgence) by repeat-

ing and staging her own defeat at others' expense. By assuming the relatively ironic, here masculine role of specular detachment toward *their*
denied, suspected feminine desire, she forces them to accept publicly as she
has had to (or anyway has) both Sutpen and the wedding; she acts as
though she "were now bent, no longer on merely thrusting Sutpen down
the town's throat, but thrusting the wedding itself" (42).

In the series of metaphors here for regurgitation, her strategy is a kind
of displaced bulimia, a social multiplication and repetition of self-disgust
in other throats, a kind of digestive power in numbers. Susan Bordo
describes "one striking difference between the abstinent anorexic and the
bulimic anorexic: In the binge and purge cycle, the [culturally defined,
archetypal] hungering female self refuses to be annihilated, is in constant
protest (to the great horror, of course, of the male self who must negate
every indulgence with a cleansing purge)" (100 n. 90). Like the bulimic,
Ellen's aunt can manage her personal ambivalence (and her society's
ambivalence) toward Sutpen by allying herself temporarily with Ellen, then
trying to pull away with a kind of smug, hypocritical disgust at Ellen's
and the town's accepting what she herself on another level will still never
finally digest, accept, or even forgive.

It is a strategy, however, which the town heaves up not just in the
aunt's face, but also all over Ellen, since the town is positioned at one
more remove from the event. As the aunt and Ellen enter the church for
the wedding still suspecting nothing is wrong, the mob of uninvited
"riffraff" outside is "quiet yet, perhaps out of respect for the church" (43).
But if they still respect the physical church, they gag on the wedding inside,
and Ellen walks "out of the church and so into it, without any warning
whatever," into the thrown "dirt, filth, whatever it was," the "clods of
dirt and vegetable refuse" with which the crowd ushers the couple away
from the church, again trying to project this unknown and unnamed filth
("whatever it was") from out of their midst (43, 44). Still more removed
from the wedding, even from the violence of the mob's cleansing purge,
are the invited guests who sit watching from the carriage across the street,
but whom Compson recognizes as present "in the persons of" this uninvited violent mob (39). They have distanced themselves as though personally uninvolved in this "Roman holiday" of a wedding, but they have
come to be reassured by seeing Sutpen getting not themselves but the
Coldfields and especially Ellen "involved with himself" (44, 33). They have
in effect ironically withheld the mythic sanction on Ellen's wedding for
which Compson says she (naively) wished, but they have not thereby
escaped a mythic role for that of the realistic, disinterested observer. In
denying their social support to Ellen, to the Coldfields, and to Sutpen on
this occasion of their highly uncertain, risky emotional commitment to

one another, the townspeople are abandoning the Coldfields to save themselves, acting a role whose analogue in myth might be the violent sacrifice of a virgin to a social menace.

Compson grants that Sutpen himself would also have liked the town's ceremonial blessings on his marriage, but Sutpen (perhaps as a man) supposedly takes those blessings less naively for granted, he being more "watchful" than either the aunt or Ellen about "measuring and weighing event against eventuality" (41). He is also represented here as taking the marriage ceremony itself less seriously or superstitiously than the townspeople who make a point of staying (slightly) away. He earns here Compson's qualified respect for his longer, higher view of these events in the light of "eventuality" even if that relatively longer view still seems to Compson ignobly practical and ambitious. Sutpen calmly foresees the town's reaction to the aunt's attempt to thrust the wedding down its throat, its readiness to try as it has quite recently before both to vomit him (and its troubled relation to him) and also then to use its teeth if it sees a legitimate, legal (rationalized) excuse: "(there were doubtless pistols in the crowd; certainly knives: the negro would not have lived ten seconds if he had sprung)" (44). But Sutpen is willing to weather and try to control this public outburst if only, as Compson says, for the sake of "the two names, the stainless wife and the unimpeachable father-in-law, on the license, the patent" (39). With regard to the license, Compson of course minimizes the lesson of Coldfield's credit, the actual power exercised by such symbols of social legitimation, with or without the moral conduct, "known past," or preexisting social goodwill on which those symbols of legitimation are supposedly based. Compson stresses instead Sutpen's almost literal faith and confidence in these symbols' apparently magical, but essentially rather hollow, merely practical usefulness, allowing Sutpen to look beyond present circumstances, but only toward what Compson sees as an uncivilized "ambition":

> compromising with his dream and his ambition like you must with
> the horse which you take across country, over timber, which you
> control only through your ability to keep the animal from realizing
> that actually you cannot, that actually it is the stronger. (41)

Sutpen may go far in the social hierarchy, that is, by skillfully weighing event against eventuality, conjuring with social symbols like the license, but this success is only a kind of trick: Compson knows better that "actually" the social position and approval Sutpen seeks is by nature beyond his manipulation and control. This suggests a tragic view of Sutpen on Compson's part which grants Sutpen his heroism and also reaffirms (in

Compson's own social interest) the "actually" unchallengeable and natural
order of things.

Ellen's wedding figures in this chapter as another instance of this
society's relations with what it defines as its outside, an outsider who
threatens to come inside, and Compson (here again like the Agrarians
turned New Critics) is describing a series of postures toward that ceremony
of personal and social initiation and union which suggest a hierarchy of
diminishing social expectations, a diminishing faith in the myth of either
a pure or a harmonious society: Compson's Ellen naively wants the "music
and turning heads" and "all the symbolical trappings" of a fancy wedding
automatically accompanied by the social approval and support those
trappings symbolize (37); her aunt wants only the physical social presence
at that wedding, forced if necessary; Sutpen will settle for even less than
the aunt, merely that the names be put on the license with or without the
ceremony, or even in the face and teeth of social objection. Although this
series pretends to temper Ellen's innocence with an increasingly ironic and
realistic sense of this society's impurities and internal divisions and contradictions, still, within this series of ironies, each party is capable only
of oppositional or patronizing contrast between its own vision and the
surprise and disappointment of the others. That is, any intimation of its
own ambiguous position not at the end of but within a series, ironically
superior toward some but innocently inferior to others, is precluded.

For example, in forcing Sutpen and the wedding on the town, the
aunt hopes to shift dramatically onto them her own apparent (and perhaps
imagined) sanctioning of what she in her purer self, smugly, privately,
ironically, "really," will never either sanction or forgive—only, she ends
up here more as the "innocently" observed than as the ironic observer.
Likewise, in withholding their presence and abandoning the Coldfields
and Ellen to the mob and the menacing beast, the town's "gentlefolk"
attempt to project their own ambivalent relations with Sutpen onto the
Coldfields, and their cruelty onto their more violent, marginalized inferiors—only, Sutpen, Coldfield, and Compson recognize these spectators'
interest in, even their representation in, the purging action of the mob,
and Sutpen is represented here as being all too well prepared for the entire
scene to serve as another butt to their spectator's irony. Thus too when
Sutpen seems to submit to the town's expression of social disgust, Compson
imagines Sutpen skillfully managing their outburst as he would the predictable unruliness of a horse—only, Sutpen's dream of continuing to control this society, Compson insists, is "actually" beyond his grasp.

And Mr. Coldfield here appears to expect from the wedding itself
less than any of these, never wanting a big wedding at all but only to use
the church "exactly as he would have used a cotton gin in which he con-

sidered himself to have incurred either interest or responsibility" (38). But in Coldfield's case this limited interest in the worldly, social business of the wedding, as in the physical or institutional church, serves to protect his greater stake in a certain "spiritual solvency," a position of more transcendent eventuality than Sutpen's, but no less vulnerable to Compson's superior irony. It is a position to which Coldfield has retreated before in order to attempt to purify himself of his involvement with Sutpen in business, in "that affair which, when it reached a point where his conscience refused to sanction it, he had withdrawn from and let Sutpen take all the profit, refusing even to allow Sutpen to reimburse him for the loss which, in withdrawing, he had suffered" (38). In permitting his daughter now "to marry this man of whose actions his conscience did not approve" (38–39), Coldfield is acting in a way Compson cannot explain except as a narrowed dedication to an unworldly spiritual solvency, placed not necessarily above the world but in retreat away from the world which Compson's more disinterested irony more bravely surveys. This process of withdrawal and retreat will eventually take Coldfield to his attic, where he will fast to death in an abstinent anorexia of self-denial and purification that takes a few steps farther his sister's more obviously ambivalent bulimia.

Less directly involved in the event than Coldfield and much more easily purified by irony is of course Compson, who describes this series of postures toward the wedding from his superior position of not moral or spiritual purity but the purity of being always undeceived and unsurprised by the social impurity and disharmony suggested by the wedding. Compson's own higher purity is not that of foolish faith in rituals, social ascension, or spiritual solvency, for he has no faith of any kind but an ironic knowledge of that impurity as if bravely without illusion. If he has acknowledged certain impurities in this society, however, he has thereby preserved the purity of his own social position in irony, and preserves as well an entire social hierarchy, though it is a hierarchy based now on people's relative preparedness for their ironic, "realistic" disillusionment. Ellen supposedly believes defenselessly in a nostalgic myth of social purity; her aunt and the town are more wary of getting soiled themselves; Sutpen is prepared to turn a temporary soiling to his longer-term social advantage; Coldfield is prepared to forsake his social hopes altogether to save the purity of his conscience; and Compson can more calmly acknowledge the contradiction between his society's conscience and the worldly ways of its power, since he was always already prepared to expect no better from that society: there remains no need for him to recoil and refuse the various profits of his own social ascendancy.

He ends the chapter by pointing to the townspeople's continuing inconsistency and Ellen's ongoing self-deception, all ironically (to Comp-

son) involved with Sutpen more than they themselves realize or admit.
The same townspeople who came to watch the "Roman holiday" wedding
return now to Sutpen's Hundred, the women "to call and (the men) to
hunt his game and eat his food again and on occasion gathering at night
in his stable while he matched two of his wild negroes against one another
as men match game cocks or perhaps even entered the ring himself" (44–45).
Compson suggests these shows are more obviously now themselves sadistic
Roman holidays aimed "toward the retention of supremacy, domination"
(21), on the part of spectators who enjoy seeing the slaves and Sutpen
assume all the pain, violence, risk, and social compromise so that they
themselves can take their profit in reassured supremacy over the blacks
and over Sutpen as well. Compson's own ambivalence and threatened sense
of social purity are here still masked, however, by the ironic distance
between himself and the entire scene of inconsistency he constructs, by
the knowing preparedness with which he faces that outside without facing
his kinship with that outside, or facing parts of himself that are only projected onto that outside.

So too in his closing portrait of Ellen: Sutpen "did not forget that
night [of the wedding], even though Ellen, I think, did, since she washed
it out of her remembering with tears. Yes, she was weeping again now;
it did, indeed, rain on that marriage" (45). Compson has purportedly
remembered, as Sutpen did, the events which he thinks Ellen as pure, weeping woman victim could not have stood to remember. But this opposition
of her devastation and high-minded repression as against Compson's own
calm, hindsighted remembering makes him seem to know much more than
he does, makes him seem to share in the knowledge both of what she experienced and repressed, and also of what Sutpen experienced and remembered, whereas for the most part Compson has actually dramatized their
greater and lesser surprises and disappointments in the event only for the
sake of the flattering contrast with his own ironic, retrospective unsurprise. While he has acknowledged "impurities" within his society reaching
higher than some would have foreseen, Compson has not acknowledged
the failure of this society (a failure reaching even into his own narration)
to deal with that outside except by more or less violent withdrawals into
increasingly narrow, asocial positions of irony toward others' surprise.
The severely narrow limits of such a narrative's ironic stagings and of the
understanding it offers of other characters and of complicated eventuali-
ties will become even clearer, even to Compson himself, as his narration
continues in the novel's next two chapters (the last two of his narration).

The logic and momentum of this series of collapsing social purities
and expectations in the cases of Ellen, her aunt, the town, Sutpen, and

Coldfield in chapter 2 seem at the beginning of chapter 3 to have called into question for Quentin the motivations not yet of Quentin's own or his father's narrative irony but of the novel's next most removed, ironic perspective so far, that of Rosa, who has acknowledged fissures of difference and impurity reaching far into her society, although she still maintains absolute, Manichean distinctions between herself and the demon Sutpen. Chapter 3 thus consists of Compson's extended response to Quentin's opening query: "If [Sutpen] threw Miss Rosa over, I wouldn't think she would want to tell anybody about it" (59). This is precisely the kind of question that provoked Freud's *Beyond the Pleasure Principle.* Why would a child want to play at being left? Why do people have and continue to have unpleasant dreams? Why are Rosa and so many others (including Compson and Quentin himself) still talking about someone with whom they profess to have so little in common? Quentin has already suggested part of Freud's explanation. Rosa's hating Sutpen for forty-three years largely avoids any renewed surprise by Sutpen, much as the town has attempted to keep its own safe distance from Sutpen through repeated regurgitations and repeated returns to the scenes of others' (the mob's, Henry's) nausea.

These more frightful repetitions may indeed somewhat avoid further surprise, by representing the threat "out there" as a particular, external trauma. But both the convulsive violence and the continuation of such representations of absolute difference (from the demon) and absolute disgust (at the vomit) have begun to seem like repetitions not so much of a pure *difference* as of an always unsuccessful act of projection and *differentiation,* signs of a *purity* and *identity* founded on continual *purifications* of oneself and *identifications* of trauma as Thomas Sutpen. This raises questions such as Quentin's about why Rosa reopens her wound now long after this particular man is dead. Her apparent compulsion suggests that all such representations have unsatisfactorily analyzed and accounted for just what it is that evidently still surprises Rosa, namely, the internal trauma of Rosa's own prior and continuing emotional involvement with Sutpen and much that he represents. Once such trauma becomes thus recognized as at least partly internal in origin, according to Freud's further explanation, it is most often managed not through fright but through a generalized anxiety, or through a generalized disinvestment or decathexis of emotion as in melancholia (or irony). Such psychological and social strategies of "managing" trauma imply their own characteristic obfuscations of its specific origins and consequences.

Beginning his response with an already knowing "Ah," Compson will attempt in this chapter to salvage for Rosa (and implicitly for himself) a more thoroughly ironic perspective on her involvement with Sutpen which will admit some of her (their) increasingly undeniable interest and involvement, but only in order to contain better the force and significance of that involvement. Rosa would want to tell about the business with Sutpen, that is, so that Quentin would not get the wrong idea that Sutpen had *really* thrown her over. As Compson narrates here the ongoing collapse of social, personal distance between Sutpen and Rosa toward the point of her eventually agreeing to marry him, Compson will also attempt to position himself at one more ironic remove from her (their) more anxious involvement, he presiding from his own supposedly more disinterested (actually cautiously decathected, melancholic) narrative irony.

To fortify Rosa's more anxious irony, Compson first resituates it now not as a strategy of retreat, secondary to her nostalgia and fright, but as a prior and original attitude to which Rosa was bound to return, a kind of inalienable birthright for someone who was born "at the price of her mother's life and [who was] never to be permitted to forget it" (46). As an explanation for Rosa's trauma, this one is only slightly less generalized and (neutrally, scientifically) biologistic than Freud's theoretical fiction of the unrepresentable birth trauma. It is an explanation that imbues Rosa's entire life with an ironic judgment either against herself or against the (male) sexuality that made her life possible only through her mother's death. Rosa's life thus seems "not only a living and walking reproach to her father, but a breathing indictment ubiquitous and even transferable of the entire male principle" (46–47). Here it is Rosa's aunt, in revenge for "the fiasco of Ellen's wedding," whom Compson blames for raising Rosa to focus that originally generalized indictment of the entire male principle too narrowly on Sutpen, as "the man who had entered hers and her family's life before she was born with the abruptness of a tornado, done irrevocable and incalculable damage, and gone on" (47).

Compson calls satiric attention to how this focusing demonization depends on a projection of melodramatic scenarios of innocence over-whelmed by evil, scenes that now quite obviously "mask" other much more complex realities. Thus Rosa learns that Ellen is "a woman who had vanished not only out of the family and the house but out of life too, into an edifice like Bluebeard's and there transmogrified into a mask looking back with passive and hopeless grief upon the irrevocable world" (47). Rosa's childhood view of Sutpen is another such unsophisticated, over-simplifying mask:

> like the mask in Greek tragedy interchangeable not only from scene
> to scene but from actor to actor and behind which the events and
> occasions took place without chronology or sequence and leaving her
> actually incapable of saying how many separate times she had seen

him for the reason that, waking or sleeping, the aunt had taught her
to see nothing else. (49)

The proof of such demonizations' impotence is that in Rosa's girlhood
her and the aunt's "grim sorties" against this mask have no effect on Sutpen
himself, who "did not even know that he was an embattled foe," any more
than he later knows he is "second party to an armistice" (50, 49, 51). As
Quentin's opening question suggests, this innocent's strategy of painting
a demon's face on Sutpen cannot possibly hope to survive the upcoming
evidence of her much greater emotional involvement with Sutpen in that
"future catastrophe in which the ogre-face of her childhood would
apparently vanish so completely that she would agree to marry the late
owner of it" (52).

Instead of analyzing the man behind the mask, however, Compson
only imagines a much larger, more vaguely defined mask, assuming that
these naive fantasies of Manichean battle and retribution will give place
again to Rosa's birthright irony. That more cautious irony will expect an
inevitable, ubiquitous defeat, and will rename and redeem such defeat as
"sacrifice." Compson imagines her as hoping to supply at least an ironic
narrative accounting of that self-sacrifice, to see herself (or at least to be
seen), "if not in herself [as] an active instrument [of retribution] strong
enough to cope with [Sutpen], at least as a kind of passive symbol of
inescapable reminding to rise bloodless and without dimension from the
sacrificial stone of the marriage-bed" (48). If she cannot have victory, then
she will accept a knowing defeat, or (less ambivalently) a defeat to be
known by someone else more detached than she. Compson imagines her,
that is, as a bloodless, flattened symbol, self-consuming before Compson's
and now Quentin's eyes much as a lyric poem would under the gaze of
its New Critical reader, not "scientifically" reporting, "polemically" questioning or criticizing anything (as nonliterary, constative symbols might),
but "reminding" readers of what they always already know: that Rosa
may show herself anxiously well prepared for sacrifice, but they can more
safely both survey and survive this sacrificial, self-referential spectacle.

As Rosa's social distance from impurity and surprise apparently collapses in her unforced agreement to marry with it, Compson is attempting
to construct for her an irony self-protective enough to guard against having
the simplifying masks of ogre and victim vanish into the less distinct
medium of air. Whereas in her girlhood she was relieved when she did
not "have to go out there and breathe the same air which [Sutpen]
breathed" (50), Compson imagines her eventually learning to feel this same
disgust more anxiously and inescapably toward breathing and life in
general:

cloistered now by deliberate choice and still in the throes of enforced apprenticeship to, rather than voluntary or even acquiescent participation in, breathing—this bound maidservant to flesh and blood waiting even now to escape it by writing a schoolgirl's poetry about the also-dead. (51)

Earlier instances of self-purifying regurgitations and anorexias have physically located "out there" and identified impurities (or others) as *vomit,* a name for the subject's own expression of supposedly constitutional and natural disgust. Compson is describing now the still more unsettling, anxious experience of an odor from which one can escape neither physically by vomiting, isolating, or avoiding it, nor even conceptually by naming it (cf. Derrida, "Economimesis"). Rosa would in her irony perhaps be able to escape her confining immersion in the vicissitudes of breathing, flesh, and blood by naming the trauma as life itself, by writing poetry about the also-dead, venturing into a lyric expression of emotional involvement or even love only with this immediate ironic qualification that she well "knows" already that both the subject and object of this love are already as much as dead. However, as Compson distinguishes her position from other more vulnerable ones, her reservations about the greater involvement and vulnerability of others begin to seem less like representations of difference than like acts of differentiation. Her ironic reservations serve as self-protective, obfuscating alibis for her (and Compson's) deep, denied interests in other more vulnerable lives. And as their obfuscations of those other lives increasingly show through their irony, Compson feels increasingly compelled to pull back and differentiate himself from Rosa's (thereby) more vulnerable position.

Compson first differentiates Rosa most sharply, of course, from Ellen, Rosa's predecessor in her own (near) marriage to Sutpen. Although originally cast as Sutpen's helpless victim, Ellen appears now rather happily married, a situation Rosa and Compson insist on seeing as Ellen's losing all moral and social perspective on the insulting marriage of Sutpen's unknown background with that of the Coldfields, "as though she has succeeded at last in evacuating not only the puritan heritage but reality itself; had immolated outrageous husband and incomprehensible children into shades" (54). Without the qualifying irony of their puritan, genteel sense of moral and social "reality," her world seems one of unself-conscious "pure illusion" (54). On the basis of their ironic sense of this reality beneath her illusion, Compson and Rosa cast Ellen's "regal" airs as those of a "swamp-hatched butterfly," rising only briefly and deludedly out of the Sutpen mud in a crass and tasteless display: because her wealth and

happiness are socially suspicious, they are rendered more simply insubstantial and unreal (54, 55).

If Compson and Rosa have thus insistently ruled out any real similarity between Rosa and her most obvious predecessor in Ellen, their ironic
reservations about Ellen's particular position cannot, however, altogether
rule out or mask all possibilities of love and happiness on the part of the
Sutpen family, nor all interest in that family and its possibilities on the
part of Rosa. These ironies about Ellen do not prevent—in a way they
rather permit—Rosa's investing her hopes instead in the much more
vaguely delineated, also much more vaguely negated, "impenetrable dreaming" of Ellen's daughter and Rosa's virgin niece Judith, no longer a wild
"hoyden" now but "the young girl who slept waking in some suspension
so completely physical as to resemble the state before birth" (56, 55).
Defining Judith's dreaming as impenetrably virgin, and, though physical,
protected in the womb and leaving (realistic, ironic, privileged) consciousness to others, allows Compson to imagine Rosa safely "projecting upon
Judith all the abortive dreams and delusions of her own [knowingly]
doomed and frustrated youth" (55–56).

Compson can even allow Rosa to contemplate the transformation of
these purely virgin, objectless, and vicarious dreams into Ellen's fashion-
able ladies' club "fairy tale" linking Judith with the elegant stranger Charles
Bon, on the condition that that embodiment of the dream be defined ironically as Ellen's delusion and Rosa's abnegation, Ellen's delusion because
it was not to be, and Rosa's abnegation because she would have known
better than Ellen could that it could never be (and so she would never
have risked the love's embodiment herself): "The spinster [knowingly]
doomed for life at sixteen, sitting beneath this bright glitter of delusion,"
hears Ellen with "peaceful despair and relief at final and complete abnegation, now that Judith was about to immolate the frustration's vicarious
recompense in the living fairy tale" (59–60). Likewise, Rosa and Compson can appreciate the relative refinement of Bon just so long as they keep
in mind the "shadowy" background which renders that refinement
unfounded, therefore top-heavy and exaggerated: "a swaggering gallant
air in comparison with which Sutpen's pompous arrogance was clumsy
bluff and Henry actually a hobble-de-hoy" (58). It is in this same spirit
of ironic abnegation and disillusionment that Rosa tells Ellen that they
"deserve" Bon—deserve him not by dint of their family's adequate social
standing (as Ellen assumes she means), but as a hollow compensation for
their family's actually more profound moral and social shame (76).

Compson attempts to prove the superiority of Rosa's (and his own)
prophetic irony over Ellen's delusion in terms of what Compson would

call their realism but which is more fairly described as their relative preparedness for surprise: Ellen fails to rise to "actual stardom in the role" of matriarch to her family because she lacks "the fortitude to bear sorrow and trouble," so that she has to turn "at the last to the youngest member of [that family, Rosa, to ask] her to protect the others" (54). Thus Compson says Ellen's vision of the family's portraits has been "smoothed of all thought and experience" (59), and when "something happened" between Sutpen and Henry to disturb that insufficiently troubled vision, Compson rather parenthetically and arrogantly calls it "the shock of reality entering her life: this the merciful blow of the axe before the beast's throat is cut" (62). Compson dismisses the question of what that reality is—a question he cannot answer—with only the assurance that Ellen would know no more than Rosa or he would, and that she would be more surprised: Ellen "would have been told nothing in the first place and would have forgot, failed to assimilate, it if she had been—Ellen the butterfly, from beneath whom without warning the very sunbuoyed air had been withdrawn" (63). By contrast with this "moth caught in a gale" (67), Rosa, of course, has been carefully trained to smell the approaching tornado in every breath. Whereas Ellen supposedly languishes in "baffled incomprehension" for two years after this buffeting and dies, Rosa, on the other hand, "continued to sew on the garments for Judith's wedding," undaunted in her supposed abnegation, perhaps even thriving on this further stay of her bloodless love's eventual loss in its unavoidable consummation (63).

But again, Compson's emphasis on Ellen's and Rosa's relative readiness for this surprise unsuccessfully obscures the fact that Compson himself at this point knows nothing of what the "reality" was that entered Ellen's life, other than the generalized reality of surprise (the tornado, the blow of the axe), against which he believes himself and Rosa to be protected by their talismanic irony. Instead of admitting his ignorance of Ellen's painful (two-year-long) experience, he congratulates himself and Rosa for being realistically unsurprised and relatively unmoved. It begins to appear, however, that Rosa continues to sew on the wedding garments not in spite of what happens—she having known all along that this was a fairy tale and would never come true—but because, like Compson, she knows *less* well than Ellen what actually happened and what it meant to those more immediately involved. Rosa's supposed abnegation and unsurprise appear now to conceal her more protected, secretly more insistent hope and belief.

Thus when Rosa is paupered and orphaned by the civic apostasy and death of her father, she does not move out to live with Judith, "the natural thing for her or any Southern woman, gentlewoman" to do; Compson explains this decision as her presuming on no such vulnerable social claim as the Southern lady's "old blood that crossed uncharted seas" (as Ellen has presumed — 67, 68). But even while Compson tries to explain Rosa's staying away in terms of her ironic "final and complete abnegation" — that is, as another instance of her standing back from too direct a role in Judith's love with the Ecclesiastes attitude that the folly of this war too shall pass — at the same time Rosa's abiding hope shows through, her hope that the other folly (of love) should not just pass away:

> Although Ellen had asked her to protect Judith, possibly she felt that Judith did not need protection yet, since if even deferred love could have supplied her with the will to exist, endure for this long, then that same love, even though deferred, must and would preserve Bon until the folly of men would stalemate from sheer exhaustion and he would return from wherever he was and bring Henry with him — Henry, victim too of the same folly and mischance. (68)

Her being completely resigned to that love's actualization, consummation, and likewise its deferral only half conceals here a guarded, secret hope and desire: it is *not* all the same to her whether that love's consummation be completely ruled out either for Judith or for her own continuing hope and desire.

Here near the end of the chapter Compson has begun to pull back to save himself from that next catastrophe of Bon's death, a death apparently not by cause of a vague "folly and mischance" but at the hands of Henry, this other supposed "victim" of that "same" folly and mischance. Compson stops his narration in this chapter just short of letting Wash announce this surprise to Rosa of Bon's death. It is a surprise which effectively calls the bluff of Compson's narrative fiction of Rosa's bloodless, resigned, disinterested, disembodied love, which should have been proof against this inevitable loss, of course, of love's object (a man in this case whom Rosa had never even met). But the ironic position Compson has provided Rosa apparently cannot confront this last most undecidable and ambivalent surprise without revealing her previously obscured interest in that still obscured, specific, other life.

Throughout the chapter, Compson has tried to explain Rosa's personal, psychological movement toward acquiescence to Sutpen as a realistic abnegation of resistance, a "sacrifice" redeemed by her and especially Compson's ironic consciousness of the loss. But he has unsuccessfully averted a growing sense both of her (and Compson's own) personal interest in that involvement and of the obfuscations of other lives required for their alibi in irony. So too in his parallel treatment in this chapter of the townspeople's less personal, more social relationship with Sutpen, Compson stresses the town's nonplussed posture toward unexpected turns of events (again by contrasting their nonplus with the irony of others less surprised). Again the effect is to block further examination both of the other subjects with whom the town becomes increasingly involved, and of their own thus guarded interests in those other lives.

Ten years after the snubbed wedding between Sutpen and Ellen Coldfield, now Sutpen is "the biggest single landowner and cotton-planter in the county," and although some of the townspeople "believed even yet that there was a nigger in the woodpile somewhere," and though "he was not liked . . . but feared," still "he was accepted; he obviously had too much money now to be rejected or even seriously annoyed any more" (56–57). Their reservations about his surprising ascendancy are represented here as limited to the vaguest unconfirmed suspicions of a "nigger in the woodpile somewhere," suspicions whose vagueness serves to block further examination of his ascendancy and of their own interest in accepting, even legitimizing it; the unconfirmed nature of those suspicions serves as an alibi for that (impotently qualified) legitimacy. They might have reflected that this proverbial "nigger in the woodpile" represents better than they think the source of much of Sutpen's wealth in cheap black (slave) labor and cheap Indian land, and that their own legitimations and acceptances of Sutpen by way of Coldfield's "credit," Sutpen's marriage into the Coldfield family, and the amount of Sutpen's money, have collaborated in relegating questions of force and unfairness into a shadowy, quite other realm of unconfirmed (and unconfirmable) secret crime. But the possibility of such reflections on Sutpen's wealth and on their own part in "accepting" it is obscured in Compson's narrative, as usual, in favor of his emphasizing their shortsighted, helpless surprise at this unexpected turn of events.

From his own ironic distance Compson imagines Sutpen rubbing their faces in his ascendancy's direct affront to their former expectations, hiring as his overseer, for example, "the son of that same sheriff who had arrested him at his bride-to-be's gate on the day of the betrothal" (57). Whereas this might have served to emphasize the town's complicity after all in those matters of illicit (unlaundered) money and power which they had tried to project onto Sutpen ten years before, for Compson's irony the emphasis is always instead their vague, unwitting helplessness and shortsighted inconsistency, so that they are reduced, for example, to being their own former fool's fools (Ellen's fools): "the same ladies . . . whom the aunt had tried to force to attend the wedding twenty years ago" are visited frequently now by Ellen and Judith. Even the men (less naturally foolish) are victims now of Ellen's "bland and even childlike imposition upon [their] sufferance or good manners or sheer helplessness": the "merchants and clerks" would "fetch out" to Ellen's carriage "the meager fripperies and baubles which they carried and which they knew even better than she that she would not buy but instead would merely finger and handle and dis-arrange and then reject" (54, 57–58).

Compson represents this social comeuppance by the Sutpens as partial confirmation of Sutpen's earlier faith in social "eventuality," but instead of outlining yet the implications of Sutpen's apparently successful plan, instead of commenting on the muddied foundations of their particular society, Compson and his Rosa insist that these are still shifting sands on which to build one's mansion, offering mere general commentary on the nature of human endeavor. Compson says Sutpen has been deluded by the same ambition with which he has now "corrupted" one of their own, Ellen, so that like her he was

> unaware that his flowering was a forced blooming too and that while
> he was still playing the scene to the audience, behind him fate,
> destiny, retribution, irony—the stage manager, call him what you
> will—was already striking the set and dragging on the synthetic and
> spurious shadows and shapes of the next one. (57)

Whereas Sutpen may have looked more successfully than many some distance into the social future (actually the social fabric), Compson, on the other hand, has claimed for Rosa the more metaphysically prophetic (also backstage, secret) "rapport with the fluid cradle of events (time) which she had acquired or cultivated by listening beyond closed doors . . . to the prefever's temperature of disaster" (51–52). By so defining the course of history as a tendency toward disaster, Compson has no trouble (retro-actively, modernistically) predicting the historical destiny of the Sutpen family and the town alike:

> the time now approached (it was 1860 . . .) when the destiny of
> Sutpen's family which for twenty years now had been like a lake
> welling from quiet springs into a quiet valley and spreading . . . felt
> the first subterranean movement toward the outlet, the gorge which
> would be the land's catastrophe too. . . . (58)

Another figure of unsuccessful regurgitation, this one again is successful for Compson only insofar as he can quietly remove himself from this society which he positions now *in* the vomit, in order to stage-manage the war as forcing to crisis and contradiction the town's accumulating series of uneasy compromises and accommodations with Sutpen's family.

As in his narration of the personal, family crisis that blasted Ellen's blossoming, however, here too Compson's striking one stage set to supersede it with another one ("the shock of reality" here as war) shows less understanding or knowledge than ironic power. His attention to scene shifting emphasizes dramatic blows at the expense of any sense of how one scene might lead to the next: he shows the generic, repetitive crisis, the fever here, rather than the particular social disease that may have invited or provoked that war, because he is himself more easily removed from the historical, past fever than from the ongoing disease. Thus when he introduces Sutpen in the role of raising and commanding the local regiment alongside Colonel Sartoris, Compson jumps almost unaccountably ahead of his story to a time when the "shape of [Sutpen] that people knew" and that "the negroes and Wash Jones, too, called the fine figure of a man" would seem to have (already at some time before) "reached and held its peak after the foundation had given away." This eventual collapse into fat suddenly, retroactively reveals for Compson's narrative purposes "the uncompromising skeleton of what [Sutpen] actually was" (63). That this "fine figure of a man" was not what a Compson then or certainly a Compson now (as opposed to blacks, or poor whites like Wash Jones) would mistake for what Sutpen "actually was" is more important to Compson's narrative than why that figure *was* taken, in the event, by many others in the town and regiment, as second only to Sartoris, and eventually as second to none. That the society might have recognized in this crisis its thorough dependence on Sutpen's kind of iron hand beneath a more genteel glove of velour is an insight blocked by Compson's ironic disengagement.

Goodhue Coldfield does pose one obstacle to Compson's easy narrative disengagement since Coldfield apparently tried to force some confrontation with this social contradiction. Compson acknowledges that "before war was actually declared and Mississippi seceded, [Coldfield's] acts and speeches of protest had been not only calm but logical and quite sensible" (64). Why, then, when the town's compromises became impossible to continue as innocently and uncritically as Compson has made them seem, why was this man of "uncompromising moral strength," this voice of the community's reason and conscience, ignored in favor of the "uncompromising skeleton" beneath Sutpen's "fine figure of a man" (65, 63)? Rather than imaginatively inhabit the townspeople's position with the admitted sympathy and self-criticism it would take to explore this presumably uncomfortable, official bow to Sutpen's money and violent power, Compson focuses instead ironically on the realistic "fact" of Coldfield's defeat and especially on his shocked reaction to that (repetitive, generic) defeat: "after the die was cast he seemed to change overnight, just as his daughter Ellen changed her nature a few years before" (64). Thus the differences between Coldfield and his social butterfly daughter, as between Coldfield and the rest of the town (even the soldiers from whom Coldfield most stridently differs) are unimportant to the overriding logic of Compson's differentiation of himself from all of them: *their* differences are reduced here by Compson all to a common victimization by the incontrovertible fever's temperature of disaster. Compson ironically pictures Coldfield declaiming at passing soldiers from his family Bible's "violent vindictive mysticism" with a militancy (as described by Compson) that makes him another soldier ("a picquet on post") despite himself and despite whatever "sensible" arguments he might have advanced had Compson let him speak (64).

Compson thus grants Coldfield a certain moral courage, but at the same time denigrates the efficaciousness and even the content of that morality, not really willing to grant Coldfield even the higher moral ground in exchange for the realism of Compson's own irony. Like the ambivalence of Melville's Captain Vere so often appreciated by the New Criticism, irony wants it all, both the finest sentiments and the privilege of overruling the riskiness of those sentiments' embodiment with its (safer but no less heroically moralistic) "realism." Compson finally portrays Coldfield's morality, in fact, not as overly pure but as insufficiently pure compared with Rosa's and Coldfield's irony. It is a petit bourgeois storekeeper's fastidiousness in the keeping of both his spiritual and terrestrial accounts, Compson always insinuating Coldfield's petty, penny-pinching confusion of the two: "his conscience may have objected, as your grandfather said, not so much to the idea of pouring out human blood and life, but at the idea of waste: of wearing out and eating up and shooting away material in any cause whatever" (65). Such observations are designed to flatter and absolve the more gallantly unstinting, patriotic, and aristocratic Compsons—those aristocrats who in the Faulkner canon tend to be sardonically wasteful, even reckless, of material and human life as well, for the sake of a cause, incidentally, from which they have much more to gain than Coldfield does. But such observations on the materialism of Coldfield's morality are also designed to flatter and absolve the more purely spiritual Rosa, the object of Compson's current transference. Compson explains the spirit of Coldfield's capitalism along the lines of Max Weber's analyses, emphasizing the simultaneous denial of material motives and the expectation nevertheless of material reward (even if only for interpretive, symbolic purposes):[5]

> doubtless what hurt him most in the whole business with Sutpen was not the loss of the money but the fact that he had to sacrifice the hoarding, the symbol of the fortitude and abnegation, to keep intact the spiritual solvency which he believed that he had already established and secured. (66)

5. Faulkner will later extend his analysis of this Protestant ethic to include an analysis of structural anti-Semitism (see Chapter 3 below).

The implied beneficiary of this second description of Coldfield is particularly the more selflessly antinomian daughter, who supposedly places not even symbolic importance on the fruits of her worldly conduct: when her father dies, Compson repeatedly calls her a pauper and orphan both, as if she admirably expects nothing from the world. And he has earlier described her knowledge of money as limited to "the progression of the coins in theory," as if to make her even more purely aristocratic than the better-fixed "gentlefolk" who are concerned in those less theoretically neatened, more conflictual material and human realms in which money and profit are extracted and ideologically purified from the labors and desires which they usually still rather uneasily represent (60).

Besides contributing toward supporting the Agrarian and New Critical myth of a leisurely Southern aristocracy "above" material concerns as against (the immigrant Coldfield's and Sutpen's) Northern capitalism,[6] Rosa's lack here of even symbolic worldly wealth and security has, of course, its secret compensation in irony's higher, more secure sense of the world's inherent insecurity. Coldfield's mistake, from this perspective, was to expect too much, to expect his moral ideas to bear fruit in the material world. It is not that he understands less well than Compson the realities of their society's deep compromises with someone like Sutpen, but that he understands less well the reality of compromise "itself," the reality of principle's inevitable defeat.

Compson says it is during her father's "voluntary incarceration" that Rosa begins her odes to the "also-dead" Southern soldiers: these odes are the equivalent on a social scale of her more personal, similarly guarded love of one of those soldiers, Charles Bon. In ironic reaction against her father's fanatical moral principles now that he has become an onerously material burden on her, she can venture this idealized but apparently patriotic commitment to her society, even in this its most feverishly violent state, by simultaneously invoking its death and defeat, praising it only in eulogy, as if these soldiers fought for their own fine sentiments (here unexamined, uncompared with Coldfield's) at an automatically ennobling, higher (or highest) cost. Her own emotional investment and her society's economic and political investments in those soldiers and in that violence are thus overshadowed. Historically, this was a strategy in which Rosa was to be (and is still) by no means alone: O'Brien notes that "the idea of the South was strengthened, ironically, by the destruction of its political expression, the Confederacy" (5). I would add that this effect of stronger

6. This is an Agrarian and New Critical reading of *Absalom* endorsed and exemplified especially by Cleanth Brooks's "On *Absalom, Absalom!,*" but persuasively refuted by Carolyn Porter in *Seeing and Being.*

idealization in defeat is "ironic" especially in the sense that irony plays a significant role in preparing this particular effect.

As the chapter approaches its end, this guarded, elegiac involvement of Rosa's in the South's war effort heads for the same revealing disaster as her guardedly virgin, vicarious personal love for Charles Bon. Compson has tried to construct for her the town's most cautiously failsafe position of uninvolved involvement with all that the Sutpen family both represents and obscures for her, only to break off that construction to foresee its failure himself as he considers again the effect on Rosa of Bon's death, that shock which will reveal both how little she knows of this man she never has and never will meet, and yet how deeply she is interested, despite her alibi of disinterested ironic abnegation. Compson has spoken earlier of "that point where man [always] looks about at his companions in disaster and thinks *When will I stop trying to save them and save only myself?*" (58). Pulling back from his Rosa at the end of the chapter as he does, when she is about to receive the shock of Bon's death, Compson can partially, temporarily save himself, but in the novel's following chapter he will be harder and harder put to save his narrative irony's assurance that everyone else ("man") will always reach "finally" this endpoint of ironically realistic self-protection in disaster, as if they are not themselves inextricably invested in those others they would "finally" thus, of course, abandon: Bon, it will seem, did not, nor did Judith, nor perhaps even did Rosa, who is at this point in Compson's story about to rush out to Sutpen's Hundred to learn or admit she is more involved with Bon, Judith, Sutpen, and the rest than she has thought, or than Compson has tried to think. Compson will in the coming chapter be increasingly harder put to save even his own narrative voice from letting those other more directly involved voices speak for themselves.

Compson has balked in chapter 3 at letting Wash Jones announce Henry's murder of Bon to Rosa, because the shock of this news so obviously compromises Compson's laborious portrait of Rosa's unshockable abnegation, as if one more ironic position close to his own threatens now to be pulled into the soup. In chapter 4 Compson will back up again to attempt another approach to the same ending, this time eventually letting Jones complete his announcement, but only after Compson has lost Quentin's attention and confidence to the voices of Judith and of Bon's "dead tongue speaking" in the letter to Judith which Compson delays giving Quentin for most of the chapter (102). Compson makes here one last attempt to remain the ironic author of the Sutpen story before his characters begin to speak up for themselves and before Compson becomes another character in Quentin's own rememberings and retellings of the tale. Compson rebegins his story by half acknowledging the precarious ambivalence of his own position, but only as a mastered state, as an ambivalence which he surveys knowingly as if from above, and which he acknowledges only in order to introduce the turning of his narrative's attention to a realm of neater distinctions between ironic authors and innocent victims, between himself and Quentin on the one hand and, on the other hand, people

> of that day and time, of a dead time; people too as we are and victims too as we are, but victims of a different circumstance, simpler and therefore, integer for integer, larger, more heroic and the figures therefore more heroic too, not dwarfed and involved but distinct, uncomplex who had the gift of loving once or dying once instead of being diffused and scattered creatures drawn blindly limb from limb from a grab bag and assembled, author and victim too of a thousand homicides and a thousand copulations and divorcements. (71)

Compson is self-protectively distancing himself from these axiomatically and reductively more transparent victims of a now "dead time," to reserve for himself instead this "modern" position not so much of ambivalent author-victimhood as of a vague cosmopolitan foreknowledge of and diffuse indifference to any particular homicide, copulation, or divorce. As if to reinforce this distinction between himself as author and these heroic figures as victims, Compson will go on in this chapter to attempt to project the same (ambivalent, internal) distinction "out there" among his characters, casting Bon as ironic author and Henry as innocent victim of the action and relationship between them, and Judith as blankly neither author nor victim but an impenetrable mirror for either. It will become increasingly clear, however, as these "dead tongues" begin to speak, that none of these transferences of Compson's work: Henry will seem not so provincially simple and victimized as this (especially in his actively and deliberately murdering Bon), nor will Bon seem so sophisticatedly, indifferently self-conscious and in control (especially in his being murdered), nor will Judith seem so blankly ambiguous: she will rather seem ambivalently and uncontainably complex, a figure mixing much of what Compson is still trying to keep asunder, notably, author and victim, irony and innocence, soul and soil, present and past, and, more subtly, male and female, white and black.

Compson explains Henry's championing of Bon against his father's unspecified slurs (when "something happened" in the Sutpen family) as an instantaneous, doomed, but noble, heroic choice between friend and father: Henry is here being fit right into the increasingly powerful postwar nostalgic myth (later the Agrarian myth) of a nonindustrial, noncapitalist, even nonmaterialistic, and therefore doomed, romantic antebellum South, as he chooses between "that where honor and love lay and this where blood and profit ran, even though at the instant of giving [his father] the lie he knew that it was the truth" (72). With a similarly ennobling, chivalric fatalism, Compson imagines the probation Henry grants Bon as a "vain" hope, and his admiration of Bon as a source "not of envy but of despair" (72, 76). Whereas his sister might hope to make Bon's image "hers through possession," to Henry the image and the attraction come "with the knowledge . . . of the insurmountable barrier which the similarity of gender hopelessly intervened" (75–76). Both Henry's homoerotic attraction to Bon and his defense of his sister's virginity are everywhere defined by their hopelessness, in spite of elaborate fantasies of hedging against the necessary defeat of either:

> the pure and perfect incest: the brother realizing that the sister's virginity must be destroyed in order to have existed at all, taking that virginity in the person of the brother-in-law, the man whom he would be if he could become, metamorphose into, the lover, the husband; by whom he would be despoiled, choose for despoiler, if he could become, metamorphose into, the sister, the mistress, the bride. (96)

Henry's love of Bon through Judith and of Judith through Bon here is as purely and self-protectively vicarious as Rosa's love supposedly was in chapter 3, but there is an even greater self-denial and fatalism in Henry's love of "the single friend whom, even [then] he must have known . . . that he was doomed and destined to kill" (72). It is precisely this most extreme proof of Henry's "doom" as innocent victim that Compson will be trying to keep from being construed instead (or as well) as the act of an "author" responsible for his and others' fates.

Bon's role as author opposite Henry's role as victim in Compson's narrative depends less on innocent nostalgia and fatalism than on the preemptive minimization of emotional risk through the ironic poses of satiety and cosmopolitan indifference, the spectator's "air of sardonic and indolent detachment like that of a youthful Roman consul making the Grand Tour of his day among the barbarian hordes," his emotional defenses armed with "a certain reserved and inflexible pessimism" (74, 75). Thus in the courtship of Judith, Compson says the suitor's role more properly belonging to Bon is "usurped" by Ellen, Henry, and Judith, who are all naively and vulnerably more interested in the fairy tale than Bon (more detached) is himself. This construction reserves in Bon a close, but safe, ringside spectator's seat for Compson; when Compson then considers, however, that this indifferent suitor supposedly "without volition or desire" will come eventually "to force the brother who had championed [the marriage] to kill him to prevent it" (79, 80), Compson must himself admit (and then deny) the failure of this interpretation: "It's just incredible. It just does not explain. Or perhaps that's it: they don't explain and we are not supposed to know" (80). This quick attempt at a recoup by means of epistemological fatalism and narrative resignation is a characteristically ironic gesture on Compson's part: he is trying to limit expectations, as usual, only in order then to try nevertheless (at considerable length) to shore up his interpretations at their weakest point, namely, that murder when the purported author of all the action, Bon, is killed (or authoritatively victimized) by his purported victim, Henry.

To explain the cosmopolitan Bon's loving provincial Henry and Judith so imprudently to the point of "forcing" Henry to kill him, Compson frames Bon's attraction to them as a jaded, voyeuristic nostalgia for a state before surprise and self-division. In watching Henry's more frightful loss of innocence, Bon supposedly enjoyed a retrospective, jaded, ironic insurance against the renewal of his own surprise, effectively managing that actually continuing risk by projecting it safely into his own past and onto the stage of another's more naive life. "Who knows," Compson asks rhetorically, what Bon loved in Henry and Judith, "what alleviation and escape for a parched traveler who had traveled too far at too young an age, in this granite-bound and simple country spring" (86). Bon's apparent victimization by Henry, then, is mediated and subordinated as only a seasoned ironist's dalliance with the naive: Bon's own contrasting position as ironist is not really threatened by this dalliance but only thereby reconfirmed. Compson will try to explain, on the other hand, the violence of the victim Henry's act of murdering Bon (and the delay that makes that act seem incongruously deliberated) as Henry's eventually explosive reaction to Compson's and Bon's having much more carefully and authoritatively staged Henry's loss of innocence during their visit to New Orleans.

Compson admits that as an explanation for Henry's murder of Bon, the mere "existence of the eighth part negro mistress and the sixteenth part negro son, granted even the morganatic ceremony, . . . is drawing honor a little fine even for the shadowy paragons which are our ancestors" (100). Without recourse, then, to this simpler explanation of a romantic innocent's outdatedly prudish sense of honor and purity, out of which Henry would have struck Bon in unthinking outrage (both too simplistically and too soon, given the facts), Compson explains Henry's delayed violence instead as the result of Bon's skillfully but dangerously protracted foreplay with Henry's more deep-seated, Southern, and especially Coldfield "puritan heritage which must show disapproval instead of surprise or even despair and nothing at all rather than have the dis-

approbation construed as surprise or despair" (88). Surprise and despair
here (like fright for Freud) would open a point of breach in a system which
presumes easily and calmly to disapprove of absolutely everything it wishes
to exclude. Compson has called repeated attention to his own and Bon's
superior skill in delaying and preparing for this eventual moment of shock,
which becomes thereby more focused for Henry's several voyeurs:

> I can imagine. . . . And I can imagine. . . . Yes, I can imagine how
> Bon led up to it, to the shock: the skill, the calculation, preparing
> Henry's puritan mind as he would have prepared a cramped and
> rocky field and planted it and raised the crop which he wanted.
> (86–87)

However, such a long foreplay with Henry's relative innocence also knowingly risks his eventually more explosive reaction. As Bon "corrupts" Henry
"gradually into the purlieus of elegance" (87), carefully avoiding any
chances for Henry to digest these experiences and frame his disapproval
in ways that would not betray surprise or despair, Henry can only attempt
(and Compson using Bon as his ironic alibi attempts) to affect for as long
as he can a cosmopolitan, ironic "nothing at all": Henry follows Bon as
far as he can (in Bon's ironic extenuations and rationalizations of greater
and greater involvement) into what Henry ultimately feels he must absolutely reject, no matter what may show of violent surprise or despair.

Bon supposedly knows all along that the *ceremony* between himself
and his octoroon slave-mistress-wife "would be what Henry would resist,
find hard to stomach and retain" (90). The ceremony would acknowledge
and institutionalize what Henry's "granite heritage" would more likely
repress altogether or minimize as a disapproved exception to the rule, an
occasional lapse from grace. Henry will admit that men of his class and
culture do consort sexually with the lower third and second castes of
women in their society, those "slave girls and women [prostitutes and other
"trash"] upon whom that first caste [of ladies] rested and to whom in certain
cases it doubtless owed the very fact of its virginity" (87). Henry can even
countenance Bon's argument against hypocrisy and in favor of

> the principles of honor, decorum and gentleness applied to perfectly
> normal human instinct which you Anglo-Saxons insist upon calling
> lust and in whose service you revert in sabbaticals to the primordial
> caverns, the fall from what you call grace fogged and clouded by
> Heaven-defying words of extenuation and explanation, the return to
> grace heralded by Heaven-placating cries of satiated abasement and
> flagellation. (92)

But the ceremony in question is especially disturbing for Henry not just in its acknowledgment of such desire; Henry himself (as a man) is presumed to be less innocent than the "white sisters" of his class, with their "moral and outraged horror" (92). This ceremony not only acknowledges the "female principle" of "ancient curious pleasures of the flesh," but also accepts it as "perfectly normal," even enthrones it—not as outside or beneath some enduringly pure realm of "grace" and "virginity," but as precisely "all: there is nothing else," since "a woman's sole end and purpose [is] to love, to be beautiful, to divert" (93). Thus Compson's octoroon alternative to her prudishly outraged "white sisters" is redefined not as a woman subject of fuller human possibilities but rather as one of "the only true chaste women, not to say virgins, in America" (93). Bon has unpuritanically made not a wife of a slave, but a slave from the (already sexist but not precisely enslaving) current idea of a wife.

That is, whereas Bon's (Compson's) ironic arguments against the puritan hypocrisy and repression of Jefferson might have called revealing attention to certain human and sexual relations and feminine possibilities more often obscured by that tradition, Compson is compelled cynically and decadently to insist instead on merely turning that heritage revoltingly "upside down" (91), much as if only voyeuristically to force Henry's revulsion:

> this grim humorless yokel out of a granite heritage where even the houses, let alone clothing and conduct, are built in the image of a jealous and sadistic Jehovah, put suddenly down in a place whose denizens had created their All-Powerful and His supporting hierarchy-chorus of beautiful saints and handsome angels in the image of their houses and personal ornaments and voluptuous lives. Yes, I can imagine how Bon led up to it. . . . (86)

Bon's applied "principles of honor, decorum and gentleness" turn out to be merely "that pessimistic and sardonic cerebral pity of the intelligent for any human injustice or folly or suffering" (91). Bon calculates that he and others like him save perhaps not even one thousand such "sparrows" out of a thousand thousand, but their formalization of their relations with these one thousand serves as a liberal's rationalization and exoneration for their accepting without qualm or indigestion the lot of those other 999,000, and for their accepting the rest of a larger, more generally, thoroughly corrupt social system which Bon can invoke at need (his "trump") even to make of this (otherwise exonerating) ceremony merely "a formula, a shibboleth meaningless as a child's game," since it is never forgotten, after all, that "this woman, this child, are niggers" (93–94).

Henry can follow Bon's cynical rationalizations as Bon pretends to tidy up such contradictions by only ironically ceremonializing their resolution — but Henry still feels the now much more extensive contradictions almost obscured, but also represented and explosively compressed, by this ceremony, although Henry cannot himself quite recognize or articulate yet its occluded human remainders:

> 'You give me two and two and you tell me it makes five and it does make five. But there is still the marriage." . . . the despair now, the last bitter cry of irrevocable undefeat: "Yes. I know. I know that. But it's still there. It's not right.' (94)

Not even his love of Bon and his emulation of Bon's superior irony can any longer obscure or delay his sense of the contradiction within this exploitive desire of Bon's in which he may well himself be deeply involved but which he cannot so easily (or cynically) digest, stomach, and retain as (Compson's) Bon (supposedly) can.

Compson hopes at this point to have explained the violence of Henry's reaction to Bon's octoroon wife and son by tracing this process of Bon's carefully, voyeuristically adding moral insult to injured honor and knowingly risking the eventual explosion of a more general disillusionment and desperate moral outrage; Compson realizes, however, that he has still not explained the delay: "So that was all. It should have been all; that afternoon four years later should have happened the next day" (94).[7] He has to acknowledge in the generalized fatalism of his irony its troubling, characteristic (but reduced here to "curious") failure to fit closely enough those human events it is meant to explain: "that curious lack of economy between cause and effect which is always a characteristic of fate when reduced to using human beings for tools, material" (94). Henry, this puritan simple, seems after all to have been able to live in these moral complexities for another four years, and would seem to have had time to consider his act more deliberately than a mere victim or tool of fate would be expected to do. Compson, then, can explain the murder's delay only by now largely abandoning his own overdetermined, largely voyeuristic, painstaking explanation of Henry's violence as the result of a moral shock to this innocent victim. Compson proposes now on both Bon's and Henry's parts an equally fatalistic, ironic "hope that the War would settle the matter, leave free one of the two irreconcilables" (95). Rather than stretching the ancestral honor too fine, this explanation abandons the idea of Henry's

---

7. Quentin, too, is impressed (differently) with the problem of Henry's delay in Compson's narrative, as suggested by Quentin's comparison of Henry to Hamlet early in chapter 5.

honor almost completely, to retain only the fatalism, as against Compson's easy, retrospective irony at the delusion of this meager but still misplaced faith in the war to solve their problem.[8]

Unlike Rosa with her more phobic intensity of narration, Compson digresses easily from such admissions of the loose fit of his fatalism to specific human personalities and events. His portrait of Judith makes an ironic virtue of his own narrative necessity—"And Judith: how else to explain her but this way?" (95)—by projecting his own inability to explain her onto her as her own inscrutability and onto Henry and Bon as *their* inability to understand her except as their own self-consciousness: "She was just the blank shape, the empty vessel in which each of them strove to preserve . . . what each conceived the other to believe him to be" (120). As usual, irony constructs a blankness to obscure both the object of its interest and its own interest in that object. Such irony hopes, as Roland Barthes says of certain music, that "nothing occurs to interfere with the signifier [so that there] is thus no compulsion to redundance; simply [instead], the production of a music-language with the function of preventing the singer from being expressive" (*Image* 187). Compson, however, is always compelled redundantly to reiterate his blank portraits, attempting in Judith's case to contain her interesting human ambivalence and complexity by reading it as an irreconcilable contradiction in Henry's and Bon's relationships to her: she is "anything but a fatalist" like Bon, with her "ruthless Sutpen code of taking what it wanted provided it were strong enough," nor is she a moralist like her more-Coldfield-than-Sutpen brother, who screamed and vomited at the half-naked fighting she watched with "cold and attentive interest" (95). Compson himself accomplishes a vague solution to this supposed contradiction only by reducing her to the blankness of "the old virtues" (96). In her case, as Compson explains it, this means relinquishing all her personal emotion and purpose to men, this with a "true pride" that here means obedience even without understanding: "*something has happened between him* [Bon] *and my father* [and proxy father in Henry]; *if my father was right, I will never see him again, if wrong he will come or send for me*" (96).

Thus Judith waits, withdrawn from and unmoved by what Compson calls with his generalized postwar sentimentality and (exonerating)

---

8. In calling attention to the explanatory limits of Compson's irony, I do not mean to imply its worthlessness in every situation. What such irony *can* imagine, for example, is how others' similar irony might well work (as I hope mine does with respect to Compson). Here Compson's observation is supported by Durkheim's that potential (anomic) suicides often wait until after an important public event, as if to identify their particular fate with a larger one for which they might feel less personally responsible or ambivalent (Durkheim 241–76).

bitterness "the most moving mass-sight of all human mass-experience, . . . the bright gallant deluded blood and flesh dressed in a martial glitter of brass and plumes, marching away to battle" (97). She is blankly "not one of" some hundred local "unbrided widows dream[ing] virgin unmeditant" on the locks of departed lovers; rather she lives austerely alone, "the same impenetrable and serene face" (97–98, 99). Although she joins the other women, the "nurtured virgin, the supremely and traditionally idle," to clean and dress "the self-fouled bodies of strange injured and dead," as the times required, she remains always the empty vessel of unquestioning fortitude and forbearance: "while [the other women] talked among themselves of sons and brothers and husbands with tears and grief perhaps, but at least with certainty, knowledge," Judith waits too, "like Henry and Bon, not knowing for what, but unlike Henry and Bon, not even knowing for why" (100). After burying her mother, Ellen, after having her grandfather starve to death coffined in his own attic, and after then burying Bon, she brings Quentin's grandmother the letter with a face still "absolutely impenetrable, absolutely serene: no mourning, not even grief," Compson says, "doubtless knowing no more why she chose your grandmother to give the letter to than your grandmother knew" (100). Compson has done his redundant best to empty her of absolutely all emotion or purpose, but this becomes more difficult for him persuasively to accomplish as he comes to her own less completely blank, more expressive gesture of communication with Quentin's grandmother.

Assuming that Compson's rendition of Judith's speech here is at least to some degree accurate, Quentin is allowed to hear now as if for himself (as if for redundant proof) something of that same blind obedience to an inscrutable cosmic irony on Judith's part which Compson wants to emphasize. But Quentin may well hear in Judith's voice, too, traces of still another sense *she* has not of an indifferent, cosmic design, but of other, different human designs; of victims perhaps not of a fate that uses humans indifferently as tools but of other humans' cross-purposes; of humans as both authors and victims of one another's fates. Judith's figure of the loom both resembles and suggests a critique of Melville's Loom of Time in "The Mat-Maker" chapter of *Moby Dick* (a favorite novel of Faulkner's and in many respects a precursor of that twentieth-century modernism and New Criticism that revived that novel somewhat in their own image). In Melville's figure, Ishmael (in a low mood) feels himself "a shuttle mechanically weaving and weaving away at the Fates," his shuttle's "free will" rather outnumbered and overpowered by necessity and chance, necessity represented by the "unalterable threads" of the warp, and chance by Queequeg's "impulsive, indifferent sword," which "has the last featuring blow at events" (214–15). Having just buried Bon one week before, Judith also feels this cosmic indifference to human designs: "it cant matter, you know that, or the Ones that set up the loom would have arranged things a little better" (101); in Judith's somewhat different loom figure, however, she also proposes to Quentin's grandmother a rather keener, less abstractly indifferent sense of other, variously frustrated human designs besides her own, something missing in the revery of Melville's "silent sailor . . . resolved into his own invisible self" (214). Although the idea of cosmic irony assures her beforehand that human efforts cannot matter, she also recognizes the failure of such an argument either to nullify one's own desire ("yet it must matter because you keep on trying") or to repress all recognition of others' desires ("five or six people all trying to make a rug on the same loom only each one wants to weave his own pattern into the rug"—101). In place of "this savage's sword"—Ishmael's ironic reduction of (his friend) Queequeg to an Object or Otherness cosmically indifferent to one's "invisible self"—Judith's loom admits the participation of other, equally struggling subjects, with the implied possibility, at least, of specific negotiations, collaborations, and communications, as in her gesture of giving the letter to Quentin's grandmother (cf. Scherer).

Compson, on the other hand, in passing the gesture and the letter on to Quentin, has tried to suppress any such recognition of his own ambivalent feelings toward the human complexity of someone like Judith, both compassionate and assertive, just as Compson has also suppressed evidence of that same ambivalence and complexity in other personalities such as Judith herself and Henry. He has suppressed those other irrepressible designs and voices which otherwise challenge his own desire to work his narrative pattern into the rug, a pattern consisting of both his feelings for those other voices and also his ironically overruling those voices along with his own. When Judith tells Quentin's grandmother that she can keep the letter, "or destroy it. As you like. Read it if you like or dont read it if you like," Compson has remembered and no doubt appreciated the contrast Judith suggests between such a style of communication and what she describes as her father's style of carving his name in stone. Her gesture admits (as his does not) that she cannot force her design on the grandmother, that her more intersubjective, dialogic meaning can survive only by risking the passage "from one hand to another, one mind to another." It is memorable enough to survive precisely because of this risky, courageous human vulnerability and mortality in interaction and exchange (100, 101). Compson's mother, however, and Compson himself self-protectively misread her still intensely vulnerable mourning for Bon as a generalized melancholia, neither of them looking farther than "the impenetrable, the calm, the absolutely serene face" as the face of a self-destructing, unreachable suicide (101). As she rejects this mistaken idea of her suicide, the grim humor (not just irony) of her reply eludes this last, blankest Compson portrait of her. She suggests instead a grief-constricted but still continuing feeling for both the living and the dead even after the war's disaster: she will not commit suicide because her father "will want something to eat after he comes home" and "Because there wouldn't be any room now, for [suicides] to go to, wherever it is, if it is. It would be full already. Glutted" (101).

As Compson finally lets Quentin read Bon's letter to Judith, one more supposedly deadened and contained voice begins to speak up as if from within and also against Compson's narrative irony. Bon's voice is both prefaced and followed by Compson's irony and laced heavily with his own, but also pointedly contradicts and explicitly rejects that same (only) authorial role of cosmopolitan identification with a blank, cosmic indifference, a role which for Bon, Compson, and Quentin here (and Faulkner) is gradually losing its persuasive force and its authority over other voices. Quentin begins to read Bon's letter hearing both these competing voices, the irony and its attempted rejection: on the one hand, "Mr. Compson's voice speaking on while Quentin heard it without listening," "without having to listen," Compson speaking on compulsively, redundantly about "the blank face of the oblivion to which we are all doomed," and on the other hand (ambivalently and so ambiguously), Bon's own "dead tongue speaking after the four years and then after almost fifty more, gentle sardonic whimsical and incurably pessimistic," but in that pessimism also trying to argue himself out of his pessimism as his final word (102). He begins his letter, for example, by remarking that he does *not* begin *"by claiming this to be a voice from the defeated even, let alone from the dead"* (129). Bon's letter is a litany of such protestations against the strong temptation of irony: he says he will not say he is hungry—*"that word would be sheer redundancy, like saying that we were breathing"*—nor ragged, nor shoeless, nor that only he and not Judith too has waited long enough. He is no more (ironically, insultingly) assured of his particularly unwavering persecution by the fates than he is sure of when Judith can look for his return. He is neither assured in his irony, that is, nor therefore, alternatively, deludedly naive. The almost double-negative constructions of his protests against his irony make quite visible here what Kierkegaard describes as the usually invisible mastery of what remain mere moments of visible irony in, for example, Shakespeare (*Concept of Irony* 336). Here, on the other hand, Bon's attempt to master irony is everywhere visible and incomplete, though unmistakable, as he resists a postwar rigidification in melancholia and despair in order to gather his emotional strength to commit himself and his fate (as both author and possible victim) to Judith, Henry, and Thomas Sutpen.

The force of resistance to irony in Bon's letter is represented as that of the unreconciled body to the mind and soul, Bon taking courage from the consideration that man "*really does not become inured to hardship and privation: it is only the mind, the gross omnivorous carrion-heavy soul which becomes inured; the body itself, thank God, [is] never reconciled*" (103). As opposed to the mind and the soul's feeding their despair on hardship and death, and becoming inured to experiences like the war by conceiving of those experiences ironically as man's cruel fate or his indifferent reality, the body reserves the ability to suffer, to complain, to desire, even to extract an unpredictable laughter from disaster. When in Bon's company's utter "*desperation*" there seemed "*absolutely no room for alternative*" to their last-ditch, ironic salvation by the boxes marked with "*that U. and that S. which for four years now has been to us the symbol of the spoils which belong to the vanquished, of the loaves and the fishes*" (103), and when those boxes turned out to contain not the desperately needed miracle of food or ammunition but the unmiraculous, banal reality of stove polish, here again as repeatedly in this chapter, the climactic focusing moment of irony in disaster leaves an anticlimactic human remainder: the men's laughter and then the use to which Bon puts this story and even the stove polish itself (as the ink, the material "body" of the letter) in committing himself to Judith.[9]

One might say that Faulkner himself is revising his sentimental-ironic, modernist mode of "*polish[ing] the stove before firing the house*" (as Bon and his men imagine General Sherman doing), transmogrifying that mode gradually by overextension and redundancy into the ink of a different mode which calls attention to what that irony omits or obscures, its human remainder in humor, involvement, ongoing communication, commitment, and desire, a mode prefigured here in this chapter especially in the speech of Judith and in the writing of Charles Bon. In this unreconciled view the war's four years of repeated hardship, danger, and death have not resulted in its digestion by a toughened generation of veterans; the "*body*" at least, is still not inured to the "*loud aghast echo*" of the war's first fusillade, but is instead "*obliviously bemused in recollections of old peace and contentment*" (104). Such unreconciled recollections in the midst of the war's nearly deafening echo prompt Bon to decide he and Judith have (either obediently or ironically) waited long enough on fate or chance to make their harder decisions for them.

9. Cf. Porter, *Seeing* 265, who discusses this letter as a "churinga," or a material proof of continuity between past and present, and between one mind and another. In Chapters 3, 4, and 5 I will discuss such material continuities in terms of money, trading, gifts, symbolic exchange, a mother's touch, and writing.

These memories, Bon insists, are not romantically, nostalgically a confusion of what was with what is; his memories are not nostalgically the
same as hopes, not an identification with the innocent victim as opposed
sentimentally to its ironically authorized destroyer. In other words, he is
not another of Quentin's "back-looking ghosts . . . looking with stubborn
recalcitrance backward beyond the fever and into the disease with actual
regret" (7); his memories are what Bloch describes as a "selective nostalgia"
for what was only more violently obscured during the fever than during
the (now continuing) disease: for example, the tenuous, material (not
absolute, metaphysical) comfort of "something between the sole of the
foot and the earth to distinguish it from the foot of a beast" (103). Now
that "the old South . . . is dead," Bon's irony toward "the new North"
(later the New South) that has survived it, is similarly selective and
tentative, as if the prewar South is not the one and only stubborn form
in which such memories of peace and contentment might survive.[10]

When Bon concludes that he and Judith are now *"among those who
are doomed to live,"* he may be invoking the familiar ironic idea of a life
in the shadow of "doom" (105). But the reversal in the phrase "doomed
to live," with which he concludes his proposal of marriage, suggests one
last pointed rethinking of Bon's (and Compson's) ironies. Bon's formulation
(like Sartre's phrase "condemned to freedom")[11] steals irony's thunder by
conceiving of human life as always already engaged with death, with
suffering, with hardship, with beastliness, and with that earth from which
it distinguishes and erects itself only through acknowledging and dealing
responsibly with its always uncertainly vulnerable and interdependent
situation.

Compson is still attempting to separate the innocent victims of life
from authors identified ironically with their own doom. Thus even at the
moment before the Sutpen gate when Bon in the role of author is murdered
by his supposed victim, Compson characterizes Bon as authorially "calm
and undeviating, perhaps unresisting even, the fatalist to the last; the other
[Henry] remorseless with implacable and unalterable grief and despair,"
as if Bon authorizes that unalterable, remorseless (presbyterian) fate and

10. Faulkner's differences with the Agrarians' nostalgia for the Old South certainly do
not imply a wholesale acceptance of the "New North" or New South, which is in some ways
what New Criticism effectively did accept in its ironic oppositions between literary fictions
on one side and another social "reality" unalterably "outside" the text on the other. Nor
of course can Faulkner's increasing criticisms of New South capitalism be read retroactively
as uncritical nostalgia for the Old South (this is partly Jehlen's tendency). Faulkner develops
a critique that stresses continuities obscured within Agrarian (and New Critical) oppositions
of Old South and New.

11. See Harvey 81–94.

Henry merely enforces it with his unmastered, victimlike grief and despair
(105). Committed to his separation of roles at this moment of that separation's greatest jeopardy, Compson refuses to see here what he has earlier
considered in a similar situation (91), that Bon is less likely to be authorizing
an impersonal fate to end his life than to be entrusting to Henry himself
(riskily, out of his love for Henry and Judith) the opportunity to act not
according to his inflexible puritan conscience but less exoneratingly, more
responsibly out of his personal love for Bon and Judith. Bon loses this
gamble in most respects, much as Judith loses her gamble in trusting her
father and Henry, and then again in trusting Quentin's grandmother to
read and appreciate her gesture and Bon's letter. These gambles by Bon
and Judith, unlucky in the immediate event, and still largely misunderstood in the next generation by Mr. Compson, must depend for their
appreciation all the more powerfully now and increasingly for the rest of
the novel on Quentin, not as autonomous author of a repetitive tale but
as another of its heteronomous, responsible addressees. It is he who must
come to understand and appreciate the acts of love and risk involved in
Judith's acts of trust as in Bon's.

Quentin again here wanders in his thoughts from his father's narration
(Quentin another victim becoming an author as well) to imagine the murder
scene at the gate himself:

> It seemed to Quentin that he could actually see them, facing one
> another at the gate. Inside the gate what was once a park now
> spread, unkempt, in shaggy desolation, with an air dreamy remote
> and aghast like the unshaven face of a man just waking from
> ether. . . . (105)

The figure of the etherized patient, aside from its possible resonance with
the artificially deadened world of Prufrock, recalls also Compson's repeated
attempts earlier in this chapter to characterize Bon's "surgeonlike" relation
to Henry and the Sutpens as "the detached attentiveness of a scientist
watching the muscles in an anesthetized frog" (88, 90, 93, 74). In Quentin's
revision of Compson's figure this pure victim of a frog is a person and
waking, regaining consciousness and sensitivity to pain, much as Compson's blankly obedient Judith is, as maybe the puritan Henry is (if too late
for Bon), as perhaps the scientifically, authorially detached Bon also is,
and perhaps as Quentin is himself. None of them seems to Quentin now
either inured to the war in general—even the house itself is "a skeleton
giving of itself . . . to help to die torn and anguished men who knew, even
while dying, that for months now the sacrifice and the anguish were in
vain" (105)—nor anesthetized to the particular violence about to happen

at the house's gate. Quentin imagines the two soldiers' "old eyes," their "gaunt and weathered" faces, and calm, unraised voices, but he also knows they are "young, not yet in the world, not yet breathed over long enough, to be old." His reference to their "unkempt hair" associates these two with the figure in the sentence before of the man waking from ether, about to *feel* this murder and death, which Quentin himself breaks off imagining, to listen in an aghast, unreconciled silence of his own, as Compson announces with Wash Jones's harsh violence the turning of Bon into "beef" (105, 106).

As Compson's calmly detached narrative distance continues to fail, Jones's account of Bon's murder is one last carrion even Compson's irony seems unable easily to swallow. Quentin will turn in the chapters that follow to Rosa and other more inextricably involved narrators than Compson, others who will extenuate or deny their involvement and participation in what they observe and narrate, only with an increasingly obvious and revealing violence to the other voices involved.

Rosa's nostalgia and Compson's irony, representing here the "two courses" of Southern narrative Faulkner felt were available to him as he struggled to write the story of Sutpen and the South, have both repeatedly failed to understand either the characters they discuss or Rosa and Compson themselves. Rosa's nostalgia for the Old South asserts a social and personal purity which attempts and repeatedly fails to focus all threats to that purity in the person of Thomas Sutpen. Her own and others', especially Compson's, more ironic response to these collapsing purities is to pretend to acknowledge all such collapses and impurities beforehand, but only by anxiously generalizing and thus subordinating and excluding those impurities again from a newly purified, detached position in irony. The series of such retreats to higher ground in the first four chapters of *Absalom,* toward the point when Compson's narrative authority over his characters and his audience in Quentin fails, has shown each such attempt at defining the South — either nostalgically or by the bitterness that serves as alibi for the same sentimental nostalgia — to be an ambivalent act of differentiation and exclusion with its own motives and consequences. Each failed position of purity becomes in this series an object of the next exclusion, each detached, ironic author becomes in turn another innocent victim. Compson's last transference in Bon, for example, becomes the victim of Henry's violent murder, and victim too of the narrative violence of Wash Jones's announcement, a violence which Compson has tried to avoid repeating but finally has to admit as the frightened violence toward others and toward himself which is obscured but also inherent in his irony.

The exemplary experience of fright, the modernist "horror," the violent threat to the closed and exclusionary spaces of their society and selves, has reached here as far or as high as what Barthes would call the expressive "grain" of Compson's supposedly calm narrative voice (what I. O. Snopes might call your old frog in the throat). Even the novel Faulkner is trying to write here threatens to deconstruct on the model of Bon's letter's crumbling pages and improvised ink. But Faulkner does not go on to generalize this failure of social purity and narrative authority into the weary, cosmopolitan irony current in Western literature and society after World War I. With the critical advantage of his Southern exposure to an older, more historically specific version of that dominant postwar irony, Faulkner examines more closely the social and emotional motivations and the extreme costs of this irony—which may resist nostalgia but also effectively resists change and any attempt at change. While it may avoid the reclusiveness of Rosa's innocence, it also effectively ignores difference and any desire for difference. Thus Quentin will turn from Compson and his supposed detachment now to attend more closely to other voices of both the ambivalently excluded and the ambivalently excluding parties—Rosa, Sutpen, Henry, even Quentin himself now—not as a potential modernist author impatient to close out and leave the South for the "literary profession" of exile and alienation, but as undeniably one of those Southerners himself, author and victim both of his own version of their self-castrating, suicidal nostalgia and irony.

2 Willfulness and Irony's Other Voices in *Absalom, Absalom!*

THE first four chapters of *Absalom* have shown the failing distances between the two alternative moods of Southern narrative: a toughened modernist irony and the romantic nostalgia to which it is strenuously, impotently, and revealingly opposed. These first four chapters have also shown the failure of this structuring opposition to distance and dispel other insistent voices from out of the Southern past and present. Hoping to leave such a deadened South behind him for Harvard and adulthood, Quentin has turned from one unstilled, nostalgic ghost in the person of Rosa in chapter 1 to his ironic father in chapters 2 to 4, in the skeptical but defensive attitude of "Why tell me about it? What is it to me?" (7). This voice of his father, however, the one which he might have expected to stand protectively between him and all those other insistent voices of his "barracks" of Southern ghosts (cf. the "impetuous, impotent dead" in Pound's first Canto), has been unable to beat those other voices back from the mouth of this underworld, and so those voices begin to make themselves heard with an uncanny sense of now more willfully barred, rejected recognition. His father's ironic distinctions between their narrative circle as modern authors of their already (abstractly) foreknown fates and, on the other hand, the vulnerability of their innocent, "shadowy" forebears as objects of a narrative and poor blinded victims of fate, have come to seem like defensive distinctions overly simple at best and cynically, deliberately unfeeling at worst. Quentin's aroused, dissatisfied attention therefore turns now from his father's detached authorial narrative back to the remembered, now italicized voice of Rosa, another author-narrator who is undeniably also a victim or character in her tale, or who is rather neither simply author nor simply victim. Quentin returns, that is, to the voice of Rosa as he remembers it from his session with her earlier that afternoon. Thus too

79

Faulkner himself, having written those first four chapters, looks again, more critically now, at both the nostalgia and the irony of modernism and Southern memory, looking especially for those other voices both have together excluded (though Faulkner is still not altogether ready to let those other voices speak).

As Quentin recalls Rosa's narration of her more personal, closer approach to the Sutpen story, her position will seem now not so naively, innocently inferior to Quentin's and Compson's irony, but rather a dialectical step beyond that irony into an admittedly contradictory, willful innocence. As Quentin remembers her story now, she seems in fact to have already predicted both their irony toward her innocence and that irony's failure, framing her story, "*So they will have told you doubtless already. . . . they will have told you doubtless . . . (so they will tell you). . . . But they cannot tell you . . .* (107–8). And in this chapter Quentin recalls especially her account of her own progression through and dissatisfaction with the two main postures of memory represented so far in the novel and her attempt at a third, in *"the death of hope and love, the death of pride and principle, and then the death of everything save the old outraged and aghast unbelieving"* (136). This last, new position of willful innocence corresponds to what Lentricchia calls conservative fictionalism (28–60), neither naively deluded by hope and love, nor proudly, cynically above desire, but uneasily, contradictorily believing in versions of Rosa's *"might-have-been which is more true than truth"* (115). Instead of rationalizing and hypostatizing an external reality as below and outside a contracting zone of still untouched, internal purity, the willful innocence of Rosa, Sutpen, Henry, and of Quentin himself in the rest of the novel acknowledges the alibi function of such perfunctory, still subordinating gestures toward a "reality" which they instead try to reject more openly, defensively, violently. This is not to say that this more blatant, damn-the-torpedoes rejection of "truth" does not serve still as an alibi of self-consciousness for a personal and social fiction believed in as "more true than truth," but only that the contradiction between this fictional truth and the one it bars is here more tightly screwed. The Sutpen story will represent now the aristocratic, hierarchic Southern ideal not just demonically threatened or ironically qualified as a narrative viewpoint in accelerating retreat (as in the novel's first four chapters), but as a full-blown social ideal put relentlessly to its historical, social, and emotional test in the context of other competing (if still inarticulate) voices.

The collapse of Rosa's (retrospectively) first, naive position of *"hope and love"* exposes her to insights and connections which she will try desperately to avoid first by wielding the innocent's blinding scenario of fright, then by adopting another higher posture, likewise soon to collapse, in an ironic *"pride and principle."* Rosa recalls riding out to Sutpen's Hundred with Wash Jones just after the murder in the naive attitude of a *"self-mesmered fool who still believed that what must be would be, could not but be, else I must deny sanity as well as breath"* (110). In retrospect, then, her breath and sanity, her personal and social identity, seem completely, purely (purifyingly) defenseless against what she obscurely invokes as those *"dark turnings which the ancient young delusions of pride and hope and ambition (ay, and love too) take"* (110). She says these still unnamed "dark turnings" are what the walls of Sutpen's house and all other houses are built to hide. In a novel whose working title was "Dark House," this is certainly a comment, too, on Rosa's own lifelong seclusion, both in her own dark house and in the deliberate obscurities of her narrative. Thus when Clytie verbally then physically stops her at the darkened foot of the stairs, Rosa's idealized, vicarious love of Bon and the other "also-dead" of her poetry is a hope and love barred here and protected not just from a frightful darkness but from the actual dead body now lying upstairs in Judith's room to be mourned. Her idealized identity and love are barred and protected by fright, that is, from the more complex, fearful process of self-exposure and suffering involved in the love and loss of another particular mortal subject.

Clytie's touch, then, is a crucial experience for Rosa, both restrictive limit to, also extreme extent of, her emotional involvement in this love of Charles Bon, both defensive bar against and revealing contact with this self-compromising love of another subject. As Rosa approaches the house she imagines Clytie sympathetically as one of *"two young women"* (like herself) in love with the man just killed, and as she rushes into the house, her similar sympathy for Sutpen's innocent *"two accursed* [legitimate] *children"* (108) (Judith and Henry) goes out mistakenly in the dark to his illegitimate, black, other daughter Clytie. But Rosa quickly repudiates and represses these fearful, groping insights into emotional, sexual, and familial connections among herself, the other Sutpens, and Clytie in order to regain with a vengeance her more myopic personal and social night vision of fright, so that Clytie becomes the alien *"cold Cerberus of* [Sutpen's] *private hell,"* the *"sphinx"* of *"absolutely rocklike and immobile antagonism"* (109–10). Frightened at losing her breath and sanity in the face of what Clytie hides physically and emotionally "within" in her too darkly defined *"brooding awareness and acceptance of the inexplicable unseen,"* Rosa strains her rhetoric to refix Clytie at an absolute moral and social (racial) distance (Clytie as Sutpen's *"own clairvoyant will tempered to amoral evil's undeviating absolute by the black willing blood with which he had crossed it"*) and at an absolute conceptual distance (herself and Clytie as *"two abstract contradictions"* — 110–11).

Defending herself from fear and grief by means of a focusing, "comprehended terror," Rosa is still dimly aware of much of what she only clumsily, imperfectly suppresses in these objectifications of Clytie as unswerving, inhuman *"instrument"* of Sutpen's, the house's, or Rosa's own will to bar Rosa from the *"inexplicable"* darkness within. Incompletely obscured here is Rosa's recognition of Clytie as, also, subjective emotional and social *"owner"* of *"that black arresting and untimorous hand on my white woman's flesh"* (111): this is the Clytie who even in her tabu disrespect nonetheless unforgettably *"did me more grace and respect than anyone else I knew"* by addressing Rosa (as "Rosa"), then by touching her, neither as black woman to white child (permissibly), nor as black woman to white woman (frightfully, outrageously), but as one (black) woman to another (white) woman (fearfully, intimately):

> *Because there is something in the touch of flesh with flesh which abrogates, cuts sharp and straight across the devious intricate channels of decorous ordering, which enemies as well as lovers know because it makes them both. . . . let flesh touch with flesh, and watch the fall of all the eggshell shibboleth of caste and color too. Yes, I stopped dead—no woman's hand, no negro's hand, but bitted bridle-curb to check and guide the furious and unbending will—I crying not to her, to it; speaking to it through the negro, the woman, only because of the shock which was not yet outrage because it would be terror soon, expecting and receiving no answer because we both knew it was not to her I spoke: 'Take your hand off me, nigger!'* (111–12)

Making this gesture of outraged racism but knowing she thereby speaks not to Clytie but only to the dimly delineated bar to her further entry and insight, Rosa can still feel with Clytie *"twin sistered"* in grief, but as she admits it, she is already moving defensively past this moment of fearful exposure of herself and of those class and race distinctions which insulate and define her identity (112).

In the now familiar rhythm of innocence and irony in *Absalom*, Rosa's betraying fear takes next the example of Clytie's white half sister Judith's apparently colder, less personal voice like that of *"not Judith, but the house itself speaking, though it was Judith's voice,"* a voice constructed like the house, that is, to hide more elaborately, in irony, her own love's "dark turning" of loss (114). Thus Rosa is turning away from her near involvement in a fearful experience which she has reduced (though incompletely) to apocalyptic, frightful terms: "*one constant and perpetual instant when the arras-veil before what-is-to-be hangs docile and even glad to the lightest naked thrust if we had dared, were brave enough (not wise enough; no wisdom needed here) to make the rending gash*" (114). She turns instead toward an ironic transcendence and (still tellingly queasy) detachment: "*Or perhaps it is no lack of courage either: not cowardice which will not face that sickness somewhere at the prime foundation of this factual scheme from which the prisoner soul, miasmal-distillant, wroils ever upward sunward*" (114).

In the issue of courage and cowardice (her own, but also, of course, her culture's), Rosa's hope and love have reached their dark turning and turned away, in order to save her breath and sanity, personal and social identity, in a distilled "pride and principle" on the model of Judith's apparent indifference here and akin to Compson's earlier, less obviously forced, easier pleasure in ironic disillusionment: her new version of irony is obviously just as extreme and strained as her earlier version of nostalgia and fright. Rosa here is not just morally disgusted with her shocking social inferiors but trying instead conceptually, metaphysically, to reduce "*to a fragile evanescent iridescent sphere . . . all of space and time and massy earth*" (114). Thus she adopts something of Compson's superior, retrospective tone in framing as fairy tale ("*Once there was—*") her own brief, deluded virgin's "*summer of wistaria,*" casting herself as love's forestalled possibility, the gnarled, forgotten "*root and urge*" of love, with no real chance of leaf or bloom (115). She stresses this love's isolation from and ignorance of reality, and its compensatory abstraction and concentration, so that her love of Bon, without contact with Bon himself, without "*even parents' love*" to go on in her experience, becomes for her the abstract occasion for her solicitude in the role of "*all polymath love's androgynous advocate*" (117). As this fairy tale nears its dark turn, her irony at its unreality modulates predictably into her pride in its ironic abstraction (her "*know[ing] already more of love than [Judith] will ever know or need*") and in its principled caution ("*waiting, watching, for no reward, no thanks, who did not love him in the sense we [usually] mean it because there is no love of that sort without hope*"—119).

Again, her irony here is extreme and strained, and leaves blatant remainders of former innocence and of other less guarded voices. Her higher, prouder, more principled love is her self-congratulatory, prophetic retreat from vulnerable, particular love: "*Because he was to die; I know that, knew that. . . . But not love, not faith itself, themselves*" (120). By seeming to have expected and thus accepted Bon's death as part of a larger scheme ("*the murdering and the folly*"), she tries to say "*That was all*"

but has to admit she suffers still, if not from the now qualified, distanced
"blow," then still *"from the tedious repercussive anticlimax of it, the
rubbishy aftermath to clear away from off the very threshold of despair,"*
those stubborn remainders of this particular love in Bon's body and in
the *"maddening"* business of building, carrying, and burying his coffin
(120–21). These last remains she cannot so easily digest into her rationalized
abstraction of "love itself" and must more adamantly and willfully refuse:

> There are some things which happen to us which the intelligence
> and the senses refuse just as the stomach sometimes refuses what
> the palate has accepted but which digestion cannot compass —
> occurrences which stop us dead as though by some impalpable
> intervention, like a sheet of glass through which we watch all sub-
> sequent events transpire as though in a soundless vacuum. (122)

She cannot keep down her sense that her ironic pride and principle, her
abstract refusal of her desire, is self-protective self-deception, appearing
strange in Judith, but gradually recognized in her own unweeping *"serene
suspension"* of feeling toward that dead *"abstraction which we had nailed
into a box,"* as though *"three women put something into the earth and
covered it, and he had never been"* (122–23). Thus supposedly divested of
all desire, they await now Sutpen's return not in the virgin's bloom, leaf, or
even root or urge of love, but *"in an apathy which was almost peace, like
that of the blind unsentient earth itself which dreams after no flower's stalk
nor bud, envies not the airy musical solitude of the springing leaves it
nourishes"* (124). This is the actually yearning but chastened dread heard in
Eliot's "Burial of the Dead" in *The Waste Land,* the dread of "mixing /
Memory and desire, stirring / Dull roots with spring rain" (ll. 2–4).

Ironic apathy is even more obviously precarious in its social expression
in those around Rosa. Judith and Clytie, instead of facing the Reality of
Ruin and learning from Rosa the logic of *"that first principle of penury
which is to scrimp and save for the sake of scrimping and saving,"* succumb
to personal appeals for food by *"anyone, any stranger in a land already
beginning to fill with straggling soldiers who stopped and asked for it"*
(126). Instead of seeing such strangers as another part of the general threat,
even Rosa herself can recognize the human motivations and dehumanizing
consequences of these soldiers' similarly ironic postwar transformations
*"into the likeness of that man who abuses from very despair and pity the
beloved wife or mistress who in his absence has been raped"* (126). This
is another case of irony's self-punishment: the soldier repeats against
himself (and/in his *"beloved"*) an injury he has been unable otherwise to
prevent or control. Rosa can see dimly, too, beyond Clytie's *"false seem-*

ing" of fidelity and docility Clytie's own similarly self-protective, self-punishing Sutpen will, "the silent unsleeping viciousness of the tamer's lash" (126). Thus, beyond what Rosa tends to see as the war's general "*debacle*" that has ruined her and Judith in order to "*emancipate*" Clytie in an ironically complete reversal, Rosa can also see, with a vision less metaphysical and more historically complex, Clytie's own formerly incomplete enslavement, along with Clytie's own now (rightly) guarded suspicion of the false hope of instant, complete freedom: "*as though presiding aloof upon the new, she deliberately remained to represent to us the threatful portent of the old*" (126). In all these cases irony's principled denial of one's own and others' desires unsuccessfully obscures its motivation in protecting one's own desire, most clearly in the three women's talking of a thousand things but not once mentioning Charles Bon or the mound "*beneath which we had buried nothing.*" Making the sound of the shot "*merely the sharp and final clap-to of a door between us and all that was, all that might have been,*" they obliterate their love of Bon in a "*retroactive severance of the stream of event: a forever crystallized instant . . . which, preceding the accomplished fact which we declined, refused, robbed the brother of the prey, reft the murderer of a victim for his very bullet*" (127). By obliterating it, they protect their love.

It is with this sense of acknowledged denial in irony of their contradictory desire that Rosa suddenly announces Sutpen's return and her engagement to him in an uncharacteristically paratactic formulation, conspicuously omitting for now any sense of her own involvement in such objective matters of fact: "*And then one afternoon in January Thomas Sutpen came home; someone looked up where we were preparing the garden for another year's food and saw him riding up the drive. And then one evening I became engaged to marry him*" (127). Sutpen's return and his accepted, or unopposed, proposal will spell the death by exposure of Rosa's supposedly stoic "*pride and principle.*" Sutpen offers her and Judith and perhaps Clytie the chance to identify with their willfully ironic pride and principle's paradoxical perfection in his more absolute and successful, willfully *innocent* repression of doubt, fear, and desire. Thus when Judith tells him about the murder, she shows her grief briefly only to transfer its denial into his fiercer keeping, bursting into tears

> as if that entire accumulation of seven months were erupting
> spontaneously from every pore in one incredible evacuation (she
> not moving, not moving a muscle) and then vanishing, disappearing
> as instantaneously as if the very fierce and arid aura which he
> had enclosed her in were drying the tears faster than they
> emerged. . . . (128)

It is an all-consuming aura which leaves of Sutpen himself only a possessed shell which talks not really to them but *"to the air, the waiting grim decaying presence, spirit, of the house itself, talking that which sounded like the bombast of a madman who creates within his very coffin walls his fabulous immeasurable Camelots and Carcassonnes"* (129). His apparently addressing the house itself as if from the dead perfects their own attempted ironic self-denial and abstraction from particular desires, while also the sound of what he says suggests a mad, Poesque hiding place in darkness and death for a concentrated, willfully innocent rededication to desire. By adding their own consciousness of loss to his in the context of a general ruin beyond his coffin walls, they can (with this alibi of ironic self-consciousness) at the same time dedicate themselves to his more willful version of their nostalgic prewar "might-*have-been*": his *"undertaking to restore his house and plantation as near as possible to what it* had *been"* (129, my emphases). Having so thoroughly idealized and abstracted her *"might-have-been"* in opposition first to particular threats, then to a generally bitter devastation, and seeing Sutpen much more fiercely repudiating their general wartime suffering and defeat, Rosa can equate his cause with her own, both parts of the one willfully idealized (postwar) Cause of the defeated South.

Taken thus to their extremes, both innocence and irony have tended to collapse before threatened losses of personal and social identity which they have pointed toward but not signified, threats against which they have tried and failed to establish their own identity by metonymic strategies of contrast, displacement, and retreat, until that threat has become now inescapably interiorized within that same contradictory identity (cf. Kristeva, *Powers* 90–91). So pressing a threat can seem to have pursued Bon (as the idealized object of Rosa's love) beyond the metonymic displacements of innocent fright and ironic avoidance all the way into his coffin, to that apparent endpoint where his idealized, abstracted identity (unless it is actively and specifically mourned) must be imagined as resurrected and transfigured in a kind of violent metaphoric sacrifice, taking altogether new form as Sutpen's coffined, willfully innocent denial of death and change for the sake of his dream of restoration, and as Rosa's (also now willfully innocent) intended sublimation of Sutpen's once-abominated dream into her own. That is, once Bon is dead and his coffin metaphorically emptied, Rosa will without grief love Sutpen instead. Once Sutpen's defeat becomes metaphorically a coffin, Sutpen will create a new dream within its walls. And once Rosa's social ideal is metaphorically defeated, she will rename its former curse as its new champion. Both Sutpen's denial and Rosa's sublimation imply the metaphoric ($a = $ not a), contradictory logic of utter transfiguration without remainder, instead of the metonymic

logic of fright's Manichean contrasts ($a \neq b$) or irony's hierarchical sub-
ordinations (a/b).

Sutpen having himself undergone, interiorized, and denied his own
exclusion and defeat, his willful innocence is a synthesis veiling a contradiction; there are traces of both the single-minded concentration of
innocence and the generalized anxiety of irony in his denial of any and
all possibility of opposition to his design: *"for all he ever told us, there
might not have been any war at all, or it on another planet and no stake
of his risked on it, no flesh and blood of his to suffer by it"* (130). At a
time when others are focusing their fear of the war's and Reconstruction's
threats to their way of life by frightening *"each other with tales of negro
uprisings,"* Sutpen will recognize no more threat from that quarter than
from anywhere, believing somehow that *"if every man in the South would
do as he himself was doing, would see to the restoration of his own land,
the general land and South would save itself"* (161). Instead of unsuccessfully attempting either to focus or to generalize an external threat, he
interiorizes and willfully denies the threat, refusing to recognize any threat
whatever. In social terms, as we will see later, he subscribes here to a Jeffersonian agrarian idea that the yeoman farmer can be transformed (self-
made) into the aristocratic (exclusive) Southern planter without reference
either to surrounding circumstances (wartime defeat, a plantation
economy) or to other people (the necessarily excluded and exploited poor-
white and black tenants and slaves). He believes the contradictory American, especially Southern myth that every man can be an aristocrat, or as
Huey Long later sang, "Every Man a King."

Like Sutpen, Rosa has also briefly interiorized before repressing the
experience of the excluded, for example in Bon's death and Clytie's touch.
So while she acknowledges threats to Sutpen's dream, she cannot quite
ironically displace those threats to a safe distance from herself. Conse-
quently she rejects that irony in order to identify all the more willfully
with Sutpen's dream, inasmuch as she believes she can transform that
dream in the sublime image of her own—transform and sublimate, that
is, what she has seen heretofore as Sutpen's unseemly, physical, violent,
materialistic, ambitious design or cause, into the image of her ideal of a
pure, homogeneous, or at least hierarchical, aristocratic society. She can
note with heavy (almost comically forced) irony his small chance of success
against the changed times, *"as though he were trying to dam a river with
his bare hands and a shingle"*; she can even doubt now in retrospect the
wisdom of his particular goal, *"the same spurious delusion of reward which
had failed (failed? betrayed: and would this time destroy) him once"*; but
she also admits that her pride and principle, her attempted ironic distance
from and protective indifference to human desire in general, amounted

in the event to her willful identification with his desire: "*I see the analogy myself now: the accelerating circle's fatal curving course of his ruthless pride, his lust for vain magnificence, though I did not then. And how could I?*" (130–31). Although she tries to plead ironically the naive innocence then of her youth, this only delays her admitting her willfully innocent attachment even then as "*one of that triumvirate mother-woman*" to Sutpen's particular heroic fiction, as if to say: "*At last my life is worth something, even though it only shields and guards the antic fury of an insane child*" (131).

This conservative fictionalist attempt to exonerate her self-dedication to his fiction as to any fiction with the disclaimer that all such fictions are of course known by her to be false, is the general tenor of her narration of her short-lived engagement with Sutpen. Again, as formulated by Wallace Stevens, "The final belief is to believe in a fiction, which you know to be a fiction, there being nothing else, the exquisite truth is to know that it is a fiction and that you believe in it willingly."[1] Such an opposition of fiction to a known but rejected, nonfictional, completely undifferentiated truth (the "nothing else") precludes any further troubling doubts she may have about Sutpen's particular fiction. That his dream of "*vain magnificence*" might be different from her nostalgic idea of a homogeneous antebellum Southern aristocracy, or even that that magnificence along with his "*ruthless pride*" might repeat especially that same aristocracy's cruel underside (cruel even to herself), are possibilities she cannot metonymically confront, displace, or subordinate, but which she attempts therefore to transfigure or sublimate altogether.

With the willful innocence of her fictionalism, she casts herself (magnificently) as all-redeeming sun illuminating his dark swamp, admitting in retrospect but transfiguring in the event the troubling lack of love:

> standing there in the path looking at me with something curious and strange in his face as if the barn-lot, the path at the instant when he came in sight of me had been a swamp out of which he had emerged without having been forewarned that he was about to enter light, and then went on — the face, the same face: it was not love; I do not say that, not gentleness or pity: just a sudden over-burst of light, illumination. . . . (131)

If perhaps his own fiction denies (by calculating, instrumentalizing) her humanity and subjectivity, hers equally transfigures (by spiritualizing) his. By some "*metabolism of the spirit*" which she distinguishes from that of

---

1. *Necessary Angel* 36, quoted by Lentricchia 28.

the entrails, she loses her (metaphorized, spiritualized) maidenhead here
to his . . . idea—"*yes, lost all the shibboleth erupting of* [her nostalgic
fright's] *cannot,* [her ironic, superior pride's] *will not,* [her ironic, indifferent principle's] *never will in one red instant's fierce obliteration. This
was my instant, who could have fled then and did not*" (132). Although
wary of her involvement with Sutpen and of all it suggests of compromise
of her previous attitudes toward him, she is also for the moment determined
to suppress those reservations except as an exonerating but uncritical alibi
of self-consciousness for her submission and betrothal (nonetheless) to his
fiction. "*I might have said then, To what deluded sewer-gush of dreaming
does the incorrigible flesh betray us: but I did not*" (132): she does not
because she tries to believe both sewer-gush and flesh can be "transformed
utterly" (Yeats 178).

Rosa characterizes both Sutpen and herself in their betrothal as mad,
but with the crucially sane-making (though effectless) difference that she
is self-consciousness in that madness. This is the brief she holds for herself
while insisting she holds no brief at all: "*told myself, 'Why, he is mad
. . . and I mad too, for I will acquiesce, succumb, abet him and plunge
down.' No, I hold no brief, ask no pity*" (133). She mocks his monumental,
self-referential style, the "*serene and florid boast like a sentence . . . not
to be spoken and heard but to be read carved in the bland stone which
pediments a forgotten and nameless effigy.*" Yet this irony toward Sutpen's
style has in no way tamed her own: for example, his leaving no place for
her reply to his marriage proposal not only allows her the breathing room
of her ambiguous but utterly unresisting acquiescence, but also describes
the less than mutual speech-situation of her ongoing monologue to
Quentin, she like Sutpen talking "*to no sane mortal listening nor out of
any sanity, but to the very dark forces of fate which he had evoked and
dared*" (133). When Sutpen madly, willfully (and heroically) defies those
undifferentiated "*dark forces,*" ignoring the underlying changes in history,
personal experience, even ignoring the change in persons, it is not only
Sutpen who speaks (like Fitzgerald's Gatsby) "*as though in the restoration of that ring to a living finger he had turned all time back twenty years
and stopped it, froze it.*" It is also Rosa, who has just said she was listening
"*to his voice as Ellen must have listened in her own spirit's April thirty
years ago*" (133). In her increasingly undeniable complicity in Sutpen's mad
fiction, her only salvation (and his) is in her self-assigned role virtually
as self-consciously unvanquished uncomplicity itself:

> the absence of black morass and snarled vine and creeper to that man
> who had struggled through a swamp with nothing to guide or drive
> him—no hope, no light: only some incorrigibility of undefeat—and

blundered at last and without warning onto dry solid ground and sun and air. (166)

Although in retrospect she admits the possibility that her *"sun"* could not compete with the *"white glare"* of his own madness, she believed then that somehow she could be the guiding, saving telos of a madness which may after all be *"not so mad"* (nor vicious) because there is a method in it which might well be redirected and saved: *"there is a practicality to viciousness . . . why not madness too? If he was mad, it was only his compelling dream which was insane and not his methods"* (134). Her key exhibit in the evidence for the ultimate sanity and salvageability of his methods is his gaining herself to wive, sufficient proof, supposedly, that he is *"not madman, no: since surely there is something in madness, even the demoniac, which Satan flees, aghast at his own handiwork, and which God looks on in pity—some spark, some crumb to leaven and redeem that articulated flesh"* (134). Rather than really recognize that his madness and hers might each have its own heterogeneous gleam and attendant murkiness, she would insist she makes his madness sane, and his demonic possession divine.

Rosa admits the tenuousness of her strategy of redemption and sublimation, having forsaken the relative safety of frightened demonizing as well as of ironic forgiveness: when Sutpen *"(demon or no) courageously suffered"* under the South's flag in the war, she *"did more than just forgive: I slew it* [the demon]" (135). In identifying Sutpen no longer as threatening or low outsider but as resurrected champion of her way of life against other still more alien (Northern) invaders and utterly changed times, Rosa knowingly identifies with his *"solitary despair in titan conflict with the lonely and foredoomed and indomitable iron spirit"* (135). That sublimating identification of Sutpen's *"solitary despair"* with herself and the South, however, strictly excludes everything else of Sutpen as empty (iron) *"shell"* of *"articulated flesh"*; he is murdered, dissected, and dehumanized as *"that speech sight hearing taste and being which we call human man"* (134). Her fictionalism excludes everything of Sutpen, that is, except that *"solitary despair"* which she can equate with her idealized, uncritical nostalgia that she parades as validating self-consciousness. This appropriation of Sutpen to her nostalgic ideal is so reductive that Rosa fails or refuses to understand that his nearly mirror-image dehumanization of her as flesh to his rationalized ideal is one more denuded calculation in his design. It is thus no coincidence, as she thinks it is, that *"the very day on which he knew definitely and at last exactly how much of his hundred square miles he would be able to save and keep and call his own on the day when he would have to die,"* was the same day he called her down to speak *"the bald outrageous words* [his proposition to trial-breed for male offspring before their marriage] *exactly as if he were consulting with Jones or with some other man about a bitch dog or a cow or mare"* (136). The blind spot in her fictionalism, it turns out here (as in other modernistic and New Critical conservative fictionalisms), is that in defining its fictions only in terms of their token self-consciousness (their circumscription by an undifferentiated realm of reality transfigured by such fictions), that fictionalism is likely uncritically to mistake one fiction for another—in this case, her nostalgic, idealized fiction for that fiction of his which she feels the full cruelty of when Sutpen tries to realize his own rationalized version of her nostalgia. That fictionalism is likely, moreover, to result in solitary, exclusive fictions, absolutely reducing all other subjects to the status of objects within a surrounding objective reality, as Sutpen's fiction here reduces Rosa and as Rosa's has also reduced Sutpen, both doing so in the name of that supposedly homogeneous fiction she thinks they share, that of the Southern aristocracy, the fiction to which she shows herself still dedicated years later in her repeated narrative portrayal of Jones as *"brute"* in the chapter's opening.

After the failures of naive hope and love, ironic pride and principle, and now of her willfully innocent *"might-have-been . . . more true than truth,"* Rosa's *"aghast unbelieving which has lasted for forty-three years"* is her still fictionalist withdrawal from her failed sublimation of Sutpen's fiction. She withdraws even more reclusively into a fiction based now not on transfiguring sublimation but on repeatedly failing, willful denials of his and all other truths outside her private *"might-have-been"* (136, 115). She is conscious, as she insists to Quentin, that the town's ironic construction on this withdrawal is that she was right, perhaps, but only idealistically, ineffectually, and isolatedly right: much as her father the *"embusqué"* declaimed agaisnt the surrounding reality of war, she has embalmed and blotted the war's *"secret effluvium of lusting and hating and killing"* in her poetry. She was right perhaps even in hating her father for giving her life. But she knows the town would still invoke against her self-consciously nostalgic, untimely, even gnostically unworldly idealism *"the revenge of some sophisticated and ironic sterile nature"* (169–70). She *"knows"* they think that as mere woman she would expect from Sutpen only this ironic homage to her nostalgic rectitude, and that the unforgivable aspect for her of Sutpen's death is only the troubling lack of this ironic homage. She is prepared, however, to grant the town no such privilege as the sophisticated, ironic perspective of reality on her idealism. She is self-conscious enough to cite their view, but all the more dedicated to a fiction which attempts simply to deny and dismiss the town's supposed sense of reality along with Sutpen's:

*But I forgave him. They will tell you different, but I did. Why
shouldn't I? I had nothing to forgive; I had not lost him because I
never owned him: a certain segment of rotten mud walked into my
life, spoke that to me which I had never heard before and never shall
again, and then walked out; that was all.* (138)

In the all-or-nothing logic of metaphor, if Rosa is unable to "own" him
by sublimation or redemption, then his new name is mud, or uncreated-
ness—"*he was not articulated in this world*" (138).

This alternative strategy of outright denial, however, succeeds no
better than sublimation has in laying Sutpen's already interiorized ghost
to rest somewhere safely beneath Rosa's consciousness. Denial merely
places differently within her fiction that still irrepressible problem (and
fascination) Rosa has with recognizing this other subject's disparate reality.
This becomes clear, for example, when she is told of Sutpen's death and
still addresses her denial's representation of Sutpen as "*walking shadow*":
" '*Dead?' I cried. 'Dead? You? You lie; you're not dead; heaven cannot,
and hell dare not, have you!*' " (139). She is unable to redeem his memory
by heavenly translation or sublimation or to consign it to hellish darkness,
both these vacillating alternatives unsuccessfully designed to exclude the
possibility of love, loss, and mourning. Her remembered, italicized speech
in this chapter ends with this most curious and striking illustration of her
failure either to sublimate or deny her fascination with his living reality,
not just as object but as an other subject, here in his death as also earlier
in his shocking proposition to trial-breed. Since she is unable to sublimate
or deny, and unwilling to recognize, his difference, it makes sense that
Rosa is so convinced of, and so drawn toward, what she announces now
as "*something living. . . . out there . . . hidden in that house*" (140). She
has obscured but not completely transformed or forgotten out there beyond
the confines of her seclusion some still unrepresentable possibility of
another subject she might (already, ambivalently) recognize and love.

Until this last possibility startles Quentin, Rosa must have seemed
to him to be addressing, like Sutpen, only her own "*dark forces of fate
which* [s]*he had evoked and dared*" (133), and although Quentin is no
longer listening, the revealing defensiveness of her wounded attempts at
sublimation and denial of the subject-objects of her love (Bon, Clytie,
Sutpen) has prompted a similarly self-conscious defensiveness on Quentin's
part toward a scene from the very beginning of her narrative in this chapter.
It is as though Quentin has here remembered after his talk with his father
what he only half heard Rosa say earlier that afternoon, when he was
dwelling on this most personally resonant, transfixing scene: "there was
also something which he too could not pass—that door" (139). It is a scene

the import of which he has apparently been unable (even having enlisted his father's efforts that evening) either to displace metonymically over time in the course of a sequential narrative, as in nostalgic and ironic strategies of contrast and superiority, or more willfully to transfigure or dismiss, as in the more interiorized, metaphoric strategies of willfully innocent sublimation and denial. This scene which remains apparently resistant to any such narrativization or signification is that of Judith and Clytie watching their bedroom door after hearing the shot and the running steps on the stairs as Henry crashes into the room to announce his murder of Bon.

Significantly, as Quentin half listens to Rosa's narrative of wounded, defensive love, he has been imagining this particular scene not from Henry's side of the door, but from Judith's hidden side, from the point of view not of his own counterpart in his own family romance, but of Caddy's. In a sense, then, he is in a position inside "that door," a position where it might begin to be possible for him to understand Judith's feeling for Bon and for Henry himself—not as naively innocent, or fatalistically, blankly, indifferently ironic, or even willfully innocent, but as vulnerable in her love for Bon (a love which Henry is violently intruding upon and murdering Bon to deny) and in her love for and trust in Henry himself (a love to which he here does similar violence). If Quentin stops just short of understanding or admitting that love of Judith's, he can see here all too clearly, at least (and so cannot "pass"), both the intersubjective violence and the repressed eroticism of Henry's entry and speech with his half-naked sister, "as if they stood breast to breast striking one another in turn, neither making any attempt to guard against the blows" (132). Any notion here of protecting or saving his sister's honor, as in Mr. Compson's narrative in chapter 4, or as in most of Compson's and Quentin's own reflections in *The Sound and the Fury,* seems all too clearly now a contradictory, willfully innocent, effectively violent fiction on Henry's part to ennoble, sublimate, and idealize his own feelings for Judith by murdering (to deny) the possibility of her own love as an erotic subject. If either the sublimation or the denial would work, perhaps Quentin could "pass" this scene, but he can only imagine Henry's trying unsuccessfully to represent this murder to Judith, first, as all for the better (a sublimation: *"Now you can't marry him"*), then, when questioned, as simple confirmation of an impossibility (denial: *"Because he's dead"*), but then more candidly as a violent act toward her and toward Bon for which he can neither ennoble nor deny his responsibility (incipient, arrested recognition, grief: *"Yes. I killed him"*):

> Now you cant marry him.
> Why cant I marry him?
> Because he's dead.

Dead?
Yes. I killed him. (139–40)

Quentin is unable to "pass" this scene because it represents the willfully barred door to his own here stalled understanding of what he, like Rosa, has hidden "out there" in the realm of obscurity beyond the pale of his own fictions, beyond his ability to contain certain realities either by (metonymic) displacement in narratives of nostalgia or irony, or in concentrated (metaphoric) epiphanies of sublimation or door-slamming denials. Quentin has grown quiet and weary of listening to the two never-ending, verbose courses of Southern memory handed down to him from back-looking ghosts of his heritage like Rosa, and from cynical ironists of the same heritage like his father. What is at stake now instead is Quentin's own impatient, more violent tendency (like Sutpen's) to synthesize such innocence and irony in willfully innocent, crystallizing attempts to solve or escape the contradictions of that heritage once and for all, by leaving the South for Harvard, or by his death. His pending suicide "because of his sister" is his most desperate attempt to escape the impasse, murdering-to-deny his contradictory sense of his own and Caddy's innocent desire and the bitterly ironic, inevitable loss of that innocence in either incest or corruption (Faulkner, *Selected Letters* 78–79). Such plans for willful resolution are complicated here by the disturbing intensity, almost the violence, of his interest, despite himself, in what Rosa tells him now of something still "living. . . . out there . . . hidden in that [dark] house," and thus in the variously compelling obscurities of all these stories and images of the South (140).

Having listened in chapters 2 through 4 to his father's irony toward Rosa's innocence, Quentin has in chapter 5 reevaluated that innocence on Rosa's, Sutpen's, and Henry's parts as less naive than willful, less original purity than compensatory sublimation. In chapter 6 Quentin explores a similar willfulness in his father's, Shreve's, and his own irony, an irony consisting less of brave realism than of more or less violent denials. In the (italicized) letter from Compson which begins Quentin's meditations in this chapter, Compson's voice condescends (as it will in Quentin's memory intermittently throughout the chapter) to the now dead Rosa as having confronted death perhaps at the last, but as having lived for forty-three years before in a near delusion of *"stubborn and amazed outrage."* It is as if Compson here supplies the unamazed, unhindered, postmortem consciousness of reality and death denied to Rosa herself (142). Compson's irony is exaggerated in Shreve, who callously sees Rosa's death as that of one more "Southern Bayard or Guinevere" in the mere romance which he and others at Harvard have repeatedly tried to coax from Quentin:

"*Tell about the South. What's it like there. What do they do there. Why do they live there. Why do they live at all*" (174). In such invitations to tell or write about the South as remote curiosity Quentin will uneasily recognize both his own attempt to escape those Southern legacies ("where he had prepared for Harvard so that his father's hand could lie on a strange lamplit table in Cambridge") and also his inability so easily or so willfully to escape: the letter informing him of Rosa's death brings with it "that very September evening itself" of his father's disappointing ironic mono- logue (141, 142). Although he tries imitating Shreve's dismissive sarcasm to pass off the news of Rosa's death as that of "an old lady that died young of outrage in 1866," this is only another obviously forced, ironic denial of the fact that she has been all too alive to Quentin much more recently and unforgettably than 1866 (142).

He recognizes, then, and grows increasingly impatient throughout this chapter with his father's, Shreve's, and his own cultural, historical, habitual forced irony and its increasingly obvious, sometimes violent denials of kinship with those innocent objects to which it opposes itself in impotent contradiction. That willful irony cannot dispel the sense of a willfulness in innocence all too closely resembling its own, as in the scene which neither Rosa's nor Compson's narrative, nor time, nor distance has dispelled from Quentin's memory:

> something which he still was unable to pass: that door, that gaunt
> tragic dramatic self-hypnotized youthful face like the tragedian in a
> college play, an academic Hamlet waked from some trancement of
> the curtain's falling and blundering across the dusty stage from which
> the rest of the cast had departed last Commencement. (142)

Quentin is stuck, that is, on Henry's persistent emotional involvement in this tragedy, an involvement which is more persistent than Compson's dramatic irony (in chapter 4) has been able satisfactorily to distance and explain as Henry's innocent, moral shock. Henry's lingering and violent involvement even after the four years of war evokes, as well, Quentin's own disturbing absorption decades later in the Sutpen story and in its reminders of similar problems of his own which he has tried and failed to leave behind in the distant past and the distant South.

Quentin's attention wanders from Shreve's narration in this chapter just as it has from Compson's because Shreve sounds to Quentin "*just exactly like Father if Father had known as much about it the night before I went out there as he did the day after I came back*" (148). Shreve sounds like Compson, that is, if Compson's irony at Rosa's willful innocence had been more obviously willful and forced, since Shreve is heavily ironic

toward Rosa's believing something is living hidden out there, even though
the one thing Shreve does know that Compson did not is that she was
right. Shreve's irony willfully denies this knowledge in a chapter-long,
dilatory period: "You mean. . . . Wait. Wait. You mean that. . . .
That. . . . That. . . . And yet . . . there was? . . . Wait then . . . For God's
sake wait" (142, 143, 144, 145, 175). As Shreve talks, Quentin remembers,
attempting twice his father's surety as to the "*calm absolutely impenetrable
face*" of Judith "*(who had not been bereaved and did not mourn)*" (148,
149), as if himself to deny the need for lingering over this murder.

But these willfully ironic attempts at a blank finality confirmed by
death are situated among potentially humorous, ambivalent, dissonant,
unspoken memories of Sutpen from before and after his innocent/ironic
monumentalization in death. From before his death come scenes of his
drinking with Wash Jones, when his and Wash's heroic posturing seems
an innocence which may be willful, but which includes an acutely ambivalent sense (at least in drink) of Sutpen's quite tenuous social superiority.
And from after Sutpen's death comes the memory of his coffined corpse
in all its Confederate colonel's regalia being dumped unmonumentally into
a ditch. Together, these scenes recall the two comic chapters set in the
midst of the "horror" of *Sanctuary*—Miss Reba's social drinking and Red's
abortive funeral—suggesting the lowly origins and continuing, complex,
faltering motivations for the South's and Sutpen's social pretensions. This
ambivalent sense of those pretensions' incompletely betrayed humanity
and solidarity is what survives the supposedly final irony of death and
failure, in the joke that Quentin imagines surviving into Sutpen's and
Jones's afterlife, whatever finally "happened" to turn them fatally against
each other (which they cannot remember): "*They mought have kilt us,
but they aint whupped us yit, air they?*" (152).

Remembering Compson's speeches at the Sutpen family graveyard as
filtered through Shreve's exaggeration of Compson's misogyny and willful
irony, Quentin is growing cautious about what complexities and ambivalences a graveside irony such as theirs might deny, growing cautious, for
example, about reading into Rosa's story his own secret knowledge of her
"maiden hope and virgin expectation," reminding himself, "*If I had been
there I could not have seen it this plain*" (155). Their irony always tends
to deny to their innocent narrative subjects, especially women, any knowledge of the reality of death: "They lead beautiful lives—women. Lives not
only divorced from, but irrevocably excommunicated from, all reality"
(156). Although Compson grants women "a courage and fortitude in the
face of pain and annihilation which would make the most spartan man
resemble a puling boy," this is only to deny them any sensitivity to death's
importance next to the "incalculable importance" for them of their ritualis-

tic funerals and graves, "the littly puny affirmations of spurious immortality set above their slumber" (156). As Quentin remembers his father's
(modernist) characterization of Bon's octoroon wife's visit to his grave as
a "garden scene" by Wilde and Beardsley, he is reminded again uncomfortably of Compson's and his own denials of Judith's grief, "*who, not
bereaved, did not need to mourn* Quentin thought, thinking *Yes, I have
had to listen too long*" (157). The aesthetic perspective, even made sophisticated by an ironic invocation of death, comes at a certain cost.

If Quentin recognizes the denials involved in these narrative ironies,
denial becomes more obvious and violent on the part of characters in the
Sutpen story enforcing such ironies against themselves and others. Clytie
might be described as willfully ironic in her "fierce inexorable spurious
humility" (162) toward Charles Etienne, but she is also willfully innocent
in her compulsive efforts to transfigure his legal blackness, with an
irrepressibly ambivalent result:

> that curious blend of savageness and pity, of yearning and hatred
> . . . sometimes scrubbing at him with repressed fury as if she were
> trying to wash the smooth faint olive tinge from his skin as you
> might watch a child scrubbing at a wall long after the epithet, the
> chalked insult, has been obliterated. (161)

To an ironic Grandfather Compson, however, Clytie's and Judith's
ambivalence is a curious temporizing, now that the boy has entered "the
actual world" at the age of twelve and assumed his (biblically authorized,
ahistorical) "uniform . . . of the sons of Ham," learning somehow "that
he was, must be, a negro," if not by being told, then by examining himself
in a shard of mirror with "incredulous incomprehension" (159–60, 161,
162). Clytie's resistance to this "actual world" of empirical racial and moral
difference is to Grandfather a futile extension of Charles's childhood state
in New Orleans in "a padded silken vacuum cell . . . where pigmentation
had no . . . moral value," her resistance to his fate the equivalent of treat-
ing him as a Spanish virgin, a monk, or a celibate (161–63).

So Grandfather's role in the life of Charles Etienne is to recognize
and appreciate the (masculine) ironic gesture of his futile, self-destructive
"furious protest, that indictment of heaven's ordering, that gage flung into
the face of what is with a furious and indomitable desperation which the
demon himself might have shown," this protest part of a foregone series
capped by "that moment when [the demon's] own fate which he had dared
in his turn struck back at him" (164). Though it is Grandfather who gives
Etienne money to go among strangers and pass for a white or a foreigner,
Grandfather's irony immediately overrules this idea as "lame vain words,

the specious and empty fallacies which we call comfort, thinking *Better that he were dead*" (166). Grandfather's racism thus clothes itself in his ironic realism, since what Compson thinks of as actual, moral, heavenly ordered, immutable reality must deny the mixed, dissonant reality of someone like Etienne, if Etienne does not (like Joe Christmas in *Light in August*) violently, preemptively deny that mixed reality himself.

In his fighting always against overwhelming odds and in his marriage to that "coalblack and ape-like woman" often used to start the fighting, Charles Etienne does enact the most obviously willful, violently self-destructive irony so far in the novel. He has preemptively "denied the white" in his appearance, in his only "sixteenth-part black blood," and in his sense of himself as deserving that fuller humanity usually granted only to the legally white: he has denied the white lest it be denied to him, "and this with a curious and outrageous exaggeration" (168, 158).

The increasingly frequent, inarticulate signal in Faulkner's work that such ironic strategies fail as controlling repetitions and begin instead to resemble parody and humor is their exaggerated violence and a surviving tendency to laughter, as noted earlier in Bon's letter, as also in the potentially comic scenes in Quentin's memories of Sutpen's old age and death, and as in Charles Etienne's laughter here during repeated beatings by both black and white men who do not "grasp" his "actual" blackness so clearly as Grandfather Compson or the ironic Etienne himself, and who therefore will not believe it (164). His denying the white provokes their revealingly excessive denial of the mixed: blacks violently deny the suggestion of blacks enforcing their own oppression, and whites violently deny the suggestion, especially, of any lasting compromise to their moral and emotional whiteness in the "sexual perversion" of white men's miscegenation with black women (167). As Eric Sundquist has recently shown, the deep ambivalence of this imbalanced relationship between white males and black females derives from the widespread historical and emotional actuality of such miscegenation in the South, which is then inverted and denied in the cultural fantasy and horror of black men's miscegenation with white women, a relatively nonexistent relationship imagined not as a reciprocity, but as a violent vindictiveness that must be violently denied (*House Divided* 109).

Such failing, redoubled denials of mixed realities in the ironic invocation and violent reimposition of more familiarly ordered realities cause Quentin to balk repeatedly now at his father's and Shreve's ironic treatment of women, especially Judith (she still at the door to his own denied, mixed realities): "*Yes I have heard too much. . . . Yes* he thought *too much, too long. . . . too much, too long*" (168, 170, 171). Compson has portrayed Judith's meeting with Etienne after his wedding as an ironically, almost logically impossible attempt at sublimation of Etienne's blackness, a "moral

restoration" and "hurdling of iron traditions" which she might well contemplate "in the privacy of that house," and which might well be motivated by her love of Bon, but which involves, in its very expression in
her voice of "seduction" and "celestial promise," simultaneously, the effective denial of Etienne's own "inescapably negro" wife and son (168–69).
Her love is represented here as an absolutely impossible, fated innocence
next to that equally simplified ironic "Gethsemane which he [Etienne, and
supposedly no one else] had decreed and created for himself" (169). Echoing
Compson, Shreve in his attitude toward Rosa's gravestone similarly denies
the significance and pain of those who lead unreal lives, who are less well
adjusted and equal to facts than the ironist is:

> Beautiful lives—women do. In very breathing they draw meat and
> drink from some beautiful attenuation of unreality in which the
> shades and shapes of fact—of birth and bereavement, of suffering and
> bewilderment and despair—move with the substanceless decorum of
> lawn party charades, perfect in gesture and without any significance
> or any ability to hurt. (171)

Quentin begins to recognize the willful denial of women's realities in such
insistent projections of denial onto women: "that calm incorrigible insistence that that which all incontrovertible evidence tells her is so does not
exist—as women can" (171).

Quentin himself feels such denials both as ironic narrator and as innocent character ("author and victim"), white and black, male and female.
When Quentin's father laughs at the black Luster's fear of the house and
(the dead) Sutpen, Quentin is uncomfortable with that laughter because
of what it evokes in his own memory of being with Luster as fearful boys,
attempting to watch unobserved a profoundly innocent, black victim, "the
Jim Bond, the hulking, slack-mouthed saddle-colored boy" (elsewhere
described as epicene), only to find suddenly it is themselves being watched
by an unobserved black woman (Clytie), who is compared to a monkey
(in the racist cliché) but who also seems perhaps a (patriarchal) ten thousand years old, who smokes a pipe as a man would, and speaks "in a voice
almost like a white woman's," so that Quentin had to run to put a fence
between him and her for "the earth, the land, the sky and trees and woods"
to look "all right again" (173–74). If he can remember feeling such mixed
realities as a character, he also shares now in Shreve's willful narrative
denial and procrastination of Rosa's "something" hidden out there in the
house, still untold. Quentin has followed this chapter's entire narrative
with growing impatience and irony but with neither vocal resistance nor
participatory revision, granting Shreve his attempt at incredulous, forced

denial of what this woman knew and what they have tried to refuse to believe—that there could be recognizable, living Sutpen ghosts surviving even beneath the hard surface of Shreve's modernistic and Compson's and Quentin's postwar Southern irony.

The Southern modernist strategy of ironic repetition, with its increasingly forced resolutions in terms of innocence and irony, continues in chapter 7 to leave inarticulate but unsettling, unresolved, telling remainders of violence and twisted humor, as demonstrated here particularly in Sutpen's autobiography as told to Quentin's grandfather and passed along through Compson and Quentin to Shreve. Sutpen is in his story an innocent immigrant to the Southern plantation society, who adopts that society completely without apology, with the effect that the society's contradictions are condensed, crystallized, and made strange instead of being more gracefully displaced through the social hierarchy or over the generations: the plantation economy's lawless opportunism and lawful opportunity appear together, for example, in one person's story instead of in different social classes or different generations of a more slowly established family like the Compsons. And in its imperfection as mythic resolution of such cultural contradictions, his story also interestingly, briefly imports and resurrects in the midst of the Southern, modernist narrative of *Absalom* pungent traces of the usually humorous narratives of the Old Southwest, narratives of an ambivalently precapitalist frontier society that was more rudely confrontational, violent, heterogeneous, and unstable than that cultural and literary idea of the Southern plantation aristocracy which largely took its place—a supposedly noncapitalist, unambitious, leisured genteel culture whose contradictions were actually only more elaborately mediated by hierarchy or rationalization.

"His trouble was innocence," says Quentin of Sutpen, echoing his father's and grandfather's judgments (178). In a scene briefly discussed in my Introduction, Sutpen supposedly discovers climactically at the age of fourteen, with no previous preparation or complicity, the necessity and form of social ambition from which virtually all else in his life would follow, discovers "all of a sudden . . . not what he wanted to do but what he just had to do" (178). Quentin will repeat Sutpen's story in another attempt to make the "trouble" suddenly Sutpen's and not the society's (and thus not the Compsons' either), by reducing Sutpen's previous history to an unknowing innocence before the predictably inevitable revelation of the absolutely and monolithically overruling reality of Southern society. But before Quentin's narrative can achieve this simplifying, climactic, frightful fall, Sutpen and Quentin both recall—if only to silence or distance them—several more ambivalent scenes from before this fall, scenes marked by violence and the presence or conspicuous absence of laughter. Sutpen's famous insult at the planter's door, for example, the primal scene which he represents as the almost single provocation for his lifelong design, is preceded by at least two similar scenes for which it becomes clearly an oversimplifying, focusing repetition. The explicit contrast between these earlier scenes will suggest what ambivalences Sutpen's repetitions—also the Compsons' and Southern narratives' repetitions more generally—are meant to sublimate and deny, and what Faulkner's later returns to this primal scene (most explicitly in *The Hamlet, Go Down, Moses,* and *Requiem for a Nun*) will gradually work to excavate, demystify, and more candidly explore.

The first such scene is from Sutpen's memory of moving with his recently widowed, usually drunken father down from the mountains of frontier West Virginia toward the plantation society of Tidewater, Virginia, seeing his father repeatedly thrown out the doors of doggeries "and this one time by a huge bull of a nigger, the first black man, slave, they had even seen, who emerged with the old man over his shoulder like a sack of meal and his—the nigger's—mouth loud with laughing and full of teeth like tombstones" (182). The almost total reduction of Sutpen's father to a sack of meal and his violent ejection are accompanied here by a laughter and an exaggerated fright (in the frontier-humor Roarers' image of teeth like tombstones) which suggest that this is actually something less than an absolute, permanent loss of life and social dignity. And in fact, in what Sutpen has already said of their frontier society, any such assertion of property rights or social sovereignty is extremely tenuous, since "everybody had just what he was strong enough or energetic enough to take and keep, and only that crazy man would go to the trouble to take or even want more than he could eat or swap for powder and whiskey" (179). Even racial superiority is felt not as a natural property or right but as something to "take and keep" only by an acknowledged violence: "where the only colored people were Indians and you only looked down at them over your rifle sights" (179).

The second scene of social rejection leading up to Sutpen's own affront at the planter's door occurs in plantation country, where Sutpen notices and inarticulately regrets the absence of frontier-style laughter:

> taverns where the old man was not even allowed to come in by the front door and from which his mountain drinking manners got him ejected before he would have time to get drunk good (so that now they began to make really pretty good time) and no laughter and jeers to the ejecting now, even if the laughter and jeers had been harsh and without much gentleness in them. (183)

Sutpen's regret is signaled only by the concessive "even if," and his sympathy for the here more completely rejected, summarily degraded father is disguised (if thinly) by the parenthetical, insider's irony which could as well be any one of the three Compson narrators' irony as the now older Sutpen's adopted own. What is strangely new to Sutpen in this society is especially the stabilization or reification of social "difference not only between white men and black ones, but [also] between white men and white men not to be measured by lifting anvils or gouging eyes or how much whiskey you could drink" (183). Accustomed to the sense of mutual physical and visual vulnerability suggested by the gouging of eyes, Sutpen can hardly imagine such a sovereignty stabilized without struggle, challenge, or at least deep resentment—cannot imagine that "the ones who owned the objects not only could look down on the ones that didn't, but could be supported in the down-looking not only by the others who owned objects too but by the very ones that were looked down on that didn't own objects and knew they never would" (179), supported so completely that Sutpen's father would be ejected without so much as a harsh laugh to mark unchanneled emotion clumsily repressed.

Yet it is this same possibility of resentment which this society does repress, as Sutpen learns briefly, painfully, before he, too, represses what he learns, to adopt instead this society's stabilizing, mediating myths, especially the Southern, more generally American, and even more generally modern bourgeois notion of an abstract freedom and equality naturally and legally extended to all (men) even though the social and economic conditions for realizing that freedom and equality are available only to some: it is what amounts to an abstractly *potential* freedom and equality, as opposed to an undeniably *fundamental* freedom and equality (Marcuse 97). The obvious exceptions in the plantation South to these assumptions of an at least potential freedom and equality for all—Native Americans and blacks—usually served only to reconfirm by contrast the mythic abstraction's consoling ideological function for those poor whites who were at least legally if not socially or economically free, such as Sutpen's family, who lived in "cabins not quite as well built and not at all as well kept and preserved as the ones the nigger slaves lived in but still nimbused with freedom's bright aura, which the slave quarters were not for all their sound roofs and white wash" (185). The myth also thus served to exonerate those who did possess the social and economic conditions for a real freedom to match the abstraction, by diverting attention away from an axiomatic unfreedom toward a despotic unfreedom, or by diverting attention away from the (class) difference between real and merely abstractly *potential* freedom toward, instead, the legal (racial) difference between (an undifferentiated) "freedom" and slavery. This process of mediation, whereby real inequalities and unfreedoms between whites and whites (taking and keeping) are hidden behind an abstract, reified general equivalent such as freedom or the right to property or capital (having and owning), or whereby those same real and also abstract inequalities and unfreedoms for Native Americans and blacks are enforced on the equally abstract, reified, naturalized grounds of race, is precisely what Sutpen's and his family's frontier background, along with their real social, economic, and physical indignities in plantation society, causes to appear strange, and what is quite understandably difficult for the young Sutpen to digest and learn. Sutpen loses his "innocence" when he most directly feels and then denies the violent exclusiveness and oppressiveness of these social conventions which he learns to conceive of as simple reality. This reductive but privileged objective correlative retrospectively opposes to and overpowers his own merely uninitiated innocence.

When the young Sutpen approaches the planter's front door with a message, he expects the man lucky enough to own such a house to be pleased to show him inside, just as he would expect a mountain man to show him proudly a fine rifle and all that went with it, not conceiving

> of the owner taking such crass advantage of the luck which gave the rifle to him rather than to another as to say to other men: *Because I own this rifle, my arms and legs and blood and bones are superior to yours* except as the victorious outcome of a fight with rifles. (185)

When Sutpen does feel in his rags the brunt of the planter's real social superiority—when he is ordered by the liveried household slave "even before he had had time to say what he came for, never to come to that front door again but to go around to the back" (188)—he is caught with no way to mediate the affront. Searching his experience for "something to measure it by," and having no "older and smarter person to ask," he realizes the flimsiness of, for example, "freedom's bright aura," as he recalls "the flat level silent way his older sisters and the other white women of their kind had of looking at niggers," a gaze of attempted superiority and objectification that is turned back against them when the blacks are being (as other subjects, not just enslaved objects of this gaze) "apparently oblivious of it, too oblivious of it" (188, 189, 185, 186). He recalls, too, his worthless legal right as a white to strike blacks without reprisal, worthless because you knew "when you hit them you would just be hitting a child's toy balloon with a face painted on it, a face slick and smooth and distended and about to burst into laughing" (186). The abstract distinction between the free and the unfree projects and disguises behind a colored balloon face that real unfreedom the blacks and poor whites almost undeniably share. Unable even to invoke the mediating "good faith of business which he had believed that all men accepted," and in which he had come with his message, Sutpen cannot help feeling his own reduction from being that human ally of the rifle owner he thought he was, to being another of the planter's economic instruments, delivering lead or bullets but not allowed himself to "come close enough to look at the rifle" (188, 189), feeling himself the equivalent of his ejected father as "sack of meal," but without the suggestive remainder of laughter. Without the consoling mediation of his affront as natural, necessary, or as merely accidental to the operation of an economy in which both he and the planter participate and believe, he here resembles the slave or prostitute who scandalizes bourgeois morality because "the regulated classes [supposedly] rendered services not immediately, with their persons, but only mediated by the production of surplus value for the market" (Marcuse 115). Without a consoling mediation Sutpen concludes of his affront that he "had nothing to compare and gauge it by but the rifle analogy, and it would not make sense by that" (189). This rifle analogy will prove usefully ambiguous, however, for denying, by sublimating, these insights for which he can find no other socially extant articulation.

Uncomforted by the balloon-face distinction between abstract freedom and slavery, and rejecting (as innocent) the idea of trying to turn the insult back and away from himself as murder, the boy resorts to the now familiar strategy in *Absalom* of generalizing and repeating the insult himself against himself:

> before he knew it, something in him had escaped and—he unable to close the eyes of it—was looking out from within the balloon face [of the liveried slave] just as the man who did not even have to wear the shoes he owned, whom the laughter held barricaded and protected from such as he, looked out from whatever invisible place he (the man) happened to be at the moment, at the boy outside the barred door in his patched garments. . . . (189–90)

Thinking he has to compete only with his innocence "(not the man, the tradition)" (189), Sutpen here attempts to "escape" and deny that innocence by identifying with the planter as simply everything opposite and superior to him. Invisible, omniscient subject to his marked object, the planter is member of no analyzable class or tradition, is of no visible or identifiable place or class whatever. Thus he owns but does not have to wear those shoes the absence of which, along with the "patched garments," are a virtual class uniform for Sutpen. Under this disembodied, invisible gaze, Sutpen's family look like "cattle, creatures heavy and without grace, brutely evacuated into a world without hope or purpose for them" (190). These associations of poor whites with cattle and shit will return to the planter's door more critically and humorously on Ab's boot in "Barn Burning," and again in the fouled figure of Ike under his frightened cow in *The Hamlet,* but here they are part of a past with which Sutpen is trying to expel every connection, including the idea of *"Home. Home,"* as well as that labor which with infuriated sympathy he watches his sister doing, "brutish and stupidly out of all proportion to its reward: the very primary essence of labor, toil, reduced to its crude absolute which only a beast could and would endure" (191).

Viewing that labor from the idealized perspective of a tradition which did in fact define itself largely in terms of "leisure" (as echoed in Cleanth Brooks's distinctions between Sutpen and the typical Southern planter — "On *Absalom, Absalom!*"), thereby denying its dependence on the labor of poor whites and slaves, Sutpen, too, proceeds to the point of reducing his poor-white past to no consequence whatsoever: *"I not only wasn't doing any good to him by telling it* [the message] *or any harm by not telling it, there aint any good or harm either in the living world that I can do to him"* (192). The enraged Wash Jones, the barn-burning Ab Snopes, and his lethal cousin Mink will later challenge this denial of the planter's vulnerability to poor whites, but for Sutpen this is the point of willful innocence when denial achieves the denial even of having denied anything: "it was . . . like an explosion — a bright glare that vanished and left nothing, no ashes nor refuse: just a limitless flat plain with the severe shape of his intact innocence rising from it like a monument" (192). Having been briefly ironic in his self-divided invocation of his insulter's denial of him, he has here completely transfigured or sublimated that insulted, former innocence in decisively undivided, monumentally innocent identification not only with his former oppressors in particular but, Ahab-like, with anything over, against, or outside him (*"them . . .* meant more than all the puny human mortals under the sun that might lie in hammocks all afternoon with their shoes off" — 192).[2] Sutpen's new, monumental, willful rather than naive innocence is so complete that he can use the rifle analogy that failed him before, with the crucial shift in meaning now (without remainder, as in metaphor) from rifle as weapon used still ambivalently *against* someone else or as contestable prize won *from* someone else, into rifle as property —

2. Cf. this *them* with the *they* who persecute a thereby purified, exonerated *us* in Hemingway's *A Farewell to Arms,* a more sustainedly paranoid romantic/ironic strategy Faulkner would soon parody and critique in *The Wild Palms.*

property no longer as "taking and keeping" but "having" (and owning)—
property that marks a stable (reified) social distinction and determines
appropriate social and moral conduct: "you have got to have what they
have that made them do what he [the planter] did. You got to have land
and niggers and a fine house" (192). In a parallel ambiguity, it is this same
willful innocence which will allow Sutpen later in life to use Coldfield's
moral "credit" quite unapologetically as financial "credit" with which to
speculate for profit. Also in his use of the word *niggers* here to refer to
another item of property in the social formula, he is already repainting
those balloon faces of race, gender, and class which failed him before but
beyond which he will later refuse to recognize the faces of other kindred
subjects such as his eldest son, his first wife, and his spiritual son Wash
Jones, among other willfully innocent repetitions of his own affront.

I have dwelt at some length on this scene because it returns so persistently in Faulkner's writing, both before and after this novel, in ways
that will serve to mark the continuing progress of his critique of irony
in its Southern and modernist literary and social manifestations. Sutpen's
monumentally innocent, nearly parodic, unqualified identification with the
Southern plantation ideology is perhaps the least critical but also in some
ways the most revealing repetition of that ideology. Whereas more
practiced ironists attempt to blame contradictions within that ideology
on external or subordinate factors, Sutpen's life forces those contradictions to a crisis. The Southern plantation ideology adopted by Sutpen is
itself an extreme form of an often noted, wider, American, bourgeois
dream of an abstract, pure freedom from place, class, history, limitation,
attachment, or responsibility, as in, for example, the Renaissance notion
of unlimited self-fashioning, Franklin's idea of a nondogmatic representative personality, Emerson's self-reliant, transparent eyeball, Ahab's *non
serviam* and the Confidence Man's protean Masquerade, James's American innocence, Adams' dynamo, and Gatsby's self-named, self-made man
redoing the past.[3] The Southern, modernist, postwar irony at the cata-
strophic failures of that ideal, instead of idealizing particular blind spots
and contradictions of particular versions of it, tends to subsume it with
all others in the category of an innocence overruled by the opposed generalization of an inevitable (but still external) fate, misfortune, or darkness.
Instead of naively ignoring or willfully refusing to see, this irony names
and reifies (sees) only a general blindness, thereby preserving its own version of the originally innocent idea of a vision free of any particular limitations—free, for example, of any discomfiting sense of kinship with a

---

3. See, for example, Greenblatt on self-fashioning; Breitwieser on Franklin; Porter on
Emerson, James, and Adams; Chase on Ahab; and Feidelson on Melville's *Confidence Man*.

less self-conscious, more apparently innocent Thomas Sutpen and the Southern history he represents.

Sutpen's willfully innocent refusal of any doubt that the particular social formula, morality, recipe, schedule, or design according to which he calculates his every move might ignore any significant remainder of experience is the blind spot stressed by all three generations of Compson narrators and Shreve in their (willful) narrative irony. Sutpen goes to the West Indies because his society's schoolbook ideology says poor men go there and get rich, never mind how; his bombastic speech and gestures seem likewise learned by rote from a phrase book; his individual oral history as one of these self-made men is told as his "destiny," noticeably without regard for "cause and effect" or "logical sequence and continuity. . . . the how and the why he was there and what he was" (198, 199). When there is trouble from the plantation slaves he oversees in Haiti, the ironic Compsons, evoking Conrad's title, say Sutpen simply does not know "that it was the heart of the earth itself he heard, who believed (Grandfather said) that earth was kind and gentle and that darkness was merely something you saw, or could not see in" (202–3). Sutpen simply decides "something had to be done so he put the musket down and went out and subdued them. That was how he told it" (204). His willfully innocent autobiography is a *Rambo* to their willfully ironic *Apocalypse Now!,* the former narrowly focusing and dispensing with an American blind spot, the latter giving that blindness metaphysical status, but neither concerned with the "natives" except as the means for mastering or representing darkness.

Thus with his first wife Sutpen thinks innocently he has measured and absolutely settled the score between them according to the requirements of his design and schedule and its accompanying, scrupulously formal, logical, abstract sense of morality and justice, whereas the Compsons marvel ironically at his "purblind innocence" of "the very affinity and instinct for misfortune" they expect in any man, along with that "dread and fear of females which you must have drawn in with the primary mammalian milk" (213). Whereas Sutpen hazards but intends to master or sublimate his slaves' cannibalism and the unseemly suggestions of white slavery in the manhunt for the French architect, the Compsons accomplish virtually the same end — a transfiguring denial — by ironically aestheticizing and universalizing the captured but still "invincible" architect's "gesture that Grandfather said you simply could not describe, that seemed to gather all misfortune and defeat that the human race ever suffered into a little pinch in his fingers like dust and fling it backward over his head" (207). The Compsons thereby deflect attention from the politics and ambivalences of this particular manhunt in which Grandfather himself participated, at least until such manhunts return for a more critical treatment in *Go Down, Moses.*

At times, the Compson narrators still attempt to distance and displace Sutpen from the more perfectly established Southern ideal and society that he merely "apes" (194), as in those strategies of innocent contrast and ironic subordination more frequently met in *Absalom*'s early chapters. But at this stage of these narrators' and Shreve's growing involvement in Sutpen's story, for the most part their irony takes a more willful, confrontational structure and tone, "as though at the last ditch, saying No to Quentin's Mississippi shade" (225), saying No to Sutpen by invoking with self-betraying zeal those distantly external, abstracted forces of human misfortune and darkness with which they (too) hope to externalize and deny problems that Sutpen's example shows instead to be undeniably internal to the same ideal of all-seeing, all-knowing invulnerability. That is, their irony, based on an abstract, universal, inevitable vulnerability, is still embedded despite themselves in historical, social, and personal forms of denying this variously concrete embeddedness (cf. Shapiro 145–56).

On the one hand, Sutpen scrupulously adheres to the social formula he calls his design to the point where it reveals itself as a double bind, such that "either course which I might choose, leads to the same result," either (as in the innocent, nostalgic course of Southern narrative) to preserve the abstract purity of his design by destroying what seems its one possibility of realization (in Henry, by making Henry a murderer), or (as in the ironic, modernist course of Southern narrative) to

> do nothing, let matters take the course which I know they will take and see my design complete itself quite normally and naturally and successfully to the public eye, yet to my own in such fashion as to be a mockery and a betrayal of that little boy who approached that door fifty years ago and was turned away, for whose vindication the whole plan was conceived and carried forward to the moment of this choice. . . . (220)

To let Bon marry Judith would be to acknowledge the impurity (at this point as either incest or miscegenation) of his dreamed-of vindication and completion as someone perfectly invulnerable to social exposure, exclusion, or obligation to anyone else's design. It would be to admit his unfreedom, as in his subtle, feared blackmail by—or petition for intersubjective, heteronomous recognition by—Eulalia and/or Charles Bon. To put more bluntly this internal contradiction within the social and personal ideal, for every man to be really, purely (invulnerably) king, every other man must be really, purely a brute and vassal: every black, every white female, every other white male, and now even the past family and self of the king himself. The magic circle of purity and freedom shrinks to a vanishing point in the ideal future. In order to achieve his design Sutpen requires material means (though even these are socially mediated) and other people as means ("money, a house, a plantation, slaves, a family — incidentally, of course, a wife" — 212), yet precisely insofar as these people can subject Sutpen to others' designs (in the threat of social exposure), including their own designs (in demands for recognition and love), insofar, that is, as these people are also, like Sutpen himself, potentially free and unreliably instrumentalized and calculable according to his design, that design will remain either pure and unreal or an always impure betrayal of the ideal. Sutpen chooses in character, to preserve the ideal by destroying this possibility for its impure realization, then destroys the next possibility and the next by insulting Rosa and Wash.

Sutpen's ironic narrative counterparts, on the other hand, are less willing even temporarily to admit this double bind as an internal problem of the society Sutpen's story is imitating and crystallizing, and their narrative tendency to willful, ironic, universalized nay-saying causes a series of conspicuous misreadings. Of the scene when Sutpen sits in General Compson's office for a legal mind's analysis of where he went wrong in his design, Grandfather and Father impotently conclude that having reached his peak and done all that he set out to do, "maybe this [is] the instant which Fate always picks out to blackjack you" (194), never mind the particular peak. Although their retrospective irony stresses what Sutpen did not know and what they might have predicted, as Shreve says later, "When your grandfather was telling this to [your father], he didn't know any more what your grandfather was talking about than your grandfather knew what the demon was talking about when the demon told it to him, did he?" (220). Just as the senior Compsons' invocation of fate is an all too conveniently far cry from the shared problem of an unreal/impure social ideal, Quentin will recognize in his and Shreve's own ironic narrative postures "that protective coloring of levity behind which the youthful shame of being moved hid itself, out of which Quentin also spoke, the reason for Quentin's sullen bemusement, the (on both their parts) flipness, the strained clowning" (225). He even recognizes that this ironic denial or banalization of Sutpen's moving predicament "after all was a good deal like Sutpen's morality and Miss Coldfield's demonising" (225). The extent to which their irony merely protects their emotional investment in his dream becomes clear, first, in Shreve's ignoring several obvious clues that Sutpen's and Milly's baby was female, as if by denying that merely external, biological accident Shreve could imagine Sutpen's design might have had a happy ending for all concerned (which by its very nature it could not). Thus too when Quentin corrects Shreve's misreading at the end of the chapter, he does so in terms that echo Sutpen's own — "horse or mare?"

(229)—as if a female child would be (already, without his denial) not one of but outside the species: Quentin likewise tells Shreve, "It wasn't a son. It was a girl" (234), as if a girl child is already, almost biologically, not recognized as a daughter. It is as if, as well, Quentin himself in his willed irony at having "to never listen to anything else but this again forever" (222) wants to recognize no more than Sutpen does in his willed innocence the possibility of a daughter's—or sister's, say Judith's, or Caddy's—own unpredictable, heteronomous designs, as opposed to her inevitable ineligibility or impurity in the male's own family romance.

Sutpen's contradictory efforts at sublimating the real in the image of his ideal, and his narrators' willfully ironic efforts to deny their complicity both in his particular ideal and especially in its impure, vulnerable realizations, are thread and groove of a single screw turned even tighter in the cameo portrait here of Wash Jones as willful innocent suddenly turned willful, violently destructive and self-destructive ironist. If Sutpen has believed his abstract, potential freedom and equality can be made real in an ideal future, Wash Jones goes farther in innocence to believe that merely that symbolic, vicarious freedom and equality may be enough. The world in which he is laughed at by blacks is "just a dream and an illusion," since

> the Book said that all [white] men were created in the image of God and so all men were the same in God's eyes anyway . . . so he would look at Sutpen and think *A fine proud man. If God Himself was to come down and ride the natural earth, that's what He would aim to look like.* (226)

Wash believes not in Sutpen's station, achievement, or efficacy, but in his utterly transfiguring touch: "I know that whatever your hands tech, whether hit's a regiment of men or a ignorant gal or just a hound dog, that you will make hit right" (228). When Wash finds Sutpen's touch does not make it right with Milly, but with a joking remark leaves her outside his house and stable like one of those "brute and vassal" blacks cursed and excluded by Wash's Bible from even symbolic apotheosis, Wash turns ironist with a vengeance. He overrules Sutpen's function as "symbol . . . of admiration and hope" with the generalized, opposite function of planters like Sutpen as "instruments . . . of despair and grief" (226, 232). Sutpen's cruelty toward Wash and Milly shows the strain of its willfulness both in his uncharacteristic attempt, if feeble, at a humor which does acknowledge his cruelty, and in the extreme, eye-gouging, frontier-style, personal violence of the two blows with his riding whip to that unrecognized, exploding balloon face of "the man who in twenty years he had no more known to make any move save at command than he had the stallion which he rode" (231). Wash's irony shows a willfulness to match in his grotesque impersonation of Father Time, hearing all voices as "the murmuring of tomorrow and tomorrow and tomorrow beyond the immediate fury," that abstracted irony seeming now to overrule the merely chaotic voice of particular human losses (all sounding like Benjy's sound and fury), so that Wash can decide that it would be *"Better that all who remain of* [Sutpen's kind and mine] *be blasted from the face of* [the earth] *than that another Wash Jones should see his whole life shredded from him and shrivel away like a dried shuck thrown on the fire"* (232, 233). Wash can decide for his granddaughter and great-granddaughter that their lives and designs are reducible to the same as his, and he can enforce the ultimately suicidal, murderous tendency of his irony on them as well as himself.

Quentin and Shreve attempt in chapter 8 a kind of New Critical interpretive metanarrative of "things that just have to be whether they are or not" (260), attempting not just to negate Sutpen's flawed, particular version of the dream for its impurity or its impossibility of realization, but to correct and redeem that dream in their own interpretive fiction of honor and love, in which "there might be paradox and inconsistency but nothing fault nor false" (253). Sutpen himself has in chapter 7 suspected such internal inconsistencies in his dream, and has responded to those suspicions with willfully innocent denial, by forcing his dream repeatedly on the recalcitrant facts, until one of those facts strikes back in the offended sensibility of Wash Jones. Sutpen's Compson narrators, on the other hand, have denied with sardonic, willful irony their own emotional and social stake in Sutpen's contradictory design by calling down a general darkness over his and all other human designs. Quentin and Shreve have also been moved by Sutpen's story, and Quentin will admit uneasily now himself in chapter 8 the resemblance of Sutpen's "logic and morality" to their own "ratiocination" (225). But Quentin and Shreve imagine they are in a position to do less harm with their ratiocination in their distant college dorm room than Sutpen was, and they propose in their imaginative metanarrative of honor and love to heal contradiction in an aesthetic reconciliation of opposites. Their sense of (only) aesthetically resolvable paradox and inconsistency is analogous to the experience of poetic truth as described by I. A. Richards and institutionalized in the New Criticism: as in Paul de Man's account of that criticism in *Blindness and Insight,* Quentin's and Shreve's own decontextualizing, deliberate distance from and "blindness" to historical consequences (which are made external to their interpretation of Sutpen's dream) eventually allow them a more concentrated "insight" (than Sutpen's or the senior Compsons') into that dream's ambiguous internal structure. The internal ambiguities and ironies which they discover here, however, will turn out not to be what de Man appreciates in New Criticism's readings of literature: so many statements and repetitions of the Heideggerian cleavage of Being (20–35, 229–45). Quentin and Shreve will find not an aesthetically resolvable or philosophically recognizable "paradox and inconsistency," but a grotesquely focused contradiction unsuccessfully obscured, reified, and transcended in Sutpen's social design as also in their aesthetic one.

Starting out with Henry in his light-switch rejection of his father's particular implementation of the grand design, Quentin and Shreve, like Henry as also like Sutpen before them, in their rejection of the design enact its next repetition, having only refined and rationalized, without analyzing, its contradictory content. Their idealization of Sutpen's design, beyond their willed irony at Sutpen's willed innocence, proceeds, in what might be called a willed synthesis of innocence and irony, in two movements, directly analogous on another plane to Sutpen's own response to his affront as a boy at the planter's door: first negating, refusing to recognize behind the black balloon face the image of his own unfreedom, then hypostatizing and sublimating that denial in a synthesizing identification with, behind that same face, an idealized planter's absolute freedom. First, "before what [Sutpen] said [to Henry] stopped being shock and began to make sense" (236)—that is, in the moment of fright's stalling oppositions before the rationalizations of anxiety and acquiescence—Quentin and Shreve proceed by focusing, narrowing, and projecting "out there" the source of threat to a correspondingly pure, prior innocence. They compare this first movement to raking "the leaves up before you can have the bonfire" (253): whatever of Bon might at first be frightening as external threat is heaped instead on Eulalia Bon and her imagined lawyer. Then in the second movement Bon can be further purified or pyrified, sublimated in both the psychological and the chemical sense, directly from "meat" to spirit, without loss, remainder, or grief, yielding Bon as neither external nor even internal threat but as perfectly refined realization of the original grand design—if also, ambiguously, another of its obscurely contradictory repetitions.

In the first movement, raking leaves, Quentin and Shreve continue to imagine problems as external, accidental, and thus either avoidable or correctable in a past or future time or imagination, as in Shreve's earlier attempt to misread the gender of Sutpen and Milly's child, echoed in Quentin's more subtle attempt to make that child's exclusion a biological and not a social fact. As they imagine now Henry's denial of his father's shocking suggestion of Bon's ineligibility for Judith (because he is her brother) and possible duplicity toward Henry (because he has known or suspected this fact and concealed it), they likewise do their best to deny, by altering, both these facts of Bon's duplicity toward Henry (never mind

Judith, who supposedly wouldn't mind the duplicity) and his ineligibility
to marry Henry's sister (never mind Judith again, who supposedly wouldn't
mind the incest either). In their joint narration of denial (described repeatedly as if without any differences of time, place, purpose, or persons),
Quentin and Shreve stare at each other with "youth's immemorial obses-
sion not with time's dragging weight which the old live with but with its
fluidity: the bright heels of all the lost moments of fifteen and sixteen"
(240). To make Bon innocent of duplicity, they return nostalgically to his
childhood, where they project all vindictiveness toward Sutpen onto Bon's
mother, who they decide would not have told Bon himself, and whom
they imagine as stripped to virtually nothing else but this conveniently displaced, distant source of animosity, so that for Bon in his imagined boyhood, her demands are reduced to "an incomprehensible fury" at "the old
infernal immortal male principle of all unbridled terror and darkness" (239,
251). Thus generalized now by irony, all this meaningless sound and fury
can be further mediated and can even be made calculable, impersonal,
and nearly ignorable altogether in the imagined figure of the mother's
lawyer, dedicated only to that financial revenge on Sutpen for which Bon
himself is imagined to have a superior contempt.

In the second movement Quentin and Shreve will eventually admit
that Bon did know or at least suspect his paternity throughout his involvement with Henry, but they can accept that fact now that they have cleared
Bon of any personal motivation for revenge against Sutpen, or indeed of
almost any personal motivation whatsoever. They have identified him with
"that expression which was not smiling but just something not to be seen
through," and with "that masculine hipless tapering peg which fits light
and glib to move where the cartridge-chambered hips of women hold them
fast" (249–50). They decide that Bon escapes his one possible emotional
attachment in New Orleans without even saying goodbye, since to him
"one place was the same as another, like to a cat" (252). That is, they have
made him perfectly transfigurable, light and glib for their aesthetic design.
Just as Sutpen at the door looked through one face, the slave's, to see and
identify with only the invisible planter's face somewhere beyond it, Quentin
and Shreve imagine Bon seeing in Henry's face not just the half brother's
image of his own innocent *malleable and eager clay* or the duped
clodhopper bastard (254), but also (deeper, transfigured) the hidden face
of his own father. From that father's face he expects the transfiguring sign
"which would reveal to him at once, like a flash of light, the meaning of
his whole life, past" (250): a knowledge which would transfigure the dark,
"infernal" boyhood secret of his paternity into his absolute identification
and illumination. Just as Henry and Judith regard Bon with their own
complete "humility which surrendered no pride" (254), as if on the verge

of their own complete sublimation without remainder into "that fairy balloon-vacuum in which the three of them existed, lived, moved even maybe, in attitudes without flesh" (256), so Quentin and Shreve tell this "fairy tale" in an attempt to sublimate Bon (in his "one sublimation of passive surrender"—265) from an external threat to the Sutpen family into a harmless, all-reconciling seeker after his father and source of meaning in Sutpen. Bon here expects somehow to see through to his father's hidden, transfiguring face, without, however, the least real surrender of his own pride: he will neither expose his need for that recognition nor make those assurances to Sutpen which might allow Sutpen to risk exposing his own considerable vulnerability by recognizing Bon, assurances Bon simply expects his father to know. Quentin and Shreve imagine this lack of a sign of recognition as an inflexible stubbornness on Sutpen's part which (their) Bon would have corrected had he been Sutpen, but they refuse to consider that Bon's unwillingness to ask for Sutpen's recognition or to reassure Sutpen of his intentions is also another image of that pride and purity of the dream that, even in its refined form in Bon, entails its incommunicability and unreality except in some imaginative "marriage of speaking and hearing" (253).

Robert Dale Parker has called attention to the prototypical, often climactic Faulknerian situation in which some version of the phrase "something happened" appears, presumably an incompletely articulated experience of fright or the unknown (3). Perhaps equally typical and, I would speculate, increasingly typical in Faulkner's later career is the phrase appearing in situations in which, contrary to elaborate prearticulations, "nothing happened" (256), as here when Bon repeatedly meets his father, expecting but not receiving the reconciling, legitimizing sign. But neither of these two phrases points in Faulkner's work disinterestedly toward either a determining origin or a retroactive endpoint of meaning (or nonmeaning), or at least not without analyzable, particular motives and consequences. Reminded now, as if by Sutpen's silence toward Bon and his talk with Henry, of the other recalcitrant, "incontrovertible fact" (269) of Bon's social ineligibility (as Judith's half brother), Quentin and Shreve imagine again first Henry's attempted *denial* of both the troubling biological fact (until he supposedly confronts Bon's mother), and the troubling interpersonal fact (in Henry's "You shall not," and in their inviting the war's preemptive, impersonal solution of their problem). Then in another, second movement Quentin and Shreve imagine Henry's attempt to *sublimate* the fact of incest and reconcile it with its social prohibition. Henry invokes royal precedents as in Shreve's earlier conceit that incest is love perfected by sin (in the love that the gods themselves make and selectively condone):

the dreamy immeasurable coupling which floats oblivious above the trammeling and harried instant, the: *was-not: is: was:*[,] is a perquisite only of balloony and weightless elephants and whales: but maybe if there were sin too maybe you would not be permitted to escape, uncouple, return. (259)

The limit to coupling here (as in incest) has become not the awareness of difference in subjectivities from which the harried instant emerges (*"was-not: is"*) and to which it immediately returns (*was*); the limit here instead is only one's own sin, with which one might much better imagine becoming paradoxically, permanently coupled and reconciled. They imagine Henry deciding that, God having "quit us" without so much as a sign, salvation now might best be found in the "mindless meat" (283), to put more bluntly this sense of incest as the denial and sublimation of a problematic inter-subjective difference.

But Quentin and Shreve already sense that this second try at denial and sublimation cannot work to heal Bon's ineligibility any more than they could earlier redeem his duplicity toward Henry. Their resolution in these terms would require Henry to accept Bon's incest, Sutpen to grant Bon a similar recognition and acceptance, and Bon to renounce that same incest for the sake of that recognition. Although Quentin and Shreve can imagine Henry achieving an oedipal reconciliation of Sutpen's and Bon's opposed roles in his own psychological family romance, that achievement of Henry's requires the effective denial and sublimation of the recalcitrant fact of Sutpen and Bon (not to mention Judith) as disparate people with disparate, all too obviously conflicting desires. Just so, Quentin and Shreve's metanarrative has denied and sublimated the fact of Henry's survival as perpetrator and divided, guilty remainder of a murder. It is to this fact of Henry's actual survival hidden by Clytie out in the dark house that Shreve's metanarrative suddenly returns and to which he loses his listener and his speech as they attempt yet another (repetitive, obfuscatory) two-stage *denial* (of Bon as a black man, therefore absolutely, unquestionably unacceptable even as "meat"), then *sublimation* (of the dead Bon as a self-effacing, almost self-murdered gentleman, proven a gentleman in his gesture of changing the pictures): "the only way I will have to say to her, *I was no good; do not grieve for me*" (287).

If this is the perfect bonfire, purportedly leaving "no ashes nor refuse" (192) of grief, thwarted desire, or guilty, forced resolution, it is grotesquely so, as demonstrated by the chapter's overinsistent then overly casual closure: "'Aint that right? Aint it? By God, aint it?' 'Yes,' Quentin said. 'Come on,' Shreve said. 'Let's get out of this refrigerator and go to bed'"

(287). They have had to consider that Bon might after all have thought and acted not just for the sake of the family (Henry and Judith), but equally for the sake of himself and his violently excluded subjectivity. And they can imagine Bon forcing Henry's borrowed paternal and racial authority to show itself, parodically delegitimized as a frightened, effectively violent cliché to resolve Henry's inarticulate uncertainty and fear: "I'm the nigger that's going to sleep with your sister. Unless you stop me, Henry" (286). Less obviously grotesque as a resolution, Bon's carrying the picture of the octoroon and their son when he dies can be imagined by Quentin and Shreve as Bon's own selfless, gentlemanly endorsement of his exclusion by a social hierarchy which can in return idealize, appreciate, and accept this disembodied, aestheticized, essentializing parting gesture (even though it could not accept the living man). This final interpretation, however, depends on seeing Bon as a white man's soul in a black man's body—a tragic paradox resolved and appreciated in the spectacle of his death. What such an interpretation of Bon's tragic spectacle denies and aesthetically sublimates is Bon's own example as someone who in carrying the picture of his octoroon wife and son has *not* denied or obscured his own guiltily forsaken relationships in his socially ineligible past. Sutpen *has* repeatedly tried to deny betraying his own ineligible first wife and son. Henry has tried likewise, by murdering Bon, to resolve his guilty fear of his own, Bon's, and Judith's socially unacceptable intersubjective and interracial sexuality and love. And Quentin and Shreve repeat and refine the dream to its most essentially modernist form, that of death reduced to the perfect gesture, obviating the need for grief.

Quentin and Shreve's tour de force of interpretation unravels in *Absalom*'s final chapter to reveal a vaguely human remainder left behind after all the attempted closures of Sutpen's and the South's history by innocence, irony, and now too their "last ditch" metanarrative combining both. Having temporarily both explained Bon's ironic physical exclusion from the innocent dream and then finally identified and redeemed his essential, transcendently noble spirit, their negation and synthesis is troubled still by some version of Bon's body—that vague darkness they can neither innocently ignore as inhuman "nigger" "meat," nor rationalize and accept ironically as a general fate, nor altogether refine and translate into their spiritually aristocratic ideal. If in the moment of Bon's death they have gentrified his spirit, they are left, like Rosa and Judith before them, with the problem of burying Bon's body, tainted as it is with its ineradicable "spot of black blood" and the violence of its murder, along with the remaining emotional, familial, and social problem later of what to do with his wife and her servant, his "passable" but less conciliatory son, and later still with his unmistakably black, unrefinably, untranslatably idiot grandson, whose howl becomes at the end of the novel a vaguely humanist reification of the forever unignorable, unacceptable, inarticulately irreconcilable, dark historical realities of ongoing human suffering—for what that humanist reification is worth to the still suicidal, explosively silent Quentin.

Although the lights in their dorm room are out now, the story refuses to end in sleep, that conventional innocent, or ironic, or aesthetically transfiguring metaphor for death: "the darkness seemed to breathe, to flow back; the window which Shreve had opened became visible against the faint unearthly glow of the outer snow as, forced by the weight of the darkness, the blood surged and ran warmer, warmer" (288). This faintly glowing dark window on the outer snow serves Quentin and can serve here as a kind of insomniac writing pad for (apparently forever) rechecking *Absalom*'s different narrative sums to show the incommensurable human remainders left by each of these narrative strategies in Quentin's memory—and by these narratives as transferences for Quentin's own unresolved family romance.

He remembers how he approached the Sutpen house that night in September with Rosa, himself more frightened (more innocent, nostalgic) than Rosa was, thinking, "I just dont want to know about whatever it is [Clytie] keeps hidden in it" (293). Staring through his dorm window in December, he remembers how for a moment that other night he saw completely through the house like a darkened window, the balloon-faced reality it framed still obscured by fright, if still undeniably, vaguely human: "as if the house were of one dimension, painted on a canvas curtain in which there was a tear," until, "almost beneath it, the dead furnace-breath of air in which they moved seemed to reek in slow and protracted violence with a smell of desolation and decay as if the wood of which it was built were flesh" (293). When Rosa would have him break in the door with her hatchet, he looks aside, frightened, and reassures himself that "all he had to do now was to step through the vacant frame" of a window, telling himself he is "not afraid, he just didn't want to know what might be inside" (294). His fearful but also strong desire to enter and know who is there becomes less easily, innocently deniable (by fright) as he strains hard despite himself to see in the darkness, until he suddenly reverts to fright again when Clytie strikes a match behind him in the dark: "like an explosion, a pistol; . . . all his organs lifted sickeningly" (294).

Rosa's willful innocence only more strenuously and violently contains her (intersubjective) fear and desire, in her "terrified yet implacable determination, as though it were not she who had to go and find out but she only the helpless agent of someone or something else who must know" (292). Her repeated insistence on breaking through the door comes not

(directly) from a greater sense of other subjects in the house, but from
her narrowly aristocratic legal argument that she is now rightful owner
of the house and its unnamed contents. She risks this time no such personal
encounter with Clytie as gave her such abbreviatedly insightful pause
before, but the unmediated violence with which she "struck Clytie to the
floor with a full-armed blow like a man would have" is enough to leave
Quentin, at least, with a sense of one human remainder Rosa's innocence
ignores, in her determination to "save" her nephew Henry: the human remainder in Clytie's fragile "rag-bundle" of bones (295). The actual sight
of Henry, though, seems to have given even Rosa at least three months
of pause, as it has Quentin, as well, who remembers fleeing the memory
into sleep that night at home with "his eye-muscles aching and straining
into the darkness," then waking, and "waking or sleeping it was the same:
the bed, the yellow sheets and pillow, the wasted yellow face with closed,
almost transparent eyelids on the pillow . . . and would be the same forever
as long as he lived": the directly quoted, undigested, mirrorlike exchange
(298). The once apparently "vacant frame" through which he entered the
Sutpen house does contain, after all, another recognizable but still decidedly
inscrutable, dying subject.

"His eyes wide open upon the window," Quentin stares now at the
human remainders left by his father's letter's ironic update and close to
the Sutpen story (298). Before the Massachusetts window begins to yield
the remembered shape, then even the words of his father's letter in his
father's "sloped whimsical ironic hand" (301), Quentin imagines first the
burning window in which Clytie's face appeared undeniable and unsavable
to Rosa and to the howling Jim Bond, who still howls and can still be
neither caught and saved nor driven away and forgotten. Quentin, then,
who has been out there recently himself and has confronted these people
now just dead — Rosa, Clytie, and Henry — as well as the one still howling,
cannot persuasively (to Shreve) pretend that just because he was born there
and is still himself alive, he has a right to his father's superior attitude
of understanding the Old South and making pronouncements over its dead:
"'I am older at twenty than a lot of people who have died,' Quentin said.
'And more people have died than have been twenty-one,' Shreve said" (301).
Compson's letter, superimposed on the Harvard window, speaks of Rosa,
Sutpen, and Henry as ghosts when they were alive and expresses a
whimsically ironic "*hope, not think,*" that there might be outrage, hatred,
pity, commiseration, longing between them now as "*actual*" people in some
other "*place or bourne,*" as if their "*actual*" realities either before or after
their deaths can be so easily, ironically dismissed now that they are finally,
predictably dead in the general way: "*The weather was beautiful though
cold and they had to use picks to break the earth for the grave yet in one*

of the deeper clods I saw a redworm doubtless alive when the clod was thrown up though by afternoon it was frozen again" (302). The long, weary tradition of such an ironic reduction of Rosa's life and all others to the food chain or the life span of a worm makes it an all too banal attempt to protect Compson himself like Quentin from feeling the great remainder of loss involved in her death as in those of Clytie and Henry, as expressed more directly but feebly in Bond's unmediated, unconsoled howl.

What seems in some ways most banal of all, however, is the attempt Quentin has also participated in with Shreve to interpret and close this entire story in the metanarrative context of "some things that just have to be whether they are or not, just to balance the books, write *Paid* on the old sheet so that whoever keeps them can take it out of the ledger and burn it, get rid of it" (260). They have not attempted just to ennoble their own role, as in Rosa's supposedly naive, innocent nostalgia, or in her and Sutpen's willfully innocent fictionalism. Nor have they attempted only to foresee the defeat of others, as in Compson's irony, or to preempt their own defeat, as in the more blatantly willful irony of Charles Etienne. They have attempted instead to summarize and effectively to ordain as the nature of things ("some things that just have to be") a profoundly irreconcilable "cleavage of Being" between, for example, their consciousness of human suffering and that human suffering's substance, as focused here in Bond's howl. They have given that suffering a human face and vocal cords, but they have not allowed it to speak for itself: by hypostatizing and reifying it humanistically as the substance of human suffering, they have again avoided listening to recognizable, articulated, heterogeneously specific human desires, needs, and demands.

With his reduction of the entire Sutpen story to the formula that "it takes two niggers to get rid of one Sutpen," Shreve announces the balancing of the books and still admits quite openly the remainder left in the figure of Bond, a remainder of not just worm meat but undeniable, unsublimated human suffering (302). It is the particular virtue of his formalist "blindness," as de Man might say, that he can always welcome such paradoxes into his "permanent parabasis" or "*comique absolu*" of unending ambiguity and irony (de Man 229–45, 187–228). He can easily, self-parodically propose another "reconciliation of opposites" whereby Bond as the one excluded "nigger Sutpen" bleaches out in "a few thousand years" to "conquer the western hemisphere" and become Shreve himself ("But it will still be Jim Bond") "sprung from the loins of African kings" (302). Although his parodic exaggeration does admit the extreme abstraction of such a solution, Shreve is not nearly so personally haunted by Bond as Quentin or even Compson is. Shreve here is still insisting that this is all a distantly Southern and not a New England or Canadian story, insisting that Bond is a peculiarly Southern ghost, so that Shreve can make him over into a hemispheric hero or into the poor who are always with us. He can taunt Quentin: "You still hear him at night sometimes. Don't you?" (302).

Quentin has stood with Clytie in the position of the other human subject his and Rosa's innocence willfully ignores. He has stood with Rosa and Henry in the position of the other human subjects his and his father's irony willfully ignores. When Shreve asks him why he hates the South, he is now in a position to recognize what his and Shreve's and the formalist New Critic's metanarrative ignores: the motivations and consequences of his and his father's often contemptuous irony toward those ghosts who haunt them personally day after day and night after night. He has successfully, self-critically resisted, as Shreve has, and as de Man says the best New Critics have (229–46), an important bridging of the cleavage of Being in either nostalgic, naive, or utopian readings of a story like that of the Sutpens. Still, Quentin's insomniac writing pad's superimposed, repeated juxtapositions of an ultimately reified human suffering like Bond's and various failing efforts to deny, frame, or transfigure that suffering is a modernist aesthetic solution (cf. Conrad's "the horror") insufficient for helping Quentin past that suicide Faulkner has already written into his near future. Suicide must now begin to seem the only way out of his impasse, the only way he can imagine stopping both his own intolerable, apparently unmediatable suffering and desire as well as his equally intolerable, cornered consciousness of that desire and suffering both in himself and others: that consciousness is intolerable because it seems only endlessly to repeat futile efforts to escape, mediate, or transcend a hopelessly reified suffering and desire. As an emblem of suffering, Bond demands, like images of starving children in an unnamed place or time, only the vaguest humanist sentiments of pity and helplessness.

Quentin, like Faulkner at this point in his career, does not appear to believe that juxtaposing human suffering and its repeatedly failing denials will necessarily help alleviate that suffering, as perhaps the great humanist metanarratives of Marx and Freud largely do presume or hope. As Jean-François Lyotard says in *The Postmodern Condition,* "our incredulity is such that we no longer expect salvation to rise from these inconsistencies, as did Marx" in his "blind positivity of delegitimation" (xxiv). Our embeddedness in structures of suffering and denial extends more deeply, we have found, than can be changed or cured by a strong, nauseating dose or charge of Jim Bond's howl (cf. Shapiro 145–56). Quentin's suicide looms like a verdict at the end of *Absalom, Absalom!* Having demonstrated that the two courses of Southern, modernist narrative are on the one hand a nostalgia for a social disease, and on the other a freedom from that disease which its practitioners are unaware is a

freedom of impotence (7), Faulkner proceeds now, as he already has pro-
ceeded in odd moments and "minor" works, to revise his course in the
direction of neither concentrating nor generalizing human suffering and
desire in images for helpless contemplation such as *Absalom*'s Jim Bond,
but trying to give Bond's suffering and desire a personal, social, historical
voice, or rather many different voices. Without first "bleaching" his skin
or transfiguring him directly into a monumental Thomas Sutpen or a
sophisticated Charles Bon, he has him instead mount the steps and enter
the big house as Ab Snopes in "Barn Burning," with an "attitude" and a
lame, shit-smeared step, or as Flem Snopes and V. K. Ratliff in *The Hamlet,*
with their puzzling ways of doing business and law, or as Lucas and Molly
Beauchamp in *Go Down, Moses,* a black man and woman articulating
their differences especially in terms of love and grief in a white-dominated
economy, or as Nancy Mannigoe and Temple Drake in *Requiem for a Nun,*
singing and speaking across boundaries of class, race, gender, and time.

3   From Irony to Humor and Rage in *The Hamlet*

WITHIN a year of publishing *Absalom, Absalom!* (1936) Faulkner was writing again about Sutpen and the Old South in "An Odor of Verbena," the final, key story which confirmed his sense that the series of largely nostalgic Civil War stories he had written in 1934 for the *Saturday Evening Post* could be turned effectively into a novel, *The Unvanquished* (1938). Faulkner had been determined "to keep the hoop skirts and plug hats out" of *Absalom* (*Selected Letters* 75), and he accomplished that aim primarily by subordinating that nostalgia to Quentin's qualifying irony, but perhaps also by shunting into the Civil War stories of *The Unvanquished* his own less ironically qualified nostalgia and that of his intended readers in the *Post*. As he wrote "An Odor of Verbena" and revised the series in 1937, however, the discoveries Faulkner had made in writing *Absalom* about the impasses of Southern modernist nostalgia and irony urged him toward other, more modest and productive alternatives, which he would continue to pursue in *The Wild Palms* (1939) and which would blossom and bear fruit in the peculiarly critical, revisionist humor of *The Hamlet* (1940).

The arriviste, "underbred," "counterfeit" Sutpen dream and the more established Old South Compson or Sartoris dream are the subjects of a dialogue in "An Odor of Verbena" between two characters named Bayard and Drusilla (cf. Shreve's "one Southern Bayard or Guinevere" in *Absalom* 142). Drusilla argues that Sutpen's dream was "just Sutpen" (selfish, capitalist ambition) whereas John Sartoris was "thinking of this whole country which he is trying to raise by its bootstraps" (256), thinking, that is, of the good of everyone throughout the feudal, supposedly organic social hierarchy, rich and poor, black and white. Bayard knows as well as any reader of *Absalom* the function of such a patriarchal ideology and the divisive tendency of such hierarchical class distinctions, and his ironic counterposition is to recall a scene (as if from *Absalom*) when Sartoris challenges Sutpen to join the "night riders to keep the carpet baggers from organising the Negroes into an insurrection" (256). Bayard remembers hearing how Sutpen resisted this postwar attempt by the threatened plantation hierarchy to scapegoat and terrorize, as if in preemptive revenge, this frightening but focused black balloon face of racial rebellion, a campaign with the clear function of shoring up only a narrowly restricted, nostalgic fragment of the ideologically whole, organic society. Bayard remembers and prefers Sutpen's less feudal, more democratic, Jeffersonian, yeoman farmer version of the Southern dream—that each man would rehabilitate his own land and that the whole country would then take care of itself. Although Bayard would recognize the historical innocence and the effective cruelty of Sutpen's dream in practice (as an inalienable part of a racist, peripherally capitalist, plantation economy), he insists too on pushing Drusilla to the limits of her willfully innocent defense of the alternative, Sartoris dream (because it is a "good dream") as easily worth the cost of taking "one human life or two dozen" (257). In the ironic view that results from this standoff, one such version of the Southern dream—agrarian (but white) aristocracy, or agrarian (but still white) populism—is as arrogantly, inflexibly doomed as the other.

David M. Wyatt has argued temptingly that "An Odor of Verbena" ironically reverses the tendency of earlier stories of the series (and the tendency of their intended audience) to demand of Bayard another repetition of the Sartoris dream in all its original honor and cruelty, a cruelty that would be mythically excused yet again as tragic necessity, reality, growing up. Ironically, says Wyatt, instead of repeating his dead father's violent arrogance by avenging his death and (oedipally) taking his place, Bayard will refuse the pistols and the love offered him by his father's seductive young wife, "realizing" when he kisses her (the first of two times) "the immitigable chasm between all life and all print—that those who can, do, those who cannot and suffer enough because they can't, write about it" (262). In a long tradition of Faulkner criticism, Wyatt argues that this decision between life and print, deeds and words, (innocent) action and (ironic) reflection was crucial to Faulkner's own sense of his career as an artist, as confirmed by his statement and achievement in this story (92–116).[1]

1. Wyatt's opposition of deeds and words here invokes especially the work of Olga Vickery, who is more attuned than Brooks is to the restlessness of experience in Faulkner's fiction, an experience never accounted for or captured by any one perspective, tone, epitomizing event or moment, an experience constantly challenging every form, however mythic. Kartiganer has a similarly modernist and New Critical admiration for the "supreme fiction" achieved by Quentin and Shreve in *Absalom,* for their having imposed Apollonian forms on the chaos and change of reality, only to have those Apollonian forms ironically destroyed by the very Dionysian forces which have given those forms their power. Yet Vickery and Kartiganer, like Brooks, are more concerned with this recurring general tension between deeds and words than they are with any particular succession of such changing or revised deeds and words. Wyatt also invokes John Irwin's reading of Faulkner in order to protest the "tyrannizing unity" of Irwin's view of an unchanging "logic of internal struggle" in the nature of the narrative act itself, a self-perpetuating and self-destructive struggle through

Faulkner, however, has already called into question, with an increasing frequency and rigor, this somewhat clichéd, ironic "realization" of an "immitigable chasm" (or cleavage of Being) between life and print. Bayard in fact invokes this cliché only as momentary defense against being overwhelmed by the oedipal temptation, and only moments later he rejects this spatial, metaphysical opposition between all life and all print in order to serialize it instead as an unending process of thought revising deeds, then deeds necessitating renewed thought: "So again it was like it had been before. No. Twice, a thousand times and never like— . . . each time both cumulative and retroactive, immitigably unrepetitive, each wherein remembering excludes experience, each wherein experience antedates remembering" (263–64). Bayard's refusal of the oedipalized action of revenge does not amount to a substitution of art for action, as Wyatt claims, "of passive for active resistance, of the words of the Book for the deeds of the code," or of "symbolic" for "literal" action (Wyatt 115). Although Bayard's resistance to his father's and father's friends' and enemies' code of repetition and revenge is indeed creative and imaginative, as art is, it is "passive resistance" only in the most politically strategic, active sense of the term. Bayard refuses the code's binary alternatives of either revenge or cowardice, but he does so by articulating another alternative for action, not by an escapist suicide or an effort at transcendent irony. Bayard challenges the dominant code from a particular, vulnerable position within that same

strategies such as repetition and revenge to dissipate or defy that irreversibility of time whose authority such strategies only serve (ironically, timelessly, modernistically, in Irwin's view as in Quentin's) to reconfirm. Wyatt would both escape and resolve this dilemma by reference to Faulkner's career decision in favor of art, as against repetition and revenge as they have been played out in his family history. After this gesture of decisiveness, however, the question remains of what he will *do* with his art.

John T. Matthews gives this debate a crucially important turn by first disagreeing that *The Hamlet,* for example, represents a departure from the "ground" of traditional, humanistic moral authority invoked by Brooks and Warren Beck. Matthews also disagrees with Vickery's invocations of natural centers known only to children, blacks, and women. *The Hamlet* "displays a world unalterably established on the discourses of society; there are no natural centers from which to measure the fall into civilization" (*Play* 164). I would strongly agree, but Matthews seemed in his early work less concerned with differentiating and tracing the movements and transactions of these differing "discourses of society" than in opposing them to the absent "centers" so often invoked in Faulkner's fiction and Faulkner criticism, centers which would have afforded more absolute (but surely not the only) measures of motivation, consequence, and change. The humorous "freeplay of meaning" Matthews applauds in *The Hamlet* seems to derive at least in its ironic function, then, from Kartiganer's supreme fictions and Wyatt's decision for art as against action. But Matthews' ground-breaking emphasis on all these centers and noncenters as different "discourses of society" has been one of the inspirations for this and other socially oriented studies, not to mention Matthews' own work since *The Play of Faulkner's Language.*

society, knowing he is himself now "the Sartoris" but wagering that he is also "one still young enough to have his youth supplied him gratis as a reason (not an excuse) for cowardice" (250). Instead of repudiating the trace of his marginal status as youth, he makes strategic use of that marginal status, much as Ab Snopes and Lucas Beauchamp would later, in order to expose and use the code's internal contradictions as a lever to make way for other alternatives. When Bayard manages to avoid both repetitiously murderous revenge and cowardly escape by confronting his father's murderer with the undeniable cowardice of further murder (especially of a youth), Bayard's father's formerly vindictive friend George Wyatt has to admit with relief and humorous appreciation, "I wouldn't have done it that way, myself. . . . But that's your way or you wouldn't have done it. . . . Well by God, . . . Maybe you're right, maybe there has been enough killing in your family without—Come on" (289).

Bayard's action embodying and provoking this humorous reconception of the apparent double bind comes only at the end of the novel, so that what I am prospectively calling humor (looking ahead to the humorous fiction that follows in *The Hamlet* and *Go Down, Moses*) is here still deeply ambiguous. It can indeed be read retrospectively (as Wyatt does, looking back at *Light in August, Sartoris,* and Faulkner's genealogy) as another imaginative resolution of paradoxical contraries (like Quentin's and Shreve's in *Absalom*), to be appreciated especially by a New Critical reading as a mythlike resolution and artistically perfect closure to the novel's action, a creative triumph of words over deeds. But it is not enough to say that Faulkner thus redeems with a single crowning gesture a popular fiction (and family tradition) of revenge by lifting it into a higher realm of art. Everything that makes Bayard's gesture dramatic also sets it apart, aestheticizes it as words triumphing over deeds and words as apart from deeds. This ending indicates with a dramatic gesture of resolution—but does not yet set into motion as a functioning narrative, social, and political procedure—the possibility of an alternative to the oedipal, repetitive pattern of repetition and revenge.

Two other reasons for reading this ending as only ambiguously, prospectively humorous, a promise of humor as yet unfulfilled: one revised passage on youth and several passages on the nature of Drusilla's laughter. As he revised the story series for publication as a novel, Faulkner added a sentence in "Retreat": "There is a limit to what a child can accept, assimilate; not to what it can believe because a child can believe anything, given time, but to what it can accept, a limit in time, in the very time which nourishes the incredible" (75). The form of this sentence's expression is dilatory, repetitive, in keeping with the insight it suggests about the function of repetition, whether as fright or irony, as a means of negating, perhaps dramatically, perhaps vindictively, as unacceptable or as incredible, what might also, in time and narrative, be more resourcefully assimilated, digested, and adapted to unforeseen possibilities. But Bayard's insight here is retrospective — "And I was a child then" — and the implied adulthood of his narrative perspective is, again, ambiguously, simultaneously indicated and occluded beyond his final gesture in the novel. Similarly, Drusilla's laughter, when she realizes that Bayard will not avenge his father, is a laughter which can be imagined as verging on humorous appreciation of his unexpectedly singular, differing response, but her laughter verges on such humor only somewhere beyond the end of the novel, as suggested by the sprig and odor of verbena with which she *indicates* (though she does not voice) her appreciation. For now, perhaps because she too is young, her laughter within the story is repeatedly compared to vomit, in the familiarly reactive style of willed innocence: she has not had time to digest the unacceptable. Like Charles Etienne in *Absalom,* she is herself a mixed reality willfully denying the mixture. Having lost her fiancé to the war, she has assumed his masculine, martial role for herself in a melancholic stalling action against the painful recognition and articulation of her loss. Thus she can believe in but cannot accept yet, and so refuses to recognize or appreciate, Bayard's own "becoming-woman" (Guattari), as he embraces the woman's and child's role as another, more candidly bereaved victim of that martial role, in order to challenge and transform both roles from what they were. Her willed innocence is thus still a vomiting denial, if also a partly disarmed, vomiting laughter.

The story series that became *The Unvanquished* was not Faulkner's only foray during this period into the realm of popular literature. After six years of working on and off in and for Hollywood, boiling the pot had become not just an economic necessity but a necessary subject for exploration in his fiction. His next work was *The Wild Palms* (published after "Barn Burning," but written before it), in which he returns from the Southern antebellum and Reconstruction settings of *Absalom* and *The Unvanquished* to the less peculiarly Southern setting of twentieth-century American capitalism and its attendant (nationwide, worldwide) culture industry. In the relatively distant, demarcated past of the antebellum South someone like Sutpen could be imagined as attempting to resolve his own paradoxical status as ideologically free but economically enslaved by concentrating and negating in the dramatic image of the black slave's balloon face the despotic, double slavery of economy and ideology.[2] And

---

2. "For the affirmation of self [such a dialectic] substitutes the negation of the other." Deleuze, *Nietzsche* 196.

in the still distant Reconstruction South someone like Bayard's father (and Bayard himself) could be imagined as taking dramatic revenge for the disintegration of a supposedly once whole culture on carpetbagging aliens and their poor-white collaborators (including Ab Snopes). These were both nostalgic versions of Southern "hoop skirts and plug hats" Faulkner knew to be popular well into the twentieth century, and well beyond the geographical borders of the Old South, as shown by the international novel and film success of *Gone with the Wind,* published the same year as *Absalom* and produced as a film in 1939. If Faulkner seems to have elevated his potboiling *Unvanquished* stories with a flourish to the level of highbrow art by finally refusing his *Post* audience the (willfully innocent) revenge he had let them expect, he would in the title story of *The Wild Palms* investigate much more persistently such highbrow, aestheticized refinements of popular culture's melodramatic, climactic gestures of resolution (in the substitution of a superior, passive resistance for active revenge, and of well-turned words and gestures for bloody deeds). And in the counterpointed story "Old Man" Faulkner would also investigate the widespread twentieth-century disillusionment and boredom with all such repeatedly spurious and dispersed attempts by the culture industry (both highbrow and low) at dramatic climax and resolution. He will examine both in the (high) internalized aestheticizations of revenge and in the (low) standardizations of revenge the underlying rationale for "how the pain of others can be a satisfaction of revenge, a reparation for revenge," in terms of "the pleasure which is felt in inflicting pain or in contemplating it," or in other words, "the external meaning of pain" (Deleuze, *Nietzsche* 135).

Charlotte Rittenmeyer consciously models her affair with Harry Wilbourne in "The Wild Palms" on modernist creeds and works such as Hemingway's *A Farewell to Arms* (1929) and "The Snows of Kilimanjaro" (1936). Her "amorous destiny" is as willfully innocent a project as Sutpen's dynastic destiny was; she is just as determined as he was that her triumph will be unambivalently "all honeymoon, always" or nothing, "Either heaven, or hell: no comfortable safe peaceful purgatory between" (83). She and Harry attempt to deny and transcend in the name of their love all "bourgeois" concerns with respectability, language, money, food, and finally children, but their protracted honeymoon is largely defined by (or inflexibly, fatally fixated on) this very negation of everything they associate with the dull pain of everyday life. So they reconstruct in a displaced form the very impoverishment of everyday life which they reject, such that Charlotte, like Sutpen, ends by choosing the purity of the dream over any possibility of its realization. These impossibly innocent, willfully self-destructive alternatives—all honeymoon or nothing, heaven or hell—lead toward an important mediation in Harry's final, revised choice when Charlotte dies and the honeymoon is no longer the option opposed to nothing: "*Yes* he thought *between grief and nothing I will take grief*" (324). But like the ending of *The Unvanquished,* this mediation represents a dramatic gesture of resolution and closure more precisely than it represents any significant revision of Harry's way of thinking. Although the scene does *represent* the beginning of a process of mourning and working through his loss in personal terms, with the possibility of gradual healing and reinvestment of emotion (so that Faulkner could appreciate and quote this closing line of "The Wild Palms" later), still, the scene's *function* at the end of Harry's story in this novel is to inaugurate that process of mourning but in the same stroke also prematurely to resolve it into something resembling less mourning than melancholia, a retrospective, imprisoning, self-flagellating repetition of his loss.[3] This is partly why this ending strikes so many readers as at once an affirmation of love and a masturbatory exercise. Harry's melancholia perpetuates by again displacing the fierce opposition between the nostalgic purity of their love and everything else of life that seemed to persecute, survive, and thereby exonerate their purer love. Like this love, his grief functions as an aestheticized, modernist refinement of revenge, carefully inflicting and contemplating his pain.

"Hegel wrote of the 'beautiful soul' who denounces the world in order to maintain a personal sense of moral purity and innocence. Others refuse to pass judgment because they are most comfortable when they are submitted to judgments, especially when that judgment condemns them as guilty" (Schneiderman 99). To the willful innocence of Charlotte and Harry in "The Wild Palms" Faulkner counterpoints the willful irony of the tall convict in "The Old Man." The stolidly disillusioned poor-white convict has already fallen for one of the culture industry's more popular images of melodramatic transfiguration and freedom in his failed imitation of the train robberies of detective fiction magazines. Now he thinks he knows better. He is determined not to believe in or to attempt escape from the prison-farm existence where he at least knows for sure that it makes no difference whether he plants seeds or stones. Like the briefly ironic young Thomas Sutpen and the finally ironic Wash Jones, the convict attempts to resolve in this way his contradictory status (as, for example, ideologically free but economically, socially, culturally enslaved): by renouncing

3. Harry's closing line may also allude to the last lines of Baudelaire's "Le jeu," about a gambler "qui, soûl de son sang, préférerait en somme / La douleur à la mort et l'enfer au néant!": the poem is cited by Walter Benjamin in a discussion of the compulsive gambler's addiction like the city dweller's to sensations and shocks as impatient substitutes for a lost possibility for lived experience among people who would return the jostled city dweller's gaze (180).

all desire and claim to freedom, he hopes to escape alienation in his slavery. The convict identifies himself with slaves, as Ab Snopes will insist on doing in "Barn Burning," but unlike Ab, the convict does not yet get any leverage from this admission, except to tell his tale. The convict takes to such incredible lengths the renunciation of this desire and claim to freedom in the face of so many real invitations and possibilities for escape, that his story begins early to resemble an exceedingly long and tall tale on Faulkner's part, with the forced attitude on the part of the speaker that is characteristic of the tall tale. The system of oppression and enslavement from which this convict is so determined not to attempt escape comes increasingly to sound simply not so inescapably monolithic as his irony stubbornly insists—or at least it is not so inescapably monolithic as his own irony is, that inexhaustible, straight-faced narration which everywhere invites the escape, at least, of a laugh. His final attempts to reduce his whole, wild story to merely following orders (278) or to draw a jaded moral of foresworn desire—"Women[: shi]t!" (339)—exhibit an irony so doggedly willful and forced as to invite in both instances (as in many others) a commentary on his "cold humorless eyes" in a face "saturnine, humorless, and calm" (278, 339). It is the mask of a humorless "straight face" through which Faulkner continually invites our daring to laugh in the convict's face, recognizing and appreciating his tale's lively defiance of the convict's own ironic exclusion of humorous reconceptions of possibility, a tale that resembles in many ways the humorous fiction called for again and more clearly in "Barn Burning" and set variously into motion in The Hamlet.

Absalom, Absalom!, The Unvanquished, and The Wild Palms each ends ambiguously with a frozen frame. Each novel ends not by functioning as a configuration of living, heterogeneous desire, but by representing a revelatory (hypostatized, metaphysical) secret truth. Absalom's inarticulate Jim Bond is the image of that object and victim that the Sutpens' willful innocence finally cannot ignore or sublimate in others, and at the same time he is the (still inadequate, inarticulate) image of that subject and that desire and loss that the Compsons' willful irony finally cannot deny or overrule within themselves. In The Unvanquished Bayard's repudiation of willfully innocent, violent revenge, with his invocation of that higher truth "Thou shalt not kill" (249), at the mere reminder of which his opponent is supposed to have fled, only raises that same one-sided revenge to the epistemological level of an ironic coup. Once Bayard has thus sacrificed his oedipal desire and almost his unarmed body as well for the sake of this higher truth, he is rewarded by having that same repressed desire return in the safely (?) sublimated form of the strong, lingering odor of (Drusilla's) verbena.[4] In *The Wild Palms* Harry's willfully innocent, intensely private romance abuts finally on his private, melancholic fixation on that romance's ultimate cost in the death of Charlotte. And the tall convict's willful irony ends by overinsistently denying his reawakened desire, "Women[: shi]t!" (339). In all these cases ambiguous openings for rekindled relations and fruitfully transformed desires are simultaneously closed off by the function of these endings as endings, as retroactive revelations of previously denied truths, their demystifications remystified by the fore-closure of any possibility of further criticism.

As I have already suggested in my Introduction, "Barn Burning" is a crucial escape from this impasse, and its composition followed just after Faulkner wrote the most spurious, humorously open-ended of the above endings (the convict's obviously ambivalent misogynistic curse). Instead of placing at the *end* of "Barn Burning" the shocking truth—"the horror" of Jim Bond's pariah-idiot howl, Drusilla's vomiting laughter and over-poweringly seductive odor, Charlotte's corpse, or the convict's curse reducing women to shit—Faulkner introduces early another version of these various shits into the story and into the big house on the sole of Ab's boot, along with his disturbing silence and his destructive fire, so that these shocks function not as dramatic, ironically subversive endings but as points of departure for Ab's perverse, strategic use of such repressed truths as means of rearticulating his otherwise blocked dignity and desire. Instead of exposing his society's oppression by willfully innocent imitation and active repetition of that oppression (the Sutpen effect), or by willfully ironic hypostatization and contemplative repetition of that oppression as reality itself (the Compson effect), Ab turns this logic of exposure and demystifica-tion to purposes of active resistance and escape. And as Albert C. Smith has shown in his study of arson as protest in black-belt Georgia, Ab's strategy was relatively popular historically and was even relatively effec-tive (at least as a cathartic expression of grievances if perhaps not as a received communication): such arson was practiced especially by blacks who usually owned no property and who would likely not survive a more direct confrontation. Although Ab's exemplary strategy thus opens pro-

4. The force of this sublimation is considerably heightened by the genital connotations of the story's title, "The Odor of Verbena," with its possible allusion to the Maupassant story of the man who lifts the skirts of a woman leaning out the window of a stairway at night and is surprised, when he plants a kiss there, to smell the odor of verbena, and to find that the woman is not the maid he thought but the lady of the house ("A Bad Error" 394–97). Bayard has committed more knowingly almost the same bad error in kissing a woman nearly his own age who is also his father's wife. The strong odor of the sprig of verbena she leaves on his pillow is thus perhaps more sublimation than revision of their relation-ship's more disturbing implications of oedipal repetition.

ductive avenues of escape both from the older, aristocratic codes of his society and from its newer, liberalized legal and social expectations, his own means of escape have become dispirited and repetitive, with finally "a no-way out of [his] way out, an impasse of the line of escape" (Deleuze and Guattari, *Kafka* 36). Furthermore, his own means of escape come to represent a terrorizing barrier to the possibility of other fruitful lines of escape for the rest of his family. Partly because "Barn Burning" is at this point a short story and not an introductory story of a novel (as it is in *The Hamlet*), Ab's means of escape seems to represent the very possibility of escape itself (though less ambiguously than in the endings previously discussed), and seems at the end to leave Sarty only a spurious escapism (partly because this ending represents Sarty's *wanting* an ending, as in his assumption of his father's death). It remained for Faulkner to carry this logic of Ab's more or less successful escapes and rearticulations of his dignity and desire into the more sustained and various form of a novel, and also into the next generation of Snopeses, Ratliffs, and other traders in merchandise and tales of fear and desire. In terms of endings as I have described them here, this next novel would *not* end, would be unendingly continued and prolific, not only in the rest of the Snopes trilogy, but in the transformations of desire's various relations and articulations through the rest of Faulkner's long career. Faulkner's repetition and revision would differ significantly from the conservative process of myth described by Lévi-Strauss:

> since the purpose of myth is to provide a logical model capable of overcoming a contradiction (an impossible achievement if, as it happens, the contradiction is real), a theoretically infinite number of slates [instances] will be generated, each one slightly different from the others. Thus, myth grows spiral-wise until the intellectual impulse which has originated it is exhausted. ("Structural Study" 193)

The repetitions of "mythical thought always [work] from the awareness of oppositions towards their progressive mediation" (188), as in what Faulkner called willful innocence. Or at least, when such mediation seems impossible, mythical "repetition has as its function to make the structure of the myth apparent" (192), as in a willful irony that hypostatizes the opposition as a contradiction that is real (as above) and sets out either to deny or exhaust the originating desire. Such repetition produces only mediating resolutions or "variants" of the original opposition. Repetition in Faulkner, on the other hand, has as its critical, empowering function not only to make such oppositions apparent along with the failure of their resolutions, but also, and further, to will the continuation and elaboration of those very *differences* which Lévi-Strauss dismisses here from mythical thought as only "slightly different," or as "variants," but in which differences the very possibility of history, criticism, change, fear, and desire exists.[5]

Set near the turn of the century, *The Hamlet* begins by surveying the end of one order and its displacement by another. The Old South is represented by the decaying ruins of the Old Frenchman's Place, an enormous antebellum plantation built as a monument to a man whose name is now forgotten, whose big house is now a skeleton long picked over for firewood by his "heirs-at-large," and whose land is "parcelled out now into small shiftless mortgaged farms for the directors of Jefferson banks to squabble over before selling finally to Will Varner," the old ruin's present owner and new "chief man of the county" (3, 5). As Faulkner describes in these opening paragraphs his novel's geographical and historical setting, he signals already his revised conception of historical change in the South after the Civil War — not as a cataclysmic collapse from purity and order into chaos or fated ruin (the two conceptions of history examined and criticized in *Absalom*), but as a genealogy and bricolage, with traces of that particular older order surviving into the several forms of its ongoing dismantling and deterritorialization, and surviving also into its reconstruction and reterritorialization in other orders.

With his first-page announcement that the Old Frenchman's slaves are gone, Faulkner also signals early what will in this novel seem a conspicuous absence of the black balloon faces of slavery who served as convenient objects for the hypostatization and projection of various other complex forms of exploitation and oppression. That is, in *The Hamlet*

5. The difference between the functions of repetition in Faulkner and in "mythic thought" (as described here by Lévi-Strauss) is analogous to the distinction outlined by Deleuze between Nietzsche's and Hegel's versions of the dialectic in *Nietzsche and Philosophy* 147–98. For Lévi-Strauss's account of this distinction between myth and history see "History and Dialectic," chapter 9 of *The Savage Mind*. For a theoretical view of repetition's function in mythic and "oral" culture that is more appropriate to the role Old Southwestern humor plays in Faulkner's fiction, see Lyotard and Thébaud 32–35. In psychoanalytic terms, cf. Deleuze and Guattari's criticisms of Lacan's notion of the Symbolic for being only a realm of displacements still subordinated to a "despotic signifier" and to an original, real oedipal configuration (*Anti-Oedipus* 82–84). In Faulkner criticism, Donald Kartiganer complains of the novels after *Absalom, Absalom!* that they rely on "*mythos* as a too confining structure"—for example, that the *mythos* of community in *The Hamlet*, while amusingly flexible, is never violated. I would suggest that such a judgment risks underestimating the critical potential of such amusing flexibility, by overestimating the critical power both of modernist, New Critical, absolute oppositions of forms to their violations (as in Kartiganer's Stevensian notion of a self-conscious, "supreme fiction"), and of similarly absolute structuralist subordination of variants, change, and difference to the dialectical function of myth.

as in "Barn Burning" slavery will not function as the ever-present alibi image of the fate only of a people racially, naturally, absolutely distinct from poor whites and from anyone else otherwise apparently suffering under the South's social, economic, or judicial regime. Nor will the idea of being or becoming black function for whites as an ironic horror. Just as Ab was able in "Barn Burning" to compare himself provocatively but easily with a slave, in *The Hamlet,* the idea of being or becoming black will function as one admissible, always pertinent analogy for several other related forms of alienation and oppression. Thus, while there are virtually no black characters in *The Hamlet,* references to blacks appear every few pages throughout the novel (3, 5, 7, 10, 11, 15, 17, 25, 27, 28, 30, etc.). This is not to say, of course, that racism had vanished by the turn of the century in the South (in some ways it had become more virulent than ever), or even that it had vanished in parts of the South marginal to the mainstream of the old cotton plantation economy, as in Frenchman's Bend: "Strange Negroes would absolutely refuse to pass through it after dark" (5). But without the black balloon face, racism here, more clearly than in *Absalom,* figures as one form of a more general phobic suspicion of "anyone speaking the tongue with a foreign flavor or whose appearance o[r] even occupation was strange" (3). In an earlier time, the novel's first page explains, this suspicion included the Old Frenchman himself, so-called even though he may not have even been French (just as it also included the unknown Thomas Sutpen and his francophone slaves); more recently it has included federal officers searching for whiskey stills, who "went into the country and vanished" (to reappear as only a stray garment or weapon on a child or an old man or woman—4); and this suspicion has also included Will Varner, whose ubiquitous economic, political, judicial, even scientific authority and influence—as largest landholder and owner of the village store, cotton gin, gristmill, and blacksmith shop, as usurer, beat supervisor, election commissioner, justice of the peace, and veterinarian—are jealously denied by the villagers even while they also firmly believe that whenever he sits on the lawn of the Old Frenchman's Place he is "planning his next mortgage foreclosure in private" (6). Varner knows only slightly better than most that there is now no natural, proper value in the land or house or family itself, nor does the house have a use value as something anyone would need "just to eat and sleep in"; all it has is an exchange value as a fetish in need of a buyer (or investor): "This is the only thing I ever bought in my life I couldn't sell to nobody" (6).

Resentment against the plantation economy and its modern avatars, that is, is no longer innocently deflected away from an invisible planter idealized as absolutely free, toward the absolutely (reassuringly or horrifyingly) enslaved black balloon face; rather, that same resentment is more

openly admitted toward the planter himself (in this case the Old Frenchman) as well as his more modern, liberal capitalist descendant, Will Varner,
while at the same time Varner is rightly perceived as only one among the
twentieth-century South's (as in Faulkner's time the "New South's")
elusively dispersed sources of alienation. As an image of this new order
as genealogically descendant from the old, Faulkner offers the "stubborn
tale" of the Old Frenchman's buried money, a key image both for the elusive, abstract fungibility of modern power and privilege (as money anyone
might find and spend who knows how), and for the stubborn phobic
tendency to reduce and remystify the sources of that power and privilege
in single persons, things (caches, fetishes), or arbiters of exchange. The
most common of these arbiters of exchange are the systems of money and
law, those "banking and civil laws" which Flem (in his father's footsteps)
has understood better than any as neither mere justice nor neutral representation of good and evil but symptoms and means of wielding and gaining power. The challenge that will be taken up by Faulkner's humorous
mode in *The Hamlet* is to appreciate and to take critical advantage of openings in this order for resourcefully rearticulating possibilities for desire,
without letting his language or his characters get stuck in a way out from
which there is no way out, or in a remystification of (reified) exchange
"itself" or humor "itself," abstracted from their particular enactments of
an irrepressibly generous, involved life of fear and desire.

From the beginning of his career Faulkner had appreciated the possibilities of humor in American literature. As early as 1926 he wrote in his
foreword to *Sherwood Anderson and Other Famous Creoles,* "We have
one priceless universal trait, we Americans. That trait is our humor. What
a pity it is that it is not more prevalent in our art. . . . One trouble with
us American artists is that we take our art and ourselves too seriously"
(45). We have already seen Faulkner demonstrate in limited ways in
Absalom, Absalom! the critical potential of frontier humor to puncture
the mystified seriousness with which the young Thomas Sutpen uncritically
accepts his father's and then his own ejection from Southern plantation
society and thereby dooms himself to repeat that exclusion as a kind of
primal scene of purifying social exclusion. Sutpen's humorlessness is made
partly to blame for the way he internalizes and then enforces almost without question his new society's violently exclusive and destructive social
oppositions and hierarchies of class, race, and gender. But in general in
Absalom as in most of his earlier, more modernist work, Faulkner opposes
to Sutpen's narrowly conceived, "innocent" seriousness only the alternative
seriousness of an equally mystified modernist cosmic irony, and not the
critically "dangerous memory" (Benjamin 253–64) of a marginally precapitalist frontier humor. Faulkner's sympathetic but increasingly critical

analysis of innocence and irony as two mutually dependent, dominant modernist strategies of mystification in reaction to feelings of cultural death and defeat in the West and the American South had simultaneously defined his desire for other still more critical fictional strategies for appreciating such oppositions' violence and costs in terms of other, excluded possibilities of relationship and exchange. He had not yet found a way to put into extended practice his sense that early nineteenth-century Old Southwestern humor proposed critical escapes from both these innocent and ironic tendencies of Southern and modernist American literature, for example George Washington Harris' Sut Lovingood, whom Faulkner praised for never having "blamed his misfortunes on anyone," thereby escaping innocence, and never having "cursed God for them," thereby escaping irony (*Lion* 251). But at least the outrageousness of Sut Lovingood's practical jokes on naively serious brides (as in "Sicily Burns's Wedding") as well as on cynically serious, ironic men of God (as in "Parson Bullen's Lizards") does survive in Ab Snopes's outrageous signature in manure on Mrs. de Spain's blond rug in "Barn Burning" (1939), when Ab is confronted with much the same primal scene of social exclusion.

Ab's gesture in "Barn Burning," however, clearly lacks the high-spiritedness of Lovingood's pranks, and this difference becomes even clearer when Ab resorts to the barn burning which has become for him the grimly habitual, failed ritualization of his still largely unarticulated rage. Harris is similarly concerned with making "speech break into writing," as Neil Schmitz argues, but the "abrupt chaotic violence" of Sut's almost unwritable speech and action makes "a poetry of that destruction" (*Huck,* 54, 55), as Ab's speech and action largely do not. In Schmitz's appreciation of Sut's humor, "Here is a vandal who admires his handiwork," who "delights in special effects" and "takes an artistic pride in the beauty of his collisions," which "are designed, and yet open to improvisation" (54–56). Sut's poetry of destruction in a story like "Sicily Burns's Wedding" resourcefully articulates his own grotesque body and thwarted desire in the midst of a wedding party that has attempted (especially Sicily) to ignore that body and that desire: they do feel it, and at least "George," Sut's mostly silent interlocuter-writer, here and elsewhere relishes Sut's poetic genius (57–59). The potential poetry and humor of Ab Snopes's signature on the rug, on the other hand, is lost not only on Major and Mrs. de Spain, but even on his son, with whom he still shows some hope of communicating. The narrator has to intercede to interpret Ab's gestures in terms of what the boy does *not* understand, of what, even when thus interpreted, is still an intensely private matter of "the preservation of integrity" according to "some deep mainspring of his being" (8, 7). What might well be communicated and appreciated (by readers, at least) of resourcefulness and humor in Ab's peculiar signature on the rug becomes in his arson an enraged and habitual destruction, peculiarly silent and unpoetic, provoking at best a matching rage on the part of de Spain but little recognition from Sarty. It would remain for Ratliff in his rendition of this same story in *The Hamlet* to relish the poetry, the humor, and the political vigor in both Ab's signature and the continuing threat of fire.

Faulkner had worked this ambivalently tender, raucous tradition of Southwestern humor in odd moments of his novels and especially in many of his short stories, besides "Barn Burning," but in his previous writing as in most of the history of humor in American literature, either the humor tended to rigidify in a habitual irony like Ab's, or it remained confined to the form of an interlude or sketch, where it tends automatically, generically, to be dismissed by writers, readers, and critics as "mere" humor, an uncritical escapism, a way out with no way out (Deleuze and Guattari, *Kafka* 36). The most successfully sustained use of Southwestern humor in a nineteenth-century novel is in *Huckleberry Finn,* which lives ambivalently and ambiguously on this border between uncritical escapism from necessity and necessities for critical escape (see Schmitz 96–125). Twain's *Mysterious Stranger,* like Melville's *Confidence Man* before it, seems finally to resolve this ambiguity in nineteenth-century literary humor in favor of humor as escapism, thus relapsing into irony. Faulkner, however, undertakes in *The Hamlet* not to turn his humorous sketches into a unified novel with a traditionally universalized, ahistorical ending or grand, reductive truth, nor to group them loosely (for the sake of artistic respectability or profit) in what he would call a novel but which would function nevertheless as a collection of stories; he undertakes instead vigorously to affirm and exercise his humor (and the humor of those traditions he works), unified historically as an unending critical necessity and possibility.

On the question of unity and repetition in Faulkner's humorous mode, and in this phase of his career when he began constructing novels from separately published and unpublished stories, it may be useful to borrow from Deleuze's explanation of Nietzsche's concepts of the will to power and the eternal return: "The will to power is plastic, inseparable from each case in which it is determined; just as the eternal return is being, but being which is affirmed of becoming, the will to power is unitary, but unity which is affirmed of multiplicity" (85–86). These concepts are more related to issues of innocence, irony, and humor than they at first appear. The Nietzschean will to power shares humor's critical potential but also its generously affirmative, nondefensive involvement with its unpredictably changing circumstances (unlike irony's spurious foresight and detachment). The eternal return, like humor, dislodges the vacillating dialectic of nostalgically innocent and ironic repetition, as these alternatives are played out in *Absalom,* for example: it is repetition not in the sense of a "normative repetition of Habit and Representation" (nostalgia and irony, respectively), but as a "radical repetition of the Same and Difference."[6] In these terms the test of Faulkner's and his characters' humor will be whether it wants "to affirm its difference or to deny what differs" (Deleuze, *Nietzsche* 78): whether it actively opens up new possibilities for life, love, and desire, or whether it only mocks a lack of such possibilities.

The barn burning story virtually introduces *The Hamlet* and the Snopes trilogy, as background to another—the first—of this novel's proliferation of refracted, revised versions of the primal Faulknerian social scene of the poor-white boy insulted at the planter's door. In the case of this first, brief scene which raises the question of Ab's background, the planter's door has been displaced by the door of the Varners' store ("in which they dealt mostly in foreclosed mortgages"—7): the store displaces the big plantation house as the new center of economic power and privilege, reflecting the fact that a capitalist ideology of fair exchange and opportunity has largely (but not completely) superseded the feudal ideology of a beneficent hierarchy. And thus the poor-white boy approaching his master in "Barn Burning" has here been displaced by a somewhat stunted but full-grown Ab Snopes, as if for a meeting of equals. Jody Varner is working in the family store "when at a sound behind him he turned and saw, silhouetted by the open door, a man smaller than common, in a wide hat and a frock coat too large for him, standing with a curious planted stiffness" (7). In the ensuing interchange Jody attempts to demystify and disperse his own power, not by hiding behind the balloon face of a slave (in contrast to whom he would appear as perfectly free and leisured, in the style of the Old South planter), but in the New South liberal capitalist style, by acknowledging only that he is "one Varner" (only possibly the power Ab should address), and by using his "bland hard quite pleasant voice" (7) as if to negotiate, between two free and equal agents within a capitalist economy, what is actually a quite one-sided "share tenant" agreement (Brown 198). Ab makes that economic inequality unmistakably clear by sardonically counting himself among "his own field hands," in an arithmetic which Jody remarks is contrary to a common usage that must have falsely flattered (as slavery and racism did) many male heads of share tenant families (as if they were not themselves field workers too). And Ab's sardonicism immediately breaks another silence, that cloaking the predictably exploitative function of the cashless, monopoly store and commissary ("I see," Ab says, "Furnish in six-bit dollars"—8).

6. Robert Hurley, Mark Seem, and Helen R. Lane, translators' note in Deleuze and Guattari's *Anti-Oedipus* 393 n. 4, referring to Deleuze's *Différence et répétition* 128–67.

Jody's mistake, however, is to read Ab's sardonicism in this exchange at the door as an ironic endpoint, merely Ab's ironic representation of reality and a way of consoling himself by internalizing and contemplating his repeated victimization subject to that impersonal, economic reality (cf. Sutpen's "there aint any good or harm either in the living world that I can do to him," *Absalom* 192). Jody's mistakenly innocent belief in Ab's helplessness and in his own absolute power relative to that helplessness leads him to think, when he hears of *one* barn burning associated with Ab, that Ab "will just have to suffer the disadvantages" of his suspicious past (12). He thinks that Ab is bound to flee guiltily at the first reminder of those suspicions, even if that means forfeiting his share of his crop to the Varners. At this point, as Ratliff retells the "Barn Burning" story to Jody (who listens in "protuberant and speechless horror"—14), its revised function is to disabuse Jody of his innocence with regard to Ab's helplessness in his (imputed) irony, to focus and set that impasse of innocence and irony aside at the novel's outset in order to set into motion a much more protean relationship among Varners, Snopeses, Ratliff, and others in the rest of the novel and trilogy. Ratliff does not tell the barn burning story from the viewpoint of Sarty, who experienced Ab's tactics in the short story as a way out from which (for Sarty, at least) there was no way out. Here, on the contrary, Ab's way out surprises Jody because it does *not* lead Ab in the direction of retreat and guilt: Ab not only definitely burned one barn, but survived and dared to burn another different barn with virtual impunity, so that he poses an unknowable, unpredictable threat now to the Varners' many vulnerable pieces of property. Ab seems now neither the condemned object of Jody's innocent judgment, nor the object of Ab's own ironic recognition of that same judgment: Ab must be instead another unpredictably resourceful subject. But Jody is unprepared to recognize him as such.

Jody makes a failed attempt at the humor Ratliff's story requires: "He began to laugh. That is, he began to say 'Ha. Ha. Ha.' rapidly, but just from the teeth, the lungs: no higher, nothing of it in the eyes. Then he stopped. '. . . Maybe I can get there in time to get him to cancel with me for just a old cottonhouse'" (18). Failing at humor, Jody only reverses his formerly innocent assumption of omnipotence to adopt instead an anxiously generalized irony, approaching the Snopes cabin "as if he were approaching an ambush," watching the house "with such intensity as to be oblivious to detail" (19). Thus his attempts at negotiation with Ab and Flem are superficial, motivated not by recognition of their particular interests as other subjects but by a desire to regain through a process of rationalization his former sense of certainty and control over unknown factors like Ab and Flem—a desire for fire insurance. Jody insists that "anything that comes up, . . . just anything you dont like" can be negotiated, invoking a liberalized system of legal and economic exchange which he has had little reason himself to question (20–21). Ab and Flem, however, as long-time victims of such an economy, both maintain a critical frontier-style awareness (the "harsh" and ungentle laughter of the doggeries in *Absalom* 183) of interests such a system might well persistently, institutionally, solemnly ignore. "When I cant get along with [landlords], I leave," says Ab, and when Jody suggests to Flem that Ab might run out of new country to move to, Flem just insists again on the frontier option (implicitly also the arson option): "There's a right smart of country" (21, 22). Flem does negotiate with Jody, but knows to reject outright Jody's bland, standard agrarian offer of a farm to work and store credit: "Aint no benefit in farming" (23). For all its ideologically natural, productive use value "in itself," farming is nothing without recognition in terms of exchange. Flem prefers a piece of the action at the store, where he can take an active role himself in the going system of exchange, as neither its exploited victim nor its embittered terrorist-escapee, but alongside or in place of Jody as another of its many perverse manipulators (and rewriters). Although at first Jody thinks he has safely coopted Ab's and Flem's disruptive potential by giving the store clerk job to Flem, he soon realizes (not for the last time) that he has gained no guarantees, that Flem is his own man both within his family and in his negotiations with Jody.

In retelling "Barn Burning" in *The Hamlet*, Faulkner and Ratliff have disposed of Sarty's innocent nostalgia for the Old South (as the only alternative to Ab's bitter irony) by simply disposing of Sarty: about his absence Ratliff suggests offhandedly, "Maybe they forgot to tell him when to get outen the barn" (13). In place of Sarty as naive witness to Ab's signature in manure on Mrs. de Spain's white rug, Ratliff introduces Sarty's older brother Flem and his different, twentieth-century capitalist's way out of Ab's own now somewhat repetitive and dangerous, violent way out of their intolerable social and economic circumstances. Ratliff insists to Will Varner that Jody's own merely rationalized version of the old planter's son's assumption of privilege and power has not recognized the nature of Ab's and especially Flem's challenge. Ab is not "naturally mean," says Ratliff; "He's just soured" (27). He is not so easily typed, that is, as an unworthy, guilty opponent, but is one (rigidified) kind of challenge among others, such that Jody should not so easily assume he can make of Ab's son Flem a mere power broker in his control, a twentieth-century version of the liveried slave at the planter's door.

Before following Flem into his own eventual rigidification or reterritorialization in the New South's own capitalistic channelings of desire, Ratliff tells another tale that both foreshadows this prevalent twentieth-century tendency and also proposes the different possibility of humorous escapes from that particular rigidification. Retelling now the 1936 short story "Fool about a Horse," Ratliff substitutes the unsoured Ab (as a child-less neighbor during Ratliff's boyhood) for Ratliff's own father "Pap" in the earlier story, thereby situating Ab's later irony as one soured, habitual form of repetition within a larger genealogy of Ratliff's humor (Ratliff is also a kind of son to Will Varner—157–58). Inasmuch as this story will also repeat and revise the primal social scene at the planter's door (here the door to the tent of the unbeatable traveling horse trader Pat Stamper and his black magician-hostler assistant), Ratliff also places his own life along-side Ab's and Flem's as another possible response to the historically chang-ing form of this primal scene. Still another function of this story, in the new context of Ratliff's telling it to an audience on the gallery of Varner's store, is to warn them all against too easy a scapegoating of Ab or Flem, whose place as the new hired clerk inside the store seems to them "as unheard of as the presence of a hired white woman in one of their own kitchens" (28). Ratliff's tale urges an understanding of the motivations of Ab's violent bitterness (not just its easily condemned criminal conse-quences), and thus his tale functions as a caution against their making the same mistake with regard to the clerk that Ab made with Stamper in this story (at least in soured retrospect), that is, they must not accept uncritically and humorlessly New South capitalism's fetishized "cash money" as the arbiter of social exchange. This is a mistake which will take the positive form of their becoming Flem's dupes (taken in by an irre-sistible bargain), and the negative form of their adopting local versions of Jason Compson's self-righteously nostalgic, fascist anti-Semitism in *The Sound and the Fury*—here a structural anti-Semitism directed against Snopeses instead of Jews. That is, Faulkner's experiments with humor as a social critique lead here toward a striking articulation of the connection between modernist irony and innocence and the economic and religious motivations of anti-Semitism, with or without the (supposedly provoking) presence of actual Jews.[7]

Ratliff tells Ab's story as that of a man who has been the victim of both the land-based capitalism of the Old South and the money-based capitalism of the New, and who has kept his humor through both experi-

---

7. One exceptional, almost explicit association of Snopeses with Jews in *The Hamlet* is Wallstreet Panic Snopes's name. I. O. Snopes gave Wall his name in the hope that "it might make him get rich like the folks that run that Wallstreet panic" (266). But considering I. O.'s own peculiar way of speaking in commonplaces, this naming functions less as an identification of Wall or even of I. O. himself with Jews than as one unusually explicit, parodic reflection on the currency and inadequacy of such anti-Semitic conspiracy theories as explanations of economic fortune.

ences, although the second eliminated him from horse trading, "And so he [later] just went plumb curdled" (29). First Ab was the victim of Old South (pretended) anticapitalism, when the horse-trading partnership he formed with Colonel Sartoris' supposedly high-minded, charitable mother-in-law, Rosa Millard, ran afoul of her violent political allegiances (which otherwise condoned horse theft, forgery, and extortion): "then Colonel's boy Bayard and Uncle Buck McCaslin and a nigger caught Ab in the woods and something else happened, tied up to a tree or something and maybe even a double bridle rein or maybe even a heated ramrod in it too" (29). Ab's apparently unprincipled business sense (compared to the Sartorises') is not, however, equivalent or easily assimilable to New South capitalism either, but brings a marginally precapitalist frontier perspective to bear on the mystified violence and costs of both the Old South economy and that of the New. What provokes his defeat at the hands of the New is not a political principle (the land, the South, property, propriety) but that of "cash money," another exchange value fetishized and divorced both from the use value of the labor and products it represents and from the social relations involved in all such symbolic exchange:[8]

> That's what did it. . . . the fact that Pat Stamper, a stranger, had
> come in and got actual Yoknapatawpha County cash dollars to
> rattling around loose that way. When a man swaps horse for horse,
> that's one thing and let the devil protect him if the devil can. But
> when cash money starts changing hands, that's something else. And
> for a stranger to come in and start that cash money to changing and
> jumping from one fellow to another, it's like when a burglar breaks
> into your house and flings your things ever which way even if he
> dont take nothing. It makes you twice as mad. (34)

In the tradition of Old Southwestern (especially horse-trading) humor evoked by Ab's previous trading up and down his road, and by Ratliff's narrative appreciation of swapping horses for the gambler's "pleasure of beating a worthy opponent as much as for gain" (30), a bad trade in terms of "absolute" gain and loss can always be parlayed into gains in other later trades, or gains in humorous affirmations of social differences and bonds (see "Horse Trading"). But when Ab sets out to "vindicate" the "science

8. I use Baudrillard's term "symbolic exchange" to acknowledge the problems with classical Marxism's opposition of use value and exchange value (to be discussed later). The model of symbolic exchange does not pretend to an abolition of the abstraction necessary in any comparison or exchange, but attempts to recognize the different values and costs of such social mediations. Andrew Parker and Gregory S. Jay have recently suggested that Marx elsewhere preinscribed much of Baudrillard's critique of this (often still useful, strategic) opposition.

and pastime of horse-trading in Yoknapatawpha County" by somehow getting his countryman's eight dollars back from Stamper, he has already accepted the cash principle as final arbiter of the trade, and has thus reduced this "science and pastime" (the human science?) of Yoknapatawpha trading to a simpler (arithmetical) science (34). Ratliff's incidental, utterly straight-faced fictions of, for example, the inflatability of the entire hide of a live horse challenge his listeners and readers to remember other kinds of gains (narrative, humorous gains) besides only the kind on which Ab's blinders are here so narrowly trained: "maybe Ab was so busy fooling Pat that Pat never had to fool Ab at all" (36). Faulkner's revision of "Fool about a Horse" for *The Hamlet* makes Ab's and his wife's losses greater than in the earlier version in monetary and material terms (here they lose the very cow for whose milk Ab was originally sent to town to buy the separator);[9] but this almost inescapably *ironic* loss is here the occasion for Ab's (temporarily) regaining and proving his precurdled, loving, lovable humor, as he reminds the young Ratliff to bring another gallon of borrowed milk tomorrow for his wife to separate: " 'It looks like she is fixing to get a heap of pleasure and satisfaction outen it,' he says" (47). Sadly, Ab's effective elimination from horse trading after this episode, and his economic reliance only on tenant farming, have led him into more desperate, violent straits since, with much less room for humor than Ratliff's better circumstances provide. When Ratliff rides out to visit Ab again, Ratliff notices "that something had gone out of the eyes" (49): Ab can accept neither the (incalculable, nonmonetary) interpersonal dimensions of Ratliff's gift of a bottle of good whiskey, nor the equally good spirits of Ratliff's humorous reference to their shared past, his attempt to trade a past loss for an affirmation of renewed relationship.

Through the rest of *The Hamlet* the test of Ratliff's and others' humor, both in Frenchman's Bend and among Faulkner's readers, will be twofold. First, humor will be necessary to understand and appreciate the Snopeses' variously resourceful, perverse, funny ways of escaping the still widely mystified but changing structures of Old South power and privilege. And second, humor will be necessary to maintain a sense of the attendant risks of falling into the differently remystified, reterritorialized forms of power, privilege, and alienation in the liberalized capitalism of the twentieth-century New South.

The third and last chapter of *The Hamlet*'s book 1, "Flem," revises *Absalom*'s ending in the idiot Jim Bond's victimized, inarticulate howl, refusing that ending not for the sake of another falsely affirmative dialectical synthesis (in another version of nostalgia or irony), but to affirm

9. A change unmentioned in Blotner's notes to *Uncollected Stories*.

another, different possibility: this reprise effectively grants Jim Bond (in the new idiot Ike Snopes) a singular voice and the possibility of action in the pursuit of his singular desires (not just his generalized "needs" for which the good townspeople might provide)—grants him a voice in the language most generally understood in *The Hamlet* and the New South, that of "cash money." Ike Snopes here is only potentially the fool figure waiting near the end of every humorous sketch—the fool figure waiting *near* the end insofar as humor always opens a critical way out of such an apparently final accounting in folly. (To believe in an ending in folly would be to end with Jim Bond's howl.) Humor insists that such bottom lines are fetishes, and survives being the fool, whereas irony stops at representing and contemplating the fool, as if thereby to avoid the risk and folly of desire.

Ratliff has predicted to Will Varner earlier "that there aint but two men I know can risk fooling with them folks [the Snopeses]. And just one of them is named Varner and his front name aint Jody" (28). With this humorous parody of ironic detachment, Ratliff avoids saying directly he can risk fooling with the Snopeses himself, but Faulkner has already begun preparing the scene for Ratliff's first contest with Flem by portraying Flem's quiet defeat of Jody and standoff with Will. It is a "new life and milieu" Flem enters with his self-made, new white shirt as clerk in the Varner store, the white-collar commercial world of wage labor and monetary (or credit) exchange, the same world of cash money that outmaneuvered his father. But although this is a life "already channeled to compulsions and customs long before his advent, [Flem] had nevertheless established in it even that first day his own particular soiling groove" (51). That is, he will reproduce this modern capitalist world with a difference: he will wear its uniform, but he will not be overscrupulous about keeping that uniform white and clean. Jody has planned that his own shirt and business will be kept clean by contrast with the reputed Snopes violence and general (poor-white) unseemliness (as in the contrasts with Sutpen on which Rosa Coldfield's nostalgia depended in *Absalom*); however, Flem "abrupts" onto the Sunday morning churchgoing scene in Frenchman's Bend as disconcertingly as Sutpen once did in Jefferson, whereupon the villagers notice with "incredulous astonishment" that he wears "not only a clean white shirt but a necktie," in a singular imitation of Will Varner, who wears the only other tie in the county (57). Although Flem's tie recalls "that quality of outrageous overstatement of physical displacement which the sound of his father's stiff foot made on the gallery of the store that afternoon in the spring," its long-term effect will be altogether different, "like [that of] an enigmatic punctuation symbol" (58). Flem's version of the Varners' capitalism will serve not as exonerating contrast or alibi, the unruly "bad cop" who makes the "good cop" look good only by contrast, force as opposed to law. Flem will refuse to represent the violence or crime to be controlled by a system of law, or to be signified or repressed by another higher level of language. Instead of reinforcing such false oppositions (actually immanent to the system) by helping to represent them as oppositions between the system and himself, Flem will critically re*punctuate,* both clarifying and making "enigmatic," these and other relationships *within* the language and system of New South capitalism.

For instance, the villagers have been disturbed that in his new position at the store Flem "never made mistakes in any matter pertaining to money. Jody Varner had made them constantly" (56). Although they knew Jody's mistakes were "usually in his own favor" and that "he would correct them when caught with a bluff, hearty amiability, making a joke of it, which sometimes left the customer wondering just a little about the rest of the bill," still, their consolation is insistent: "But they expected this too, because he would give them credit for food and plow-gear when they needed it, long credit . . ." (56). This consolation leads, however, to the clumsily subordinated afterthought, ". . . though they knew they would pay interest for that which on its face looked like generosity and openhandedness, whether that interest showed in the final discharge or not" (56). In a store in which, it may be recalled, the Varners "dealt mostly in foreclosed mort-gages" (7), not being able to "catch" Flem in an error deprives them of this (balloon-face) consolation for and diversion from an actually *systemic* exploitation by the entire monopoly-store and tenant-farming system. By refusing to be that system's cheating or violent alibi, Flem effectively repunctuates that system from within in such a way as to clarify and make enigmatic how a consolation has as it were been made to subordinate and conceal a more significant afterthought.

Flem, then, is a different, white-collar breed of servant at the New South planter-businessman's (business) door. If he will not serve as a blackened evocation of the planter's necessarily violent, despotic relation-ship with racial or criminal outsiders, if he will not do the Varners' dirty work as Jody's henchman and thus exonerate the system he serves for a secret wage, then the villagers will react to this disturbing suspicion cast on the system itself, in the all too common twentieth-century style of popular fascist anti-Semitism: they will identify Flem with (and vilify him in place of) their entire system of commodity fetishism (in money) and bureaucratic depersonalization (in law) of social exchange. This is to say not that they see him literally as a Jew, but that they see him in the way Marx explains that the Jew was seen, also in the nineteenth century, as the particular appearance of a cult of haggling and worship of money that is more spiritualized and sublimated but no less actual in the Christian

state. Thus Flem serves here as what Marx would have called a "structural" Jew: "the practical Jewish spirit, Judaism or commerce, has main-
tained itself, and reached its highest development, in Christian society.
The Jew who is a particular member of civil society is only the particular
appearance of the Judaism of civil society" (60). But instead of heeding
his immanent demystifications of the Varners' own formerly smiling capitalism, the villagers suspect Flem of taking over the power and thus responsibility and blame for the store and the entire spider's web of economic
relationships it represents, as if

> not only the guiding power but the proprietorial and revenue-deriving
> as well was concentrated in that squat reticent figure in the steadily-
> soiling white shirts and the minute invulnerable bow, which in those
> abeyant days lurked among the ultimate shadows of the deserted and
> rich-odored interior with a good deal of the quality of a spider of
> that bulbous blond omnivorous though non-poisonous species. (58)

His "passing" Jody is viewed as ominously invisible and institutional, not
felt like an event when "something happened" (58), but discovered as an
established fact sometime later, too late, "when Jody begun to find it out"
(60). Flem's voice "murmuring, matter-of-fact, succinct," his back "shape-
less, portentous, without age," he has penetrated almost unobserved into
the sanctum of Will Varner's formerly private "yearly settlement with his
tenants and debtors," Will holding the cash box and Flem the ledgers,
the pair resembling "the white trader and his native parrot-taught headman in an African outpost" (60–61). In a significant revision since *Absalom*
of the white planter's black-barred door, the pair's internal relations have
changed, their difference in color compromised by the headman's having
learned to speak, read, write, and trade in the white man's money and
language. Even more striking is the change in the pair's external relations,
since the headman is of the same color as all the other poor Africans that
would approach the trader's door. Deprived of the spurious racist distinction between themselves and the system's most plainly victimized, these
villagers react defensively and ironically by revising this older racism (based
on a naturalized, ideological white superiority to black slaves), to institute
in its place a victimized, ironic, sectarian/clannish racism acknowledging
more directly (if still distortedly, simplistically) their own continuing social
and economic frustration and alienation.

Thus Flem comes to represent the mysteriously unlocalizable unknown
in the workings of their economy. In contrast to his recent poverty, he
is now the rumored source of considerable loans with security and interest
"not specified" (61). Villagers curious about a herd of cattle that disappears,

then reappears in a different field as a different, more valuable herd, "via a foreclosed lien nominally held by a Jefferson bank" (61), are referred by Will Varner to Flem, who refers them right back to Will. But they insist on associating Flem with both the profit and the mystification suggested by such examples of capital's protean power. Thus also Flem's new cousins in town, I. O. Snopes and Eck Snopes, represent two complementary, polarized aspects of the economic system as they see that system being commandeered by Flem's pervasive, secret influence. On the one hand, Eck, the new blacksmith, is a movable and malleable pawn within that system, a piece of clumsy, incompetent brawn "working steadily but in a dreamlike state" (65), "accommodating and unfailingly pleasant and even generous, yet in whom there was a definite limitation of physical co-ordination beyond which design and plan and pattern all vanished—disintegrated into dead components of pieces of wood and iron straps and vain tools" (66). I. O., on the other hand, is all (borrowed) plans and patterns, a personification of the system itself as furious energy and violent, darting motion, always appearing unrestrainably "independent of his clothing" (64), and speaking constantly in the linguistic general equivalent of that system, in universally applicable and reversible aphorisms, "his voice voluble and rapid and meaningless like something talking to itself about nothing in a deserted cavern" (65).

Somewhere between and beyond these two caricatured antitheses, their cousin Flem intercedes as if to synthesize concrete needs and abstract designs, to reconcile use value and exchange value in an efficient capitalism. Flem builds a new blacksmith shop in the village "so that people could get decent work done again" (66), but he does so as part of a series of commercial maneuvers intricate to a point where "even Ratliff had lost count of what profit Snopes might have made" (67). Ratliff imagines this is too much mystery, at least for Jody, who would want a "pure and simple" answer (and what early Americans called the set, "due price," cf. "Regulation" 442): "Just [what] is it going to cost me to protect one goddamn barn full of hay?" (67). Jody has often profited himself from surreptitiously managed surplus values (for example, in the interest he collects on the credit he gives, in the markup involved in furnishing his tenants in "six-bit dollars," and in the forfeited payments involved in his "business" of foreclosures); however, these profits have been concealed by an older landholding and newer capitalist ideology that trusts him to set and reset, unilaterally, the terms and prices of money exchange. The aura of mystery surrounding Flem's own profits in the same money economy arises from Jody's and most others' discovery that now someone else has his own skillful and unpredictable hand in the workings of that economy. This is precisely the murky awareness of "the concealment of domination in production" described by Horkheimer and Adorno as the specific economic reason for bourgeois anti-Semitism:

> The productive work of the capitalist, whether he justifies his profit by means of gross returns as under liberalism, or by his director's salary as today, is an ideology cloaking the real nature of the labor contract and the grasping character of the economic system. And so people shout: Stop thief!—but point at the Jews. They are the scapegoats not only for individual maneuvers and machinations but in a broader sense, inasmuch as the economic injustice of the whole class is attributed to them. (173–74)

Ratliff views social and economic changes in the Bend from the critical perspective of his own long experience in more reciprocal, humorous, and symbolic exchanges (in horses, mules, used odds and ends both of objects and pieces of news)—ambivalently precapitalist exchanges measured less exclusively in money terms than those in the Varner store are. This perspective helps to prevent his sharing others' exaggerated surprise at Flem's activity, for example on the occasion of Flem's first confrontation as clerk with Will Varner: "So it was very likely Ratliff alone who was not surprised, since what did divulge was the obverse of what they might have hoped for; it was not the clerk who now discovered at last whom he was working for, but Will Varner who discovered who was working for him" (53). The (demystified, observed) obverse and not the inverse: it is only the onlookers' surprise and remystifying, scapegoating suspicion that make it seem to many (both watchers and readers) that if Flem has not met his master, then everyone is now working for Flem. Actually Flem is still working for Will, but the Master has had to look his Slave in the face.

Faulkner has thus prepared the scene for the first of two major tests of Ratliff's humor. He has set two opposite traps for Ratliff to avoid, either "innocent" underestimation of the Snopeses as no more than unruly pawns or cogs securely contained within a system which he and not they can manipulate to his own advantage, or on the other hand "ironic" overestimation of Flem as the untouchable mastermind who is in control of the whole weblike system. Eck and I. O. are caricatures of these two dialectically paired, reductive, self-defeating views of the Snopeses.

Ratliff enters the Bend after a gallbladder operation, "looking forward to his visit not only for the pleasure of the shrewd dealing which far transcended mere gross profit, but with the sheer happiness . . . of moving once more . . . in the sun and air which men drank and moved in and talked and dealt with one another [in]" (67–68). Ratliff appreciates more than only profit in such "shrewd dealing"; he enjoys it as a particularly intense, symbolic form of social exchange. The question is only whether his now "delicate robustness" is up to it. Faulkner praises his "shrewd humorous voice which would require a good deal more than just illness to other than merely weaken its volume a little," but Faulkner also shows that Ratliff can be "surprised out of his own humorous poise" (69): his humor is not a possession, an intellectual or moral "sense of humor" that one either has or "should" have, it is not a safe position but a "poise," existing only as an achievement to be precariously, creatively reachieved and exercised in the midst of ever-changing circumstances and relations (see Girard).

Ratliff's attitude toward the Snopeses' progress is contrasted with that of Bookwright and Tull, whose excellent appetites Ratliff and Faulkner greatly enjoy watching even while Bookwright and Tull both cast themselves (and Ratliff) among Flem's helpless, innocent victims. Bookwright stops mid-pie to speak with a "fierce dark face" of a black debtor to Flem who has repaid over double the principal on his loan in interest payments he unknowingly considers cheap (70). Here not just the landless poor white (as in *Absalom*) but the white yeoman sees himself in terms of the openly exploited black, but blames that exploitation entirely on Flem. When Ratliff asks whether they have acted on their concern (for example by enlightening the black man, or better, offering him better terms), Tull only says, "It aint right. But it aint none of our business." Then when Ratliff says, "I believe I would think of something if I lived there," Bookwright cautions him against certain defeat, advising him to "go out there nekkid in the first place. Then you wont notice the cold coming back" (71). Bookwright and Tull's passive, defeatist scapegoating of Flem not only deflects responsibility for exploitation from the Varners to Flem, but also absolves them of responsibility for their own victimization. They are ignorant, unprotectedly naked, and therefore innocent, both of anything they have done to support this system in action or belief, and of anything they have not done once they have realized this system does have recognizable victims and have decided it is none of their business. They expect a kind of moral credit for not resisting that defeat. This is what Horkheimer and Adorno describe as the other, *religious* origin of modern Christian anti-Semitism, in "the deceptively positive meaning given to self-denial": the instinct of self-preservation having supposedly been overcome in the imitation of Christ, the church then sets that self-denial down as merit, deserving (a self-preserving) redemption. The knowledge "that the spiritual promise of salvation is not binding" is rejected by those who have "persuaded themselves with a heavy conscience that Christianity was their own sure possession. . . . The adherents of the religion of the Father are hated by those who support the religion of the Son—hated as those who know better" (178–79).

Thus when he first sees Ike Snopes, Ratliff scoffs at the ingrained Christian sentimentalization that describes the idiot's mental disability as essentially, divinely human—"And yet they tell us we was all made in His image." Bookwright, on the other hand, accepts that sentimentalization to the extent that he gives it only its simple ironic inversion (thinking Ratliff is being fooled as predicted, as if in the image of Ike)—"Maybe he was" (81). Ratliff prefers to resist such debilitating views of himself and Ike in favor of an appreciation for Mrs. Littlejohn's ability to communicate with Ike not as a representative reification of unmediated human desire and loss (like Jim Bond) but as a different subject with particular (mediable, articulable) desires; Ratliff will later trust her with the means (in money) for the further articulation and pursuit of those desires. However, Ratliff does lose sight of this relationship to another subject in Ike at the moment of his own apparent defeat in his elaborate goat deal with Flem, when Ike seems to represent the mirrorlike image and unforeseen explanation of Ratliff's own defeat. At that imbalanced moment of surprise (as in *Absalom*) the idiot inspires "something black" in Ratliff, "a suffocation, a sickness, nausea" (85), an avoidance by mythic rationalization of a particular realization Ratliff cannot now look at or think about: Ike's eyes thus seem, like those of Jim Bond or Melville's Pip, to be eyes "which at some instant, some second once, had opened upon, been vouchsafed a glimpse of, the Gorgon-face of that primal injustice which man was not intended to look at face to face and had been blasted clean and empty forever of any thought" (85). When Ratliff has recovered his humor, he can think better of Ike, and can realize his particular mistake this time in dealing with Flem.

He has underestimated Mink in something like the way he momentarily here underestimated Ike. He has avoided successfully the economic scapegoating and overestimation of Flem as another legendary Pat Stamper, perfectly invulnerable to material risks and shrewd trades. That is, Ratliff has made sure Flem is in the position of having no choice but to trade on Ratliff's terms, owning fifty otherwise unsalable goats and several flammable properties subject to threatened burning by Mink. Ratliff has also avoided Jody's mistaken initial underestimation (in Ab's case) of the desperate motivations and unignorable power of a threatened incendiarism such as Mink's. Under the influence of these two alternatives, however, and with an eye especially to avoiding the first, economic scapegoating, what Ratliff fails to avoid is the underestimation of Mink's resourcefulness as still another unpredictable player in the game and not just one more of its resentful, violent victims whose threat of violence Ratliff can himself play against Flem:

> I just never went far enough, he thought. I quit too soon. I went as far as one Snopes will set fire to another Snopes's barn and both Snopeses know it, and that was all right. But I stopped there. I never went on to where that first Snopes will turn around and stomp the fire out so he can sue that second Snopes for the reward and both Snopeses know that too. (88)

Thus in the brief coda to this last chapter of "Flem," in the midst of various signs that Flem has securely established himself in his "usurpation" of Jody's heirship to Will's economic power, Ratliff also recognizes the radically unpredictable, destabilizing presence of Mink as "a different kind of Snopes like a cotton-mouth is a different kind of snake" (91). This is not to make again his earlier mistake of opposing Mink's threatening violence to Flem's "nonpoisonous," economic power. It is to recognize not Mink's intentional or representational opposition to Flem, but his unmanageable (by Ratliff *or* by Flem) unwillingness to forsake that violence only for the sake of an economic stake in the world of which Flem has entered the door. If Flem has found a capitalist's way (in) out of his father's way out, his capitalist's way out has its own definite limits, which from now on in *The Hamlet* and *The Snopes Trilogy* not only Ratliff's humor but also Mink's rage will help to expose to critical questioning and displacement.

In the course of his goat deal with Flem, Ratliff tells the men on the Varner store gallery (and Flem, listening inside) a parable of the difference between a Northern goat rancher and his Southern counterpart, a parable which may be useful to summarize Faulkner's procedure in *The Hamlet*. The parable anticipates the influential distinction by Lévi-Strauss in *The Savage Mind* between the mentality of the modern "engineer" and that of the primitive "bricoleur"; it anticipates as well the poststructuralist objection to such dialectical oppositions. Ratliff trades "not only on what I think he knows about me, but on what he must figure I know about him, as conditioned and restricted by that year of sickness and abstinence from the science and pastime of skullduggery" (82). Ratliff therefore adopts the other villagers' simple, reductively abstract portrait of the capitalist planner-engineer and a correspondingly simple portrait of his own style as down-home bricoleur, hoping thereby to bait Flem into thinking that Ratliff is disingenuously without elaborate plans himself. "If a fellow in this country was to set up a goat-ranch, he would do it purely and simply because he had too many goats already" (79). Ratliff would see the Northern goat rancher as a godsend Yankee/city slicker/Jew scapegoat easily fleeced to save Ratliff himself from poverty after his operation. Such a Northerner "dont start off with goats or a piece of land either. He starts off with a piece of paper and a pencil and measures it all down setting in the library" somewhere up North, then comes South with only his idea and "his hand grip bulging with greenback money," the most abstract mediation possible between idea and substance (79, 78).

This brings us to the poststructuralist critique of such oppositions. Ratliff well knows Flem is more of a bricoleur than this opposition suggests. And Ratliff knows he is himself more of an engineer than this opposition suggests. But his contest with Flem results in something other than only a mediation of these antitheses, something other than Ratliff's expert synthesis of the two as the science *and* pastime of trading. As Jean Baudrillard says of the parallel opposition in classical Marxism between use value and exchange value, such an opposition is itself, from the outset, a *strategic* opposition (*Critique* 137), setting the structure and terms for events which may, however, despite this strategic preparation, fall outside or lodge disruptively within the structure, preventing the structure from accomplishing its logical synthesis without impertinent laughter, puzzlement, or rage, or without a radical restructuring of the system by those very events whose play it was meant to contain (cf. Unger on "revolutionary reform"). Ratliff's and Lévi-Strauss's opposition between the bricoleur and the engineer is structured not from above the structure but from within, and it loads the deck in favor of a certain sophisticated bricolage. Ratliff is reminded of his place *within* the structure he constructs when he discovers that not only he and his opponent Flem (whom he has lured into a premeditated position within that structure) are operating within this system, but also Mink, who is not simply the violent threat in Ratliff's deck of cards but another player-planner with his own plans that upset Ratliff's poise from out of somewhere to Ratliff's blind side. Thus too Faulkner himself is neither pure bricoleur nor pure engineer, revising not in obedience to an original idea or genius, nor from the detached perspective of his entire opus, but in continual engagement with the particular problems and limitations presented to him by each of his ongoing revisions of problematic oppositions.[10]

10. It may be helpful here to adduce a few seminal, analogous critiques of the structuralist and modernist tendency toward binary oppositions like that between bricoleur and engineer. Gilles Deleuze has studied Nietzsche's similar criticisms of the Hegelian dialectic for its fixation on the negative/opposite to the sad neglect of the different, with the consequent discounting of "dance [which] affirms becoming and the being of becoming; laughter, roars of laughter [which] affirm multiplicity and the unity of multiplicity; [and] play [which] affirms chance and the necessity of chance" (194). Jacques Derrida has a similar appreciation for Georges Bataille's "Hegelianism without Reserve," in which that reserve or remainder is always

At the risk of digression, I will say that this also helps explain Faulkner's changing narrative technique in *The Hamlet*. Instead of pretending to speak only as one character or a series of characters each with his or her own unmediated voice (occluding that character's place within Faulkner's fiction by means of an axiomatic suspension of disbelief), Faulkner here rather represents a narrative voice and also places within quotation marks not only brief, dramatic exchanges between characters but also long, sometimes tall stories told by characters to each other, calling attention to these characters' actual places within Faulkner's fiction. They are not dramatically or perspectivally independent of each other, but subject to changing blind spots with regard to other characters and events, and subject as well to the changing blind spots of Faulkner's own ongoing construction of their fictional milieu. Faulkner often writes here that "no one knew" this or that piece of information, but writes this without the automatic implication that he himself or his narrator slyly does know.

Thus if Flem has indeed skillfully demystified the workings of the modern cash economy which the Varners previously ran as a monopoly from behind a concealing combination of aristocratic privilege and a free-enterprise, liberal capitalism in which not just the planter but everyone else pretends a perfect freedom, still, Mink Snopes will not so easily find his place in the world of capitalist opportunities being opened up by his cousin Flem. Nor will he be satisfied with only the critically humorous perspective of Ratliff on his alienation from that system's tendency to fetishize certain narrow forms and measures of meaningful social exchange. When Ratliff recovers his "humorous poise" after having his plan upset by Mink's unexpectedly shrewd interference, he can appreciate Mink's difference both from himself and from Flem, appreciating especially the prospect that "that wasn't the last time this one is going to make his cousin trouble" (91); but this can afford Mink himself little consolation. Ratliff becomes something of a humorously detached observer, though I do not

---

to be heard in the burst of laughter that accompanies and upsets the Hegelian synthesis. Thus too Michael Taussig has shown how "primitive" forms of devil worship among colonialized South American tribes have not been simply adapted to or superseded by capitalist systems of agriculture, mining, and monetary exchange. Rather, various forms of devil worship have evolved continually as systems of belief alternative to and in critical relation with their changing social contexts. It is a bricolage continually retooled and reengineered among other reengineering bricolages. And finally, along lines similar to these, Renato Rosaldo has argued against structural anthropology's assurance that its interpretations of structures of ritual meaning adequately account for differences between the interpreter's stake in the structure and the variously different stakes of those apparently moving within that structure but whose grief or rage is of such singular character or *force* as to set those structures aside as only the projected, irrelevant tidiness of an unmoved observer (or of an unmoving official defending cultural order).

want to underestimate the critical edge to his observations. But he will not cause Flem much trouble again himself, whereas Mink's trouble will eventually, in *The Mansion,* be fatal to Flem. Flem will affirm that fatality with an unexpected glimmer of humor which will require Ratliff's humor to be appreciated. The crucial difference between the "hearty celibacy" of Ratliff's humor and Mink's painfully unfortunate, hard-pressed rage is that Mink's rage can find no humorous poise either in relation to the Old South's legacies of nostalgia and irony, or in relation to the New South's own polar alternatives of commodity fetishism or an anti-Semitism without Jews. He is unable to find that humorous poise because of both his extremely trying circumstances and the (related) force of his rage.

It is, however, Faulkner's discovery of Ratliff's humor and the long tradition from which it derives that will variously and invaluably inform most of the rest of *The Hamlet* and most of Faulkner's fiction for the rest of his career. The complementary presence of Mink's rage is a candid admission of that humor's own particular limitation, its instability under the pressure of constantly changing events. But Faulkner's discovery of the aesthetic and political vigor of humor will enable him to rewrite the scene at the planter's door and other scenes and complexes not repetitively but with radically transmuting difference, always with possibilities for humor along with possibilities for humor's failure.

To appreciate such humor requires citing specific instances, since it is never a finally achieved position or principle, but an event of a certain type in the context of other events. And such instances of humor are much easier to cite in *The Hamlet* than in *Absalom, Absalom!,* occurring now at the level of major (though never "central") events and not just between the lines or in "merely" minor or marginal moments, as before. In *The Hamlet*'s book 2, entitled "Eula," another ambitious, poor-white dirt farmer named Labove will negotiate with a planter figure lounging in stocking feet in a barrel-stave hammock (recalling the planter admired from the bushes by Sutpen as a boy in *Absalom*). Labove will adopt a historically and personally different route to success—schoolteaching, football, book-learning, and university liberal arts and legal training—with his "insufferable humorless eyes" fixed on the legal profession and the governor's mansion, but as he approaches "the last door" to his chosen profession and future, he cannot resist a fatally sidelong gaze, then a headlong bolt toward the sexuality and especially the obliviousness of Eula Varner, who represents a world not opposed to but hugely different from and ignored by his own *except* in a narrowly false and failing opposition (110, 116). Hers is an entirely different system of exchange from that of respectable marital offers, because of "that quality in her which absolutely abrogated the exchange value of any single life's promise or capacity for devotion, the puny asking-price of any one man's reserve of so-called love" (118). One last attempt ironically to resolve this discrepancy by getting himself shot and killed by Eula's jealous brother Jody fails humorously, as Labove has seen it fail humorously for a black man before and rightly fears it will fail humorously again for the poor white. But it is precisely on such humorous failures that Faulkner was learning to rely for opening critical ways out of these and other inadequate oppositions.

Hoake McCarron makes a more frontal assault on Eula, trying not to ignore or resist Eula's attraction, but to overcome her with his own "masculine" sexual charm and force. This man who has paid his black childhood friend and servant to be beaten at his hands, and who still wears the shiny black boots from his days at a military school, does finally succeed in impregnating Eula, where many others have only dreamed of succeeding. But he succeeds only by being supported by Eula from underneath, suffering extreme pain from an arm which he has just broken fighting off some other suitors, which he has then just had set almost without anesthesia, and which he has then just broken again in the act of reaching his own goal—reaching it, but satisfying perhaps only Eula's own desire.[11] Her own desire is also her brother Jody's blind spot. Like Quentin he has a jealous fixation on the preservation or ruin of the family's honor located in her maidenhead. But Will Varner accepts with more humor (than his son and than Quentin's ironic father) both her desire and her possible failure to conform to the virgin/whore dichotomy in which she is usually imagined, by placing the sexual humorously in the midst of other less sublime bodily possibilities: "What did you expect—that she would spend the rest of her days just running water through it?" (144). In Ratliff's imagined scenario of Flem in hell dealing this final blow to Jody's pride and thus usurping his throne as prince of this family and economy, taking possession (still in hell) of paradise (in Eula), it is Flem's humorlessly single-minded, Faustian determination to measure all such differences and desires by only the strict terms of "what the banking and civil laws states in black and white is hisn" that continues both to enlarge and to confine his power in hell (150).[12]

In book 3, "The Long Summer," the idiot Ike Snopes's previously

---

11. Cf. Schmitz on Thorpe's "The Big Bear of Arkansas": "When the bear at length consents to become a bedspread, to give Doggett [the hunter] his meat, the moment it chooses to do so, and the way it chooses to die, declare its unsubdued mastery. In the woods near his house, after breakfast, Doggett crouches, pants down, to defecate. It is then that the bear as a *black mist* walks through the fence, *arrives,* and in scrambling to shoot merely to protect his life, Doggett slips into his ordure. Only then, besmirched, does he ostensibly bring down the bear" ("Tall Tale, Tall Talk" 486).

12. Cf. Taussig on the Faust legend as a response to capitalist expansion (13–38).

unmediated, incoherent desire takes the coherent shape of a cow, in neither a purely pastoral fantasy of primitive, unopposed desire, nor an ironic or satiric portrait of love as clumsy animal husbandry. Ike's cow is another subject, and humorously so. When in a frightened fall by the cow Ike receives "the violent relaxing of her fear-constricted bowels," he has the humor to speak to her still, "trying to tell her how this violation of her maiden's delicacy is no shame, since such is the very iron imperishable warp of the fabric of love" (173, 174). And Ike's pursuit of his unsentimentalized, uninsulated desire thus leads to other discoveries of other kinds: "learning fast now, who has learned success and then precaution and secrecy and how to steal and even providence; who has only lust and greed and bloodthirst and a moral conscience to keep him awake at night, yet to acquire" (183). Ratliff's money will enable the progress of this love, though it will also effectively confine it to a stall and subject it to possible commodification (as surreptitious peep show) and moral censure (as unrighteous scandal) by Ike's community. At this juncture the toy cow Eck buys Ike to replace his beefed and ritually ingested lover becomes a meagerly consolatory, but well-meant, radical bricolage. It suggests the possibility of a changed function for art (and humor) in the mourning of a loss — as a means not just of denying or directly contemplating the loss, but also of negotiating the slow and painful transitions from irreplaceability to new and radically different emotional reinvestments.

Jack Houston is "possessed of that strong lust, not for life, not even for movement, but for that fetterless immobility called freedom" (205). Habituated to the "proferred slavedom" of his black mistress, his mother, and later the prostitute he "ravaged" from a Galveston brothel, "what he did not comprehend was that until now he had not known what true slavery was — that single constant despotic undeviating will of the enslaved not only for possession, complete assimilation, but to coerce and reshape the enslaver into the seemliness of his victimization" (211, 206–7). He might apparently enslave or geographically escape and even forget Lucy Pate, the patiently determined neighbor's girl who will eventually be his wife, but he cannot escape his own place in her independently coercive, reshaping plans — her love — as he recognizes most forcefully when the stallion which was "the actual transference" of his relinquished "polygamous and bitless masculinity" actually kills her (214). Even then she still seems stubbornly, unaccountably to live on, independent of his efforts either to banish every trace of her or to preserve her within the "black, savage, indomitable fidelity" of his suffocating melancholia (205).

Mink Snopes's life in *The Hamlet* is in many ways a poor-white version of the yeoman farmer Houston's life. Unlike Houston, Mink is less habituated to others' "proferred slavedom" than to his own slavery, but he is trapped in a similar dialectic of despotic master and slave. Like Houston he takes a prostitute as wife (Houston's first, common-law wife), but in Mink's case she functions as a transferable symbol not of his polygamous masculinity but of her own polygamous past, as "not a nympholept but the confident lord of a harem," the unpaid, privately operating, well-mounted sexual lord of her father's isolated gang of convict laborers, from among whom she picks Mink in his turn as a planter's son picks from among the field slaves. Thus each time Mink approaches her, he has to tear aside "not garments alone but the ghostly embraces of thirty to forty men . . . the constant stallion-ramp of those inexpugnable shades" (237). When Mink faces off against the aristocratic arrogance of Houston, who is armed, well mounted, and well heeled by his magnificent blue-tick hound, and attempts the "vindication of his rights and the liquidation of his injuries," the two of them become "twinned forever," Mink discovering "that he had pulled trigger on an enemy but had only slain a corpse to be hidden" (218, 217, 218–19). Having "vindicated" himself as master, that is, he has not escaped the dialectic of master and slave; he is no more successful than Houston was before him in burying the mastered slave's stubborn body. Moreover, the ghosts of his wife's past come enragingly to life, even in her attempts to help him. Worst of all, having killed an older, aristocratic embodiment of his frustration, he is forced to deal as well with the modern avatar of the old plantation legend of hidden gold—in this case the money Lump tells him is still in a pocket on Houston's hidden body, money Mink needs to make his escape. He has the chance to escape on part of the money but does not because of his determination to oppose the New South as he has the Old, outraged that Lump might profit by his mistake, and amazingly resilient in his rage. In fact, his rage is so extreme, subjected to such extreme and unbearably relentless trials, that no reader can pretend to undergo in imagination what Mink undergoes groping and running in the dark woods expecting at any moment to burst his head open against a tree. In its narration his rage passes over uneasily into the realm of an excruciating, intensely humorous tall tale, humor insisting on the possibility of some way out for the blocked force of his rage.

Book 4 of *The Hamlet,* "The Peasants," consists primarily of two stories, a revision of "Spotted Horses" (1931, itself a revision of *Father Abraham,* written in 1926), and a salted gold mine story that will serve as a segue to Faulkner's next novel, *Go Down, Moses.* In the first story many of the men in the village get caught up in a contest of masculine pride and discount prices with a shrewd, taunting Texan auctioneer, only to find that they have half-consciously ignored a third schemer in Flem. They have ignored (to their financial cost) this possibility of which their own and Ratliff's humor amply reminded them but which they preferred to set aside for the sake of the giddy pursuit of their aroused desires. Some of them then insist on blaming that repressed cost on Flem in another instance of humorlessly self-justifying bad faith, but the grandfatherly justice of the peace who adjudicates their claims with his thick Bible and copy of *Mississippi Reports* will not magically protect their innocence from above unless they venture to speak up for themselves, as Mrs. Tull does. Even then the law reveals its own stake not in the protection of their supposedly pure, self-denying, victimized innocence, but in the regulation and limitation of social responsibility and exchange in the narrowly defined terms of written contracts. They will need to speak up differently.

Ratliff's own less self-righteous pleasure in "shrewd dealing" having been thus revived by the spotted horses trades, he allies himself next with Bookwright and with the most humorless of the former losers, Armstid (also the one least able to afford to lose), as if to vindicate "the entire honor and pride of the science and pastime of horse trading in Yoknapatawpha county," as Ab once did against Pat Stamper. Ratliff does not pretend to be immune to the lure of the Old Frenchman's legendary hidden gold and the whole economy of capital it has come to represent, but when Flem maneuvers him out of his expected profit again (and this time much more damagingly), Ratliff vindicates the humor if not the skill of local trading traditions in his humorous ability to see a way out of his money loss, unlike Armstid, whose less affordable loss is part of what enrages him to the point of madness. Here again Faulkner admits, as it were, that Ratliff's more humorous ability to see a way out is also in part a more *fortunate* ability, he having been less hard-pressed by that money economy than Armstid or Mink has been. Faulkner's next novel, *Go Down, Moses,* will present even harder challenges to the humor he has developed in *The Hamlet* as the characteristic mode of his fiction. *Go Down, Moses* will test that humor in the here bracketed but ever-present context of relations across the formidable Southern and American barriers of race. What are the obstacles and the chances for humor and love there?

4 Racism's Black Balloon Face Revised in *Go Down, Moses*

WHITE Southern racism heaps onto the fantastic image of the black balloon face both the explicitly despotic and the implicit, axiomatic signs of inequality, indignity, and alienation in Southern society — both the more and the less explicit onus of labor (as opposed to leisure or to property ownership, respectively), violence (as opposed to peace or to social dignity), sexuality (as opposed to restraint or to purity), and bestiality (as opposed to nobility or to humanity). Under such prodding and pressure, when the fantastic black balloon face bursts, as it does for the young Sutpen and other "innocents" in *Absalom, Absalom!,* the Southern ideology of race may either reconstitute itself in a more willfully innocent, nostalgic form like Sutpen's monumental design, refusing the potentially differentiated, critical social implications of that explosion as only a meaningless, alien horror to be avoided at any cost; or the ideology of race may dissipate those same social implications in a willfully ironic, modernist systematization of that explosion as metaphysically inevitable but no less socially meaningless and undesirable. In "Barn Burning," Ab Snopes's frank recognition of his own social and economic circumstances in terms usually reserved for blacks or for a metaphysical despair opens up for him a way out of this social and political impasse, an avenue for the active and powerful assertion of an integrity based in the same undignified, befouled, inarticulate violence to which his society ineffectively pretends to be invulnerable and immune. Ab's own way out, however, although it asserts a certain forcefulness in terms of his myth of "integrity" as the "deep mainspring of his . . . being" — 7–8), does so at the social and political cost of scenes of apocalyptic horror. Ab's integrity can only be forced violently upon his circumstances and upon those around him, since its peculiar difference seems to inspire recognition neither in the "innocent" planter whom he defies, nor in the black servant at that planter's door, nor even in Ab's own family members, who are alternately terrified of Ab and sentimentally nostalgic for the supposedly righteous authority of his worst enemies. Ab's way out of these oppositions is thus at the same time both a promising, dramatic escape and a dead end, a way out but with no way out for anyone but himself, appropriately confined to a short story that refers to earlier novels that are apparently already closed (*Absalom, Absalom!* and *The Unvanquished*).

Under revision, however, the short story "Barn Burning" has inaugurated in *The Hamlet* a novel of a different kind. Ab's recognition of his own condition in the racist image of the black balloon face and his willingness not to deny or rationalize but to strike out from that position suggest to Sarty's more resourceful, older brother Flem possibilities not just for apocalyptic revenge against an exclusive society but for a manipulation of that society's liberalized legal and economic mystifications, in order to gain for himself and his extensive family mobile and actively participatory roles within that social machine. That is, Flem rephrases the sound of his father's stamp of the foot to assert his own more socially articulate but still critical "enigmatic punctuation symbol" (*Hamlet* 58). In the multiple plots, styles, and casts of *The Hamlet*'s form (cf. the gothic obsessiveness of *Absalom*) and in the peculiar quality of Ratliff's humor, Faulkner has demonstrated an expansive (Bakhtinian) sense of liberation from a social scene previously monopolized by latter-day aristocrats (Compsons, Varners) and marked now by a humorous appreciation of the differences between those more or less liberalized aristocrats and their variously disrespectful new competitors, especially the Snopeses. Faulkner has also demonstrated and critically explored, however, the strong temptation to respond to Flem's demystifications of the pious capitalism of the New South with historically current, local versions of newly pious antimaterialism and (structural) anti-Semitism. Faulkner shows people in Frenchman's Bend altogether blaming Snopeses (as Jason Compson had the Jews) for the kinds of exploitations most had uncritically overlooked and accepted at the hands of the Varners. Such structural anti-Semitism is more defensively judgmental (though less actively engaged) than Ratliff's humor, and it reduces the Snopeses to a simple reincarnation of the planter, as only the latest and most efficiently ruthless masters of an economic system to which everyone else becomes simply a helpless, innocent hostage. Instead of taking from Ratliff's usually humorous view of Flem's example a lesson in the profound ambivalence of capitalism's masters and slaves both, many observers in the novel (and readers of the novel) prefer simply to substitute in the Old South planter's now ironically demystified social position a newly remystified family name, still functioning in the role of omnipotent victimizer. And Faulkner provokes this same questionable suspicion by leaving enigmatic the question of whether this substitution of family names only demystifies and thus remystifies the same old system, or whether such substitutions might actually effect radical structural openings of the kind suggested by Ratliff's obviously less strictly monetary, more ambivalent, symbolic, reciprocal notions of social exchange. Or to put this another way, Faulkner opposes to the prospect of a ruthless capitalism exemplified by Flem Snopes, not only a *falsely* sentimental nostalgia for a noncapitalist Old South fantasy, but also another more critical nostalgia for certain features of a precapitalist Old Southwest, a "nonsynchronous" (Bloch), endangered and dangerous memory (Benjamin) which survives alongside the capitalism of both the Old South and the New, and which evokes from the literature of Southwestern humor critically different models of social exchange.

Thus in "Barn Burning" and *The Hamlet* Faulkner has temporarily muted his explicit treatment of racial issues in order to explore in the less immediately frightening terms (in the American South) of class just what happens when the scapegoat's balloon face explodes: by making that balloon face violent, unsavory, filthy perhaps, but white, Faulkner explores and encourages an advance beyond innocent horror and paralyzed despair to a certain possibility of recognizing difference, even though that recognition still tends to retreat to the (Lacanian Imaginary) terms of seeing either identity or opposition. Flem Snopes is reduced by many to the uncanny status of the all too familiar but usually repressed ugliness of twentieth-century American capitalism. In this view, this white balloon face speaks not another language (as Sutpen's slaves did) but this society's own normative, dominant discourse, only (or crucially) more ruthlessly and efficiently than before. Not a criminal barn burner but an ostracized though economically necessary moneylender, Flem still appears as scapegoat, though more enigmatically (ideologically) than either his father or the black slave (whose differences from the norm have been more resolutely legalized and naturalized).

While Faulkner makes this scapegoating reaction to Flem's maneuvers understandable, he is attempting himself and exemplifying in Ratliff another less ironic, more humorous recognition not only of identity or opposition but of difference (and symbolic exchanges based on such recognitions of difference). In *Go Down, Moses* he reopens the racial dimensions of the balloon-face explosion, in hopes of a more adequate understanding of what Sutpen heard in that explosion only as the "roaring waves of mellow laughter meaningless and terrifying and loud" (*Absalom* 188). Faulkner has made the recognition and appreciation of difference somewhat easier in *The Hamlet* by limiting himself for the most part to differences of class and personal style, and has narrowed the range and power of those class differences by choosing a rural setting. But he has appreciated various active resistances to, and specific alternatives to, dominant cultural forces in Ratliff's and others' unpredictably different, marginalized voices and relations, and he might well expect even more valuable (if also more threatening) differences in the group whom Faulkner's whites tended to see as at once both more different from and more involved with themselves than poor whites were. On the one hand Faulkner's white-faced representations and humorous recognitions in *The Hamlet* of such outbursts of laughter as Sutpen heard have avoided the terror of black laughter at the risk only of a bloodless, remystifying irony toward poor-white laughter instead. On the other hand, if successfully humorous recognitions of difference will be harder to come by in the interracial confrontations of *Go Down, Moses,* their greater risk will also yield what is in some ways a greater return, less often now in humor than in the related terms of love and mourning, since the recognition and appreciation of specific differences in this more difficult context often comes almost too late. Such chancy confrontations and recognitions risk a retrenchment in fright for the sake of a more humorously ambivalent sense (a more fearful but also a more powerfully desirable sense) of unpredictable, particular differences and unexpected particular movements of love and loss.[1] Thus it becomes clearer in *Go Down, Moses* that the black balloon face is recognized first as bursting into loud laughter instead of into effective action or articulate speech because even its laughter has remained largely unrecognized except in the barren categories of meaninglessness and terror. Blacks in Faulkner's South have not been able to avail themselves of the mythic, legal, and economic protections on which Ab and Flem have relied in order to act and speak their difference (with however little appreciation). Nor have they had the economic conditions for freedom of action or speech, nor the legal rights to such freedom, nor even the mythic "nimbus" of freedom on which Sutpen built his hopes. But their laughter here does hold out newly appreciated possibilities for the articulation of other humorously creative, transforming escapes from the dominant categories of meaninglessness and terror in terms of which their differences have been read, possibilities for new forms of activity and speech that neither accept nor ignore, but critically resist and reshape the dominant social codes in which their experience (in Faulkner's work) has largely been organized.

In an important essay on this subject, "Faulkner and the Negroes," Irving Howe slightly but provocatively misses the point of Faulkner's writing on race when he challenges Faulkner to complete the inner logic of that writing by creating "an articulate Negro who speaks for his people,"

---

1. On the function of specificity in mourning as a force of resistance to ideological appropriations and short-circuitings of mourning's loving labor, see Breitwieser, "Early American Antigone."

so that Faulkner might "examin[e] Negro consciousness from within, rather than as it is seen or surmised by white characters" (59). The issue Howe's essay addresses, of either the perfect accessibility to white characters or authors of an essentially human consciousness, or the "ultimate inaccessibility" to whites of an essentially black consciousness (60), lies just to one side of the focus in Faulkner's writing on the range of particular historical discourses and social structures which define such a consciousness as black or white and in which that consciousness necessarily acts and speaks. If we understand race not as an essential or biological category but as a social definition and condition, blacks in Faulkner's writing may well act and speak for their people most articulately precisely when they adopt attitudes of strategic *non*articulateness and humorous obliqueness (as in an "impertinent" laugh), neither imitating the language and social structure of a white-dominated society nor ignoring those structures, but appropriating and "signifying upon" those same structures.[2] Thus Hubert Beauchamp warns Buck McCaslin against overhastily dismissing (as inarticulate, for example) the foolishness of *Go Down, Moses*'s opening story, "Was," and its forays into a "bear-country" of racial and sexual issues: "This is the most serious foolishness you ever took part in in your life" (22, 24).

To avoid such a dismissive attitude in reading such frequently humorous (if also painful) stories demands an approach like that of Eugene Genovese toward the study of black religions in the South in *Roll, Jordan, Roll*. Genovese does not study those religions "from within" by seeking any pure statement of theological principles (a statement which might have been suicidal in historical effect); Genovese instead studies those religions in terms of their historical and cultural functions in variously appropriating a religion first offered to blacks largely by accommodationist white preachers, and variously reshaped by blacks to their own incommensurate, different social and historical needs and desires (151–284). Rather than articulate those desires directly in the masters' own uninviting, muscle-bound discourse, black slaves learned early to improvise and "signify upon" that language and its ideological codes (notably in the genre of black spirituals from which both Faulkner and Genovese take the titles *Roll, Jordan, Roll* and *Go Down, Moses*), developing a deliberately and strategically "minor" discourse with regard to the "major" discourse of their time and place.[3]

2. This colloquial, African-American phrase is elaborated on especially by Henry Louis Gates, Jr.

3. On "signifying" in black language and literature, see Cooke, Gates, and Sundquist. On the idea of successfully minor literature and language, see Deleuze and Guattari's *Kafka*, and Renza.

Likewise, "Was" can be read most usefully as a nondialectical, humorous revision — an indirect but no less radical rereading and revision — of the supposedly primal scene of the black balloon face's once meaningless and terrifying explosion into laughter. This time, in "Was," the slave does not just answer the door and unexpectedly insult the young boy of one of his master's tenants, who thinks "innocently" that he is free and that the slave is not (as in *Absalom*). This novel raises the stakes, so that the naturalized social and racial hierarchy is more radically threatened: the master himself (Buck McCaslin) waits now at a slave quarters door at midnight, confident (with a more *willful* innocence than that of the poor-white tenant boy) that he will there recapture his escaped amorous slave and half brother, Tomey's Turl, and that he will simultaneously confirm his own "masculine" freedom from that "bear-country" (22) of sexuality and marriage into which he has risked pursuing Tomey's Turl. As in Hegel's master-slave dialectic, this master expects his slave to function both as a point of contact with a dangerous reality and also as an insulation from that reality. But Tomey's Turl explodes out of the door and runs right over his master, leaving him lying on the ground wondering whether it is blood or whiskey he feels where the bottle broke in his back pocket: in either case his fouled pants suggest he has lost control of this fear-constricted boundary between master and slave, white and black, male and female, clean and filthy:

> Afterward, Uncle Buck admitted that it was his own mistake, that he had forgotten when even a little child should have known: not ever to stand right in front of or right behind a nigger when you scare him; but always to stand to one side of him. Uncle Buck forgot that. (19)

Buck's twin brother Buddy would not have forgotten to stand ironically aside: he would have avoided by cautious, anxious foresight being surprised in either innocent opposition to, or frightened identity with, any such object of his aversion or fear. But as Hubert Beauchamp says, Buddy is not as "human" as Buck, neither "woman-weak" nor a drinker, nor a gambler even when playing poker (26–27). That is how skillful Buddy is at cleanly "winning" all such occasions for social exchange (occasions otherwise based on unpredictable, reciprocal differences and desires). Buck's own much more precarious position, in relation to both this slave quarter door and Sophonsiba's bedroom door in the next scene, reflects his own more obviously ambivalent interest in what lives in this "bear-country." Although he pretends only to be pursuing Tomey's Turl (who would thus be the only one pursuing a woman) and not to be ambivalently pursuing a woman himself, still, the "freedom" won for him by his twin brother Buddy in a poker game with Hubert Beauchamp effectively calls Buck's bluff, leaving him at the story's end acting restless for another such conveniently ambiguous pursuit. Moreover, the apparently final victory of this "masculine" freedom can only be a pyrrhic and temporary victory at best. This story is only the first in a series, and that series gradually reminds readers that this opening story of masculine mastery and freedom (like those to follow) has been framed from the beginning as a story passed down to and remembered by Ike McCaslin, son of that eventual marriage of which this story is actually a courtship episode, the marriage of Buck to Sophonsiba. Meanwhile, a victory rather less hollow has already been won by Tomey's Turl, who manages to return to the McCaslin place with his future wife Tennie, by taking his own skillful advantage of Buck's and Sophonsiba's more or less ambivalent desires. In this case the black balloon face speaks with his own unexpectedly different and ambivalently *appreciated* revisions of the standard significations of victory and loss. This opening story of *Go Down, Moses* from before Ike's birth proposes Ike's twinned but different genealogical legacies and alternatives, as it were, in irony and humor, his Uncle Buddy's cautious chastity and his father Buck's and half uncle Turl's "fear all right but not fright" (329) in the dangerous but lively "bear-country" of racial and sexual relations throughout *Go Down, Moses*. These are also the novel's genealogical legacies and alternatives in Faulkner's previous work.

The next (perhaps finest) story in *Go Down, Moses,* "The Fire and the Hearth," similarly suggests Faulkner's concertedly humorous, critical revisions of his most modernistic primal scenes. His central character for this further revision of Sutpen's scene at the planter's door is another marginally white character who will also strain the dominant codes and resolutions of his society, but who will do so more rigorously and more resourcefully than the young Sutpen did. Lucas Beauchamp is marginally white, but not by being another poor-white character, socio-economically black though ideologically white: on the one hand he is more definitely black than a poor white such as Sutpen or Ab, since Lucas is legally, therefore racially, therefore naturally defined as having three-quarters black "blood," but at the same time he is also "whiter" than such poor whites, by virtue of an ambivalent, ambiguous kinship system,[4] according to which he is unofficially recognized as being more closely related to the local

4. On the conflict in the South's plantation legend between the marketplace values and the domestic values of interracial kinship (the slave regarded as the planter's property and worker versus the slave as rhetorically and/or genetically one of the planter's family), see Porter, *Seeing* 227–34.

founding father, the white planter and patriarch Carothers McCaslin, than anyone else alive is, with the exception of Ike McCaslin. In the episode here which recalls Thomas Sutpen's primal scene, Faulkner reuses many of the same phrases once used to describe the young Sutpen's ironic "realizations" of the planter's absolute superiority and invulnerability to him and his kind. Sutpen tried and failed to interpret what he heard only as "*roaring waves* of mellow *laughter* meaningless and terrifying and loud," an inchoate turbulence which builds to a kind of crisis, "it all kind of *shouting* at him at once, *boiling* out and over him like the nigger *laughing*. . . . like an explosion—a *bright glare*" (*Absalom* 188, 192, my emphases throughout this paragraph). Faulkner describes now with a critically different, defamiliarizing effect a similarly "*blinding glimpse* of the absolute" (*Go Down, Moses* 39) by Lucas, who is digging in an "orifice" in the side of an Indian mound when the whole mound "stooped *roaring* down at him"; the overhang collapsing so that it "*boiled* about his feet and, as he leaped backward and tripped and fell, about his body too, hurling clods and dirt at him, striking him a final blow squarely in the face with something larger than a clod." Then the mound loomed, "poised above him in a long *roaring wave* of silence like a burst of jeering and prolonged *laughter*" (38). The object with which he is struck turns out to be a revised, modern version of what so struck Thomas Sutpen, the white planter's barred door and its (suddenly, reactively internalized) suggestions of absolute privilege over poor whites and blacks alike; Lucas here is struck by a piece of an earthenware vessel containing a gold coin. With his "brain *boiling* with all the images of buried money he had ever listened to or heard of" (38), Lucas dreams of a modern victory as absolute and pure as the planter's aristocratic, land-based privilege, translated into the updated money-based terms of a capital which to all appearances is completely without a victim. Just so, the planter himself once seemed to Sutpen so absolutely invulnerable that Sutpen dreamed that in the planter's place he himself would not need to bar his door. This coin reminds Lucas of that twenty-two thousand dollars two white men dug up and got "clean away with" two years before. Lucas dreams that his find is likewise to be money "on which there was no sweat, at least none of his own" (123). This buried money, in other words, would be capital without connection to labor, need, or even previous desire—pure exchange value, perfectly abstracted from the specificities of intersubjective, symbolic social exchange. It would be a means not of pursuing or even fulfilling desire, but of absolutely conquering, escaping, preempting desire. Unlike Sutpen, however, Lucas already critically half acknowledges that this vision of capital's absolute purity entails costs in other terms: he knows he will have to give up farming to hunt for the gold, even though he still likes farming and takes pride in it (42). Other such costs will come to seem prohibitive later when this buried money almost entails his also giving up his wife, Molly, who has from the first called the money the "curse of God" (122). But for a time, such costs in other currencies pale before the undeniable cultural power of such visions of buried money.

Lucas' "blinding glimpse of the absolute" at the door of his supposed gold mine will seem to require (as Sutpen's vision did) that he deny and leave outside the door of privilege all his present and past relations, a requirement at which he will eventually balk, as Sutpen did not. Lucas does attempt to deny his ambivalence about such a blinding victory, before Molly finally calls his bluff. First Lucas searches his memory for a more unambivalently, decisively pure image of victory. Recalling an episode from a generation before, he evokes a time closer to that "old time when men black and white were men" (37), an era of frontier opportunism in the South when the forms of privilege may have been more violent but were also (at least in critical juxtaposition with present forms, as here) less elaborately mystified than they are under the aegis of buried money. (Thus the figure of buried money is itself an image less mystified than the topos of usury which became dominant somewhat later historically, as in *The Hamlet*—the almost unrepresentable idea of money hidden as surplus value in rented property, profit, or interest somewhere within the very workings of the system of exchange.)[5]

What Lucas remembers here from "the old time when men black and white were men" (the time of Sutpen's bloody wrestling matches with his slaves) is the episode when Lucas entered the front door of the big house at dawn armed with an open razor intending to kill Zack Edmonds, whom he had come to suspect of "taking" his wife, Molly, though this was also the man "whom he had known from infancy, with whom he had lived

---

5. Compare the same progression among the three orders of Baudrillard's *Simulations*—first the simulation in *stucco* of "Nature" (cf. a Southern aristocracy based on a despotically enforced, naturalized, racial superiority), then the multiplication of such simulations made possible by mass production and *concrete* (cf. Sutpen's and the Gilded Age's legendary self-made men with their fortunes accumulated and multiplied within the system, without reference to that system's external or prior violence done to nature or human natures), and finally the simulations in *plastic* of the models and of the digitalized code itself (cf. "usury," surplus value). The point of such progressions is not that the first order of simulation is closer to nature but that the first distinction between the simulation and the simulated becomes the least stable, because it presumes an absolute distinction in kind between the simulation and reality: it becomes the most vulnerable to reminders of other differences on other grounds, differences introduced by, for example, the critical perspective of Southwestern humor, in which the supposedly "natural" characters and events take on artful and fanciful forms, while the supposedly artful, sophisticated characters and narrative "frame" take on much of the contagious violence of their "natural" counterparts.

until they were both grown almost as brothers lived" (55). In that encounter
Lucas was especially determined not to let Zack think that "because I am
a nigger I wouldn't even mind" (53), determined not to let Zack be sure
(as the young Sutpen was) that the black balloon face would not strike
back if struck. He insists on at least a physical, "masculine" contest by
violence. But Lucas is also not satisfied to burst out of the submissive slave's
role into the (ideologically prepared) opposite role (increasingly legendary
during a paranoid Reconstruction) of "violent Negro" reprisal and
terrorism, by cutting Zack's throat while he is asleep or unarmed. Lucas
wants to feel he has beaten not just Zack but Old Carothers too, face to
face and man to man, as it were, so he discards his razor to wrestle Zack
for the one pistol between them. As in the wrestling matches and rifle contests in *Absalom,* such a contest is intended to prove a natural superiority —
in *Absalom* to confirm the racial division, here to confirm that Lucas is
the "better man" on the grounds of his closer, more "masculine" kinship
with Old Carothers (Zack is descended from Old Carothers' daughter,
Lucas from his illegitimate son). Lucas challenges the racial essentialism
with what seems a stabler gender essentialism, which Faulkner will call
into question next, especially in *Requiem for a Nun.* Lucas knows,
however, that once he has won this contest and has the gun, his gesture
will be lost on anyone but Zack (who will be dead) and perhaps Old
Carothers' ghost. His gesture, that is, will be incommunicable in his
society's language, since he will be lynched as a "Negro" murderer just
the same as if he had surprised Zack in his sleep or without a fair fight.
He briefly considers suicide so that at least Zack would live on knowing
Lucas is neither impassive "nigger" nor blindly "violent Negro." When Zack
notices Lucas' blinding rage at such limited means of articulating his
dignity — "He cant even see me right now" — Zack rightly fears that at such
moments a cornered Lucas is capable of an enraged murder otherwise
unworthy of him (as Melville's Billy Budd was). Thus when Zack springs
for the gun Lucas does pull the trigger despite his wavering decision against
it. When both Zack's life and his own life and dignity are almost incredibly
saved by the misfire, Lucas is tempted to believe that because of his (white)
McCaslin "blood" Old Carothers has "come and spoke for me" in a kind
of romance of unrecognized royal birthright (58), as if this misfire and the
unexploded cartridge he still keeps years later as a talisman prove Lucas'
secretly absolute command of a social code only superficially alien and
frustrating. But while he can fantasize an identification with the absolute
white patriarch as his natural destiny, Lucas also knows such a destiny
is a forced construction on the more shifting sands of unmeaning chance,
and as soon as he sees Molly again after his lucky "victory" over Zack,
he admits the precariousness of both his racial relations with men like Zack

and his sexual relations with Molly, since he is still no more able to ask a white man not to lie with his wife than the white man can promise he won't (59). Even though he has won in this instance both a social dignity with Zack and a domestic haven with Molly, this remembered episode serves to remind him how social dignity and love would usually seem, for all but the luckiest black males in Lucas' situation, the two horns of a dilemma: a precarious social dignity at the cost of life and love, or a precarious love at the cost of social dignity. And even trading social dignity for private love remains an unsure settlement.

Having resituated the buried money plot of "The Fire and the Hearth" in the critical context of this flashback to other now more easily demystified assumptions of privilege, Faulkner then also uses this buried money plot to reflect critically (by way of revision) on the still more modern, still less easily demystified forms of privilege in Flem Snopes's realm of shrewd trading. First, the main buried money plot in "The Fire and the Hearth" recalls the salted gold mine story at the end of *The Hamlet,* in which Ratliff's, Bookwright's, and Armstid's belief in actual buried money is merely a predictable, manipulable position within Flem's shrewder, more modern scheme, a scheme that requires only that Flem supply convincing tokens of any such actual money in order to profit from Ratliff's and the others' overly eager belief. But lest such mistaken belief seem to be finally corrected and replaced in *The Hamlet* by a simplistically innocent (structurally anti-Semitic) scapegoating of a newly demystified, delegitimated liberal capitalism — or by a simplistically ironic acceptance (and remystification) of that same capitalism — Faulkner in "The Fire and the Hearth" rewrites again Flem's apparently pure, bloodless capitalism in the effectively critical context of its relation to that more complex, reciprocal, symbolic exchange which it attempts but fails to reduce altogether to token counters or alibis within its own systematization of exchange.

More specifically, at the end of "The Fire and the Hearth," the five-cent sack of candy that Lucas gives Molly recalls the same gift given by Flem to Mrs. Armstid in *The Hamlet.* In Flem's case, of course, the gift is a flagrantly inadequate compensation for losses and injuries to Mrs. Armstid and her husband in the recent auction of the spotted horses (itself another gold mine salted with "masculine" pride and cheap prices). "A little sweetening for the chaps," Flem calls it there (317), and most of the rest of the male community's pity for Mrs. Armstid and her children is equally ineffective except as an alibi for their ideological denial of the possibility of actually doing or saying anything that would help her against either her husband's or Flem's exploitation of her. Such ineffective sweetening of the pill recurs in "The Fire and the Hearth," where Lucas' truly symbolic gift (a gift as such) of candy to Molly is preceded by a contrasting description of Roth's regular monthly gift to Molly of a tin of tobacco and a sack of candy, a gift he calls

> a libation to his luck, as the centurion spilled first a little of the wine he drank, though actually it was to his ancestors and to the conscience which he would have probably affirmed he did not possess, in the form, the person, of the negro woman who had been the only mother he ever knew. (99–100)

The quality of payoff is more explicitly transparent and unsuccessful here than in *The Hamlet;* in Lucas' case, however, such more or less successful denials of and substitutions for ambivalent, reciprocal social exchange are displaced by his gift to Molly of yet another five-cent sack of candy, signifying this time an acknowledgment and pledge of that very reciprocal exchange. In this exchange, Molly's is not a placated, minor, women's and children's world marginal or inimical to men's primary systems of exchange, but the larger world of intersubjective love and desire regularly betrayed (denied, reduced) by such narrowly conceived dominant forms of exchange.

Thus throughout "The Fire and the Hearth" Lucas in his always already marginalized position as a—man, perhaps, but a legally *black*—man, is always inclined, though often despite himself, to translate the streamlined terms of the money economy into the more ambivalent, singular terms of an endless trading in different, changing desires. He will not spend his own three hundred dollars for the Memphis salesman's divining machine, and when he cannot persuade Roth Edmonds to invest *his* money, Lucas notices that despite the salesman's urban speech and status, his way of squatting on his heels without any other support gives his rural origins away. Lucas then knows he can swap using a borrowed mule instead of cash and can trade later on the salesman's own readiness to believe in buried money. Faulkner also situates the idea of money without any of one's own sweat on it, what Molly calls the "curse of God" (122), in the same genealogy with the "curse" Roth blames for his own earlier betrayal of his foster-brother Henry (Molly and Lucas' son): "the old curse of his fathers, the old haughty ancestral pride based not on any value but on an accident of geography, stemmed not from courage and honor but from wrong and shame" (111). When at the end of "The Fire and the Hearth" Lucas decisively turns away from that curse in all three of its historically dominant forms—as naturally aristocratic privilege, monied privilege, and manipulative capitalistic privilege—he does so without denying his own ongoing temptation by all three of these social formations of desire. His gift to Molly does not place him idealistically aside from or above the curse he thereby escapes (as Ike McCaslin is somewhat inclined to place himself in this novel). Lucas' escape rather deforms those same contents it carries away (Deleuze and Guattari, *Kafka* 59); it testifies to his recognition that these particular formations of desire, to which he is not immune, nevertheless often exact too great a price in terms of his different, singular desires with regard to his mortality, his family, and especially Molly, desires he sometimes cannot, sometimes will not, subordinate or translate into the code.

Go Down, Moses repeatedly bursts the fantastic black balloon face on which white privilege variously depends, but within that series of repetitions, the novel differentiates among several distinct social forms that such white privilege and such black explosions have tended to take. Instead of subordinating those different disillusionments to one metaphysical disillusionment (as is more the case in Faulkner's and others' modernist writing), *Go Down, Moses* plays each discourse of white privilege critically against another, and places all three main forms of such privilege in the context of more reciprocal and symbolic models of social exchange— humor, the giving of gifts, and now mourning: in the next story, "Pantaloon in Black," a black man tests and exhausts the three dominant (white) discourses of his society as a means of articulating his loss. In the novel's first two stories, "Was" and "The Fire and the Hearth," the black balloon face has burst into kinds of laughter or gifts which white characters might be expected to appreciate and understand as humorous, critical revisions of dominant but inadequate forms of privilege. In "Was" Tennie's Jim has managed to play on the ambivalence of a landed, aristocratic privilege based on a naturalized racial superiority of white male planters over black slaves (with their less civilized, less "masculine" control over their sexual appetites). Buddy's gambling serves in this regard as a hollow ritual in which the best man supposedly wins his freedom, but his twin brother Buck's ambivalence about such a victory has already allowed Tennie's Jim to join his future wife, as it will also lead to Buck's own foregone marriage sometime after the story's pyrrhic ending. This first bursting of the black balloon face, represented not as a horror or as a metaphysical irony, but as an occasion for humor, serves to embolden the novel's imagination, as it were, of other more dangerous burstings of black balloons. In "The Fire and the Hearth" Lucas Beauchamp remembers bursting out of his own role as an impassive "nigger" in this same naturalized, aristocratic discourse of race, remembers that episode when he managed by sheer chance to avoid that role as well as his alternative ideological role and fate as a violent "Negro," another naturalized type, a kind of monster deserving to be lynched. Remembering the chance collapse of that discourse of a natural, aristocratic racial privilege, Lucas is better prepared than most to be critical of, and eventually to balk at, the other two dominant discourses of white power, that based on accumulated fortunes (buried money, industrial capitalism) and that of shrewd trading with strangers for a clean victory and a profit (usury, postindustrial capitalism). Forced to choose, Lucas rejects all three of these discourses of power in favor of a more precarious, more marginal investment in his relationship with Molly, symbolized somewhat privately and precariously by the gift of candy and by the fire they have kept alive on their hearth since they were married.

In "Pantaloon in Black" Rider has made a similar investment, setting out to emulate the local legend of "Uncle Lucas" and Molly Beauchamp's symbolic fire on the hearth and the correspondingly long tenacity of their marriage. When Rider's young wife, Mannie, dies, however, his domestic haven comes to seem not a chosen alternative or critical, revisionary escape from the dominant systems of power, but the one space within those systems that is allotted to his desire: when Mannie dies and that private, domestic option suddenly seems foreclosed, his inability to articulate his loss in any of his society's dominant discourses drives him to a kind of hysterical, inarticulate rage. His rage provokes, in return, the willful incomprehension and hysterical, vindictive rage of the threatened (white) structure of power (he is lynched for killing in self-defense a white night watchman named Birdsong whom Rider has caught cheating at dice). The story might be described as a crisis in interracial literacy.[6] Faulkner frames his account of Rider's various desperate attempts to articulate his loss with two instances of white incomprehension. Near the story's beginning Faulkner acknowledges his own writing's predicament by describing Mannie's grave as one which,

> save for its rawness, resembled any other marked off without order
> about the barren plot by shards of pottery and broken bottles and
> old brick and other objects insignificant to sight but actually of a
> profound meaning and fatal to touch, which no white man could
> have read. (135)

Faulkner will be writing at the edge of what a white man could see of recognizable order and meaning in Rider's attempts to articulate his loss

6. Cf. Eric Sundquist's "Faulkner, Race, and the Forms of American Fiction," which extends and somewhat recasts, as an issue of interracial literacy and thus new voices in American society and fiction, Sundquist's earlier treatment (in *Faulkner: The House Divided*) of Faulkner's writing on race as a psychological drama of "working through" a cultural repression toward a "fully realized grief" (158). I am interested here in Faulkner's shift from issues of realization to issues of articulation and rearticulation (in class, racial, and gender relations, in humor, grief, and otherwise).

in the available social forms. Faulkner will write at the edge of what his white discourse and these blacks' revisionary "signifyings" on that discourse would allow him to recognize both in the successive social forms that Rider tries to fit to his grief and also in that grief and rage which — unfit, unarticulated, apparently insignificant and hysterical — are only exacerbated by the inadequacies of those available forms. The other half of the story's frame is a reflection on Rider's story, from Mannie's burial to his lynching, by the "spent" and "a little hysterical" sheriff's deputy who was in charge of the prisoner (154). The deputy's account, too, enacts the limits of his white discourse, not only in the violence of that lynching which he has allowed to happen, but also in his insistent incomprehension of "them damn niggers. . . . Because they aint human . . . when it comes to the normal human feelings and sentiments of human beings" (154).

Rider's own desperate efforts to articulate his grief take three main forms, in accordance with the three historically dominant discourses in his society, but all of them are found to be inadequate to that grief and growing rage. From the beginning Rider rejects out of hand his grandmother's less historically dominant religious urging ("Cant nothing help you but Him!" — 150), which sounds to Rider like an acceptance of a Power either incomprehensibly unjust ("Whut Mannie ever don ter Him? Whut He wanter come messin wid me and—" — 145) or unhelpfully powerless ("Efn He God, . . . Leff Him come down hyar and do me some good" — 150). Rider is used to having more social dignity and power himself than most blacks of his time and place, so he turns in his moment of need in other, more worldly directions.

In terms of the natural aristocracy of men established by heredity or feats of physical prowess, Rider performs several almost superhuman feats of strength, for which he is generally recognized. But the repressed dimension of this same physical privilege uncannily returns in the apparition of Mannie's ghost. Though he tells her he is not afraid, and speaks "as sweet as he had ever heard his voice speak to a woman," still, when he approaches her ghost, it fades: "he could actually feel between them the insuperable barrier of that very strength which could handle alone a log which would have taken any two other men to handle, . . . the will of that bone and flesh to remain alive" (140–41).

In terms of the industrial workaday world, Rider has had his share of money and prestige: "Because he made good money: sawmilling ever since he began to get his growth at fifteen and sixteen and now, at twenty-four, head of the timber gang itself because the gang he headed moved a third again as much timber between sunup and sundown as any other moved" (137). He was "never without work even in the old days when he had not actually needed the money, when a lot of what he wanted, needed perhaps, didn't cost money—the women . . . he didn't need to buy," the clothes that didn't matter, the food and lodging he got free from his aunt (138). The money had been good only for dice and whiskey on Saturday and Sunday until he saw Mannie, and now the money figures especially in his memory of his weekends with her, begun with his entering the door on Saturdays to "ring the bright cascade of silver dollars onto the scrubbed table in the kitchen" (138). Without Mannie waiting for that weekly household money now, without such an anticipated incarnation of the mythical shower of gold into love (or of pure exchange value into meaningfully reciprocal, symbolic exchange), Rider's attempt to lose himself in his work can only temporarily help him to give some value to his time, help him to

> stop needing to invent to himself reasons for his breathing, until after a while he began to believe he had forgot about breathing since now he could not hear it himself above the steady thunder of the rolling logs; whereupon as soon as he found himself believing he had forgotten it, he knew that he had not. (145)

Again the repressed returns to upset this second discourse of supposed power over such reminders of his economically incommensurate, unrecuperable loss. So he turns next to the whiskey and dice that he knows his money *can* buy.

This third possibility for articulating his loss might be called Rider's hysterical carnivalesque, his attempt to surrender and scatter himself and his grief to the winds of drink and dice, with their bright promises of a mysterious surplus value of excitement and victorious survival that is expected to arise from the dizzying participation in one's own loss: "Ah'm snakebit and de pizen cant hawm me" (152). Rider regards his drinking after Mannie's death as a contest with a substance that has always claimed to be a "better man" than he (148), and even while he insists that his relative victory in this contest has "done me all de help Ah needs. Ah'm awright now" (149), the whiskey is already coming back up, one more repressive opposition or boundary which "cannot hold," seeming by sudden contrast to loose "mere anarchy" upon his world (Yeats): "his throat and mouth filled now with a solid and unmoving column which without reflex or revulsion sprang, columnar and intact and still retaining the mold of his gullet, outward glinting in the moonlight, splintering, vanishing into the myriad murmur of the dewed grass" (149). Here more clearly than in *Absalom*, nausea is less a representation of the opposition of order and chaos than an event, less a collapse of order into a chaotic absence of order than a predetermined, almost digitalized switch from this order into its own somewhat fantastic opposite ("still retaining the mold of his gullet"). This is so especially since in this case the order lost is one in a series of inadequate, failing orders, this one supposedly itself an escape from the orders of physical prowess or occupational success into the gay abandonment of all order in the realm of the carnivalesque. When this third realm assumes its place thus in a series in which all other options seem closed, as they do to Rider, then this supposed escape from order begins to feel more like another ordered, overdetermined escape *valve* in the same repressive machine: Frederick Douglass suspected as much long before about the drunken holidays allowed to the slave once a year, which "serve as conductors, or safety-valves, to carry off the rebellious spirit of enslaved humanity" by "cheat[ing the slave] with a dose of vicious dissipation, artfully labelled with the name of liberty" (75–77). Next to come up "out of the tremendous panting of [Rider's] chest" is "his own voice," admitting that the whiskey "aint done me no good" (150).

Thus also in Rider's turning to dice (and then to violence) his hysterical carnivalesque can only attempt and fail again to repress a loss he has still found no way to articulate or mourn. Unlike the complicatedly symbolic escapes, trades, and gambles in "Was" out of which Tennie's Jim, at least, manages to emerge joined with the woman he loves, the dice game Rider enters is fixed, allowing only minor, false winnings to blacks who always lose to the white man in the end. Rider can see through this false alternative, and challenge the white man, even kill him in self-defense and endure his relatives' rage (by being lynched), but all this is still somehow beside the point of his grief, still focusing on an inscrutable antagonist somehow responsible for his loss, rather than on the lost object he can find no way to articulate. Thus he is indifferent to the possibility of escaping capture or lynching, and in the midst of beating off a crowd of other prisoners he laughs hysterically: "laughing and laughing and saying, 'Hit look lack Ah just can't quit thinking. Look lack Ah just cant quit'" (159). His violence, like his gambling, has only a spurious, temporarily distracting shock value, what Benjamin called "the disintegration of the aura in the experience of shock" (194).[7] He can only repeat and intensify in such shocks the momentary experience of loss without the "aura" of articulate reminiscence of what it is (or who it is) he has lost, thus without ongoing symbolic exchanges and reinvestments of those reminiscences in mourning.

This compulsive repetition of a shock will perhaps be recognized as another instance of what I have been calling irony, except that Rider (somewhat like Charles Etienne) is less able to believe in his own suffering

7. "To perceive the aura of an object we look at means to invest it with the ability to look at us in return" (Benjamin 188).

than is someone (white, for example) who is less accustomed than Rider or Charles Etienne to powerlessness and suffering; the self-inflicted losses and fatalisms of these black characters tend to resemble less those of the sinner or of the recently disillusioned than those of the reckless gambler. For example, in *Light in August,* Joe Christmas, who could pass for white, seems to take his lynching, and the racial identity and generalized "blackness" it finalized, much more seriously than Rider takes his own lynching for a similar offense. The dominant discourses of race seem in this story almost hopelessly inadequate to Rider's plight, which becomes therefore almost illegible to the sheriff's deputy, as Faulkner virtually admits that it also threatens to be for him. The dominant discourses of race have apparently determined that the meaning and dignity of Rider's life must be found and articulated (if at all) in certain private, domestic circumstances—circumstances which begin to seem thus not an opening for revisionary escape from an oppressive system but a narrow, confining refuge still within that same system's inescapable control. Rider's story thus threatens to become only a story of his sensational hysteria and rage in his inability to find a way to mourn his private loss in other terms. It can be better appreciated as a story itself trying to find a way, and finding its own blocked, indirect, incomplete way, to tell something about the critically different relationship with Mannie that he has lost. Illumination of that critical difference, for example, is one effect of Faulkner's ending Rider's story with a focus on the contrastingly empty relationship of the deputy and his wife.

To a young white boy like Ike McCaslin in "The Old People," who has been pronounced a man upon killing his first buck, the difficulties of articulating and mourning the loss of the buck's life and of his own childhood under the tutelage of Sam Fathers tempt him not to hysteria or rage but to a (frightened) willful innocence of death and racial division. He has often listened to Sam Fathers' stories "about the old days and the [Chickasaw] People whom [Sam] had not had time ever to know and so could not remember . . . and in place of whom the other [black] race into which his blood had run supplied him with no substitute" (171); but despite Sam's own admission of the difficulty of translating this unremembered past into his own lived present, "to the boy those old times would cease to be old times and would become a part of the boy's present, . . . the men who walked through them actually walking in breath and air and casting an actual shadow on the earth they had not quitted" (171). When one of the last of those old Chickasaw people dies, one who "consorted with nobody, black or white," except Sam, Sam goes to the woods, someone sees a burst of flame, and "nobody ever found Jobaker's grave" (172).

Like Rider's, Sam's grief remains strikingly incommunicable to those blacks
and whites among whom he has lived, and he soon enters the McCaslin
plantation house, "without knocking as anyone else on the place except
a house servant would have done," to announce his departure to live in
the woods (172–73). Although Ike notices both this indifferent breach of
their white etiquette of racial separations and distinctions, and then the
unexpected personal separation on Sam's own terms, he nonetheless willfully rejects his older cousin's suggestion that Sam might want to get away
for a while from someone to whom he could not communicate his grief.
Ike insists instead on reading this departure as Sam's going on before to
prepare a reunion with him in another realm, what will be there a resolution on a higher level of this merely temporary, insignificant division, since
the boy is soon to enter himself into the "doored wall" of the woods and
into manhood (177). With this same willful innocence, once he is within
that door and has killed his buck and "in less than a second . . . ceased
forever to be the child he was yesterday," he trusts the "tremendous, attentive, impartial and omniscient . . . eye of the ancient immortal Umpire"
of the woods to resolve the similar paradox of his "loving the life he spills"
(181).

Ike is invoking here what Richard Slotkin has analyzed as the long-
lived American myth of "regeneration through violence," the myth of the
frontier hunter who is initiated into heroic manhood by his assimilation
of the mysterious knowledge and power of the beast (and/or the "savage
Indian") he has learned by imitation to track and kill. Faulkner's critical
treatment of the myth will show not only that the innocence of the myth
in its popular forms is a willful innocence, a deliberate obfuscation of its
historical implications in terms of the exploitation and destruction of the
wilderness, the land, the Indians, and blacks.[8] Nor will Faulkner's criticism
of the myth rest with an ironic acknowledgment of its obscured destruc-
tiveness (this will be the willfully ironic position represented by Ike's relinquishment of his patrimony). Faulkner accepts neither civilization's triumph
nor the wilderness's destruction and death as the final pronouncement of
this myth. He represents both these innocent and ironic versions of the
same myth as willfully reductive attempts to resolve a much more stubborn
ambivalence of fear and desire, an ambivalence felt in mourning as in
humor and love. It is this ambivalence that not only survives the political
uses of the myth to excuse exploitation and destruction, but survives, as

8. This is Slotkin's reading of Thoreau's and Melville's painful "probing of the depths
beneath the [myth's] surface" in their literary retreatments of the popular myth (550).

well, ironically detached literary "exposures" of the myth's often destructive political simplifications.[9]

Ike's manhood entails, on the one hand, his earning his place among the older white hunters by killing the buck, and on the other hand, his still appreciating as "part of [his] present" the huge buck that Sam salutes later in another tongue as "Oleh, Chief. . . . Grandfather," that is, as another of those immortal People "actually walking in breath and air and casting an actual shadow on the earth they had not quitted" (quitted, he realizes, largely to make way for these white hunters—171, 184, 171). Ike insists to McCaslin that "there is plenty of room for us and them too," and that he "saw" what McCaslin suggests maybe "dont have substance, cant cast a shadow" (187). But by admitting that he, too, saw the immortal buck with Sam just after killing his own first deer, McCaslin indirectly suggests that in this mysterious resolution of personal ambivalence and cultural contradiction, what they "saw" may well have had more to do with the mythic ritualization of their killing of those deer than with the immortality of the buck. For example, in the context of this rather feverish, ambiguously supernatural or tall tale of hunting and initiation, the immortal buck (like Mannie's ghost) might be understood as another uncanny return of the repressed: the return, in Ike's case, of that life he recognizes here that he has spilled, also of that fear he has willfully controlled in killing the buck, and also of the repressed impossibility of his further belief in the immortality of either himself or of the People without another willfully innocent forcing of such belief, as in the imagination of this immortal buck. It is only much later (near the end of "The Bear") that Ike will appreciate this totem buck, along with the dog Lion, the bear Ben, and the huge snake that evokes the memory of this buck and Sam's salute, not as immortals triumphing over death but as his imperfect cultural and personal means of recognizing, articulating, and mourning his loss, especially his loss of and separation from Sam.

Early in "The Bear" Ike recognizes in the sound of the dogs on Ben's scent an "almost human hysteria, abject, almost humanly grieving" (197), an abjectness he soon recognizes in a slightly less hysterical version in himself at the first sight of Ben's footprint—"a sense of his own fragility

9. Faulkner's critical treatment of the hunter myth in *Go Down, Moses* is written in the key of mourning, though with many humorous moments. For another critical treatment in the humorous mode, see his short story "A Bear Hunt." For an important predecessor in this mode see also Thomas Bangs Thorpe's sketch "The Big Bear of Arkansas," as read not by Slotkin but by Schmitz in "Tall Tale, Tall Talk" (see Chapter 3, note 10, above).

and impotence against the timeless woods"—along with a realization that
this immortal bear of local legend and of his own dreams is also, like
himself, a "mortal animal" (200, 201). The burden of Ike's mourning
(mostly his melancholia) in "The Bear" will be to repair (and still prepare
for) such collapses of willful innocence into inarticulate hysteria and fright,
by willfully repeating such shocks until, when Ike next sees the bear, "It
was quite familiar, until he remembered: this was the way he had used
to dream about it" (211). Ike has managed to repeat and focus his fright
in a particular kind of fear (207), repeating, in dreams and especially in
his hunting, dangerous losses and separations which he has thus fetishized
in Ben and the wilderness. While this fetishization of loss in Ben and the
wilderness enables a certain courage and skill on Ike's part as a hunter,
it also limits his ability to articulate personal and cultural losses and separations of different kinds, as Ike himself comes to recognize. He is not
facing and articulating different, particular dangers or particular losses
so much as he is facing and articulating all danger and loss in the more
manageable but limited terms of this one danger in particular. For example,
General Compson attests to Ike's courage and skill in finding and confronting unarmed something his elders among the white businessmen-
hunters had not been able to or perhaps had not had the courage to
approach, even to kill: "this boy was already an old man long before you
damned Sartorises and Edmondses invented farms and banks to keep your-
selves from having to find out what this boy was born knowing and fearing
too maybe but without being afraid, . . . maybe by God that's the why
and the wherefore of farms and banks" (250–51). But Compson still does
not know what it is that he here trusts that Ike knows, and Ike still can't
tell when McCaslin returns to camp a few days later to demand that Boon
"Tell the truth" about killing and burying Sam according to Sam's instructions. Boon can only begin to try to explain to McCaslin, then give up
and deny doing it, and Ike can only intervene in a hysterical burst of tears,
pleading with McCaslin to "Leave him alone! . . . Goddamn it! Leave him
alone" (254). What Ike knows is only that he and McCaslin from their
world of farms and banks do not, perhaps cannot, know what Sam and
Boon supposedly know as inheritors of the wilderness by virtue of their
race, and neither Sam, who is dead, nor Boon, who is childlike and hysterical, can tell them. There can be "room for us and them too," in other
words, but only by more or less shocking, melancholic, ironic "realizations" of an unbridgeable separation and loss, a separation and loss which
reach a narrative climax at the end of section 3 of "The Bear" with the
deaths of Ben, Lion, and Sam in an almost overwhelmingly rapid succession
of shocks.

Ike's paired tendencies in "The Bear" to willful innocence and willful irony in response to repeated shocks have recalled to many readers similarly melancholic configurations of desire and loss in Faulkner's more clearly modernist works, and the story has often thus been anthologized, canonized, and read as if it had no critical historical context of the sort provided in *Go Down, Moses* by the surrounding stories and by the story's own long fourth section, which is usually omitted (on Faulkner's recommendation) for purposes of reading "The Bear" as an independent short story. Even read thus as a short story, however, "The Bear" stretches to the limit what these tendencies to willful innocence and willful irony can accommodate of other voices. But, as in *Absalom, Absalom!* and others of Faulkner's more modernist works, these voices are made somewhat ambiguous by irony. For example, the black cook Ash's voice at the end of section 5 and the frustrated, hysterical voice of Boon are heard at the limit of Ike's own innocence and irony. They are more articulate than Jim Bond's howl at the end of *Absalom,* but still ambiguously so. They become much more persuasively articulate, however, in the context of still other marginal, critical voices to be heard soon thereafter in the novel's remaining two stories: critically different voices that will also be heard resistantly, fearfully, but with more attentiveness than irony can or will afford.

Ike's tendencies to innocence and irony are also critically defined by the larger historical context explored in the story's long fourth section in the novel, in which he tries to explain to his cousin McCaslin Edmonds and himself his own relinquishment of his white McCaslin patrimony. As in *Absalom,* the opposition of innocence and irony is tested on a vast historical canvas; that canvas is even larger here, encompassing some biblical and Old World history as well as that of the American North and South before and after the Civil War. But this larger history is also more specific in its differentiations among historical groups and movements, especially in the South, as if in greater appreciation of the historical and economic differences and changes explored in *The Wild Palms* and (more extensively) in *The Hamlet.*[10] Both the scope and the specificity of this

---

10. These historical differentiations are the particular strength of Susan Willis' reading of "The Bear" in terms of economic dependency theory. Myra Jehlen's reading of Faulkner's later work lacks Willis' sense of twentieth-century changes in the terms of contradiction in Faulkner's South, so that Jehlen still sees Faulkner's criticisms of Flem as a reaction bound to favor the aristocrats in an older opposition of yeoman farmers and planters. But the potential critical significance of these changes is blurred for both Jehlen and Willis, by their insistence on resolution as the only way out of opposition, so that they view this later work as more or less "torn apart by contradiction and frustrated by the attempts at resolution, the text produc[ing] the creative richness of myth and the gripping futility of mediation" (Willis 194).

historical context suggest the reductiveness of Ike's ironic readings of history in terms of a repeated dispossession of an Edenic innocence in the New World as in the Old. Ike does allow for the human heart's sometimes mistaken readings of the (Book's) truth, because people can "comprehend truth only through the complexity of passion and lust and hate and fear which drives the heart"—he suggests an opening here for a revision later of his own readings of history—but in his own grief, fear, and desire for certainty Ike insists that "the heart already knows" the truth (260), and he sees in the course of history since Eden one loss of innocence after another.

In a New World that might have been a New Canaan to redeem the corruption of the Old, old Issetibbeha's possession of the Native Americans' land was "tainted" by the very possibility of sale to Ike's white grandfather and his kind (259), whose curse on the land continued in the form of possession and slavery until they were deprived of some of their power by the suffering and blood of the war (286). But the abolitionists of the North were themselves only "rich descendants of slavers, females of both sexes" (283), dealing comfortably in abstractions amid "the whirling wheels which manufactured for a profit the pristine replacements of the shackles and shoddy garments as they wore out" (284). Those slaves who were given their freedom "misused it as human beings always misuse freedom"; likewise, the carpetbaggers

> in another generation would be engaged in a fierce economic competition of small sloven farms with the black men they were supposed to have freed and the white descendants of fathers who had owned no slaves anyway whom they were supposed to have disinherited and in the third generation would be back

in town jobs, leading lynch mobs "against the race their ancestors had come to save"; next would come "that other nameless horde of speculators in human misery, manipulators of money and politics and land" (289–91). Through all these surrounding permutations of the original dispossessors—slaveholders, manufacturers, and financiers[11]—Ike's patrimony in the realm of "farms and banks" has remained the same. There is nothing new under the sun even though the plantation house has been replaced by the commissary store (as in *The Hamlet*) as "not the heart perhaps but certainly the solar-plexus of the repudiated and relinquished: the square, galleried wooden building squatting like a portent above the fields whose laborers it still held in thrall '65 or no" (255). The exemplary horror and outrage

11. Cf. again Baudrillard's three orders of simulation (note 5, above).

for Ike is his discovery in this commissary's ledger books of his grandfather's incest with his own daughter by one of his slaves. Ike's thinking
"*His own daughter His own daughter. No No Not even him*" (270), and
the slave mother Eunice's suicide in "formal and succinct repudiation of
grief and despair who had already had to repudiate belief and hope" (271),
together recall from *Absalom* the two college freshmen "saying No to
Quentin's Mississippi shade" (225) and one of the two drowning himself
as if in agreement with Eunice and then with Ike that men were "all
Grandfather all of them" (283), so that Ike decides to try to relinquish "old
Carothers' doomed and fatal blood which in the male derivation seemed
to destroy all it touched" (293).

So much corruption implies a corresponding prelapsarian innocence,
and Ike's litany of ironic shocks leads toward two instances of his ahis-
torically nostalgic, willful innocence with which Faulkner suggests the limitations of this opposition as a final reading of history, however understandable and strategic it may have been in Ike's time, place, and in his
own "heart's driving complexity" (260). Although Ike would repudiate his
grandfather's race and kind, he falters at stating the "heresy" of what is
nonetheless still an essentialist, primitivist concept of blacks as a race —
that "They are better than we are. Stronger than we are. Their vices are
vices aped from white men or that white men and bondage have taught
them" (294), and their virtues include "what they got not only not from
white people but not even despite white people because they had it already
from the old free fathers a longer time free than us because we have never
been free" (295). This primitivist definition of blacks as contrasting with
whites or as immune to a white curse owes more to the emotional and
rhetorical exigencies of Ike's repudiation of his white heritage and the entire
course of white civilization than it does to any relationship with the blacks
he has lived among. Some of the inadequacy of this innocent, purist conception of blacks as an alternative to the directly opposite racism of his white
heritage (which his irony denies) becomes clear to Ike himself when in
the fifth and final section of "The Bear" he is startled out of a similar revery
about the uncorrupted wilderness as a realm without death to remember
a particular black voice that he has patronizingly ignored, notwithstanding
this antiracist position.

In retreat from a generalized corruption, Ike feels willfully innocent
nostalgia also for the beginning of his marriage as a becoming "one: for
that while, one; for that while at least, one; indivisible, that while at least
irrevocable and unrecoverable" (311). From that original state of "glory
which inherently of itself cannot last and hence why glory" (326), his
marriage suddenly collapses into barrenness. When his unnamed wife
demands that he reconsider his relinquishment of the farm, and offers her

love in symbolic exchange, his habitual opposition of innocence and irony faces a crisis: his irony, after all, has worked by preempting his own desires before they involve him in unpredictable circumstances. But his irony is no protection against her unpredictably different desires, which his love for her might well lead him to want to pursue, and then to share responsibility for instead of denying. Ike will hear again in "Delta Autumn" of the limitations of his ironic habit when it comes to the love of another subject: here he balks at these unexpectedly different desires in a relationship he prefers to think of as indivisible or lost, and instead of trying to articulate this difference he sees the "chaste woman, the wife" suddenly "changed, altered" into something "composite of all woman-flesh" in mysterious contact with the unknown somewhere beyond his man's, hunter's knowledge or even possibility of understanding: *She already knows more than I with all the man-listening in camps where there was nothing to read ever even heard of. . . . She is lost. She was born lost.*" And with such a specimen of corruption he no longer feels compelled to tell the truth, and promises what he has no intention of fulfilling. "*We were all born lost*" (315). Her desire is hypostatized as untranslatable into, or nonnegotiable in, his own language of innocence and irony, just as Boon's desire was inarticulable in McCaslin's system of farms and banks, and she collapses at the end of section 4, as Boon and Rider have in similar moments, into an apparently indecipherable hysteria.

As in those similar moments of closure on Boon and Rider, however, the closure on a note of apparent incomprehensibility effectively recalls, in order to revise, *Absalom*'s closure on Jim Bond's hopelessly inarticulate, undifferentiated howl: although Ike tends to remember his wife as the Lost Woman tempting him to an equally absolute perdition,[12] she has articulated a specific demand the nature of which will become clearer to readers of *Go Down, Moses,* as to Ike himself, in its rearticulation and amplification by Ike's cousin Roth's lover in "Delta Autumn." There Ike's wife's demand can be better appreciated as another voice out of that marginal space of symbolic exchanges represented throughout this novel in terms of singularly personalized trades, contests, gifts, fears, and loves, insofar as these function not as isolated sanctuaries, narrow refuges, or pressure valves within the dominant systems of relationship and exchange

12. This is also Faulkner's memory of her (through Ike?) years later in the class conferences transcribed in *Faulkner in the University* 277–78. But Faulkner is also quick to imagine the possibility of her being different, and of Ike's conceding to her, "You're wiser than I, let's try it your way." This attractive moral (and practical) possibility for Ike, however, betrays Faulkner's more profound understanding of Ike's peculiar character and circumstances: "That's possible, I would like to think that. But he would have stuck to his position, that I will not profit from this which is wrong and sinful" (275–76).

but as possibilities for critical revision from marginal positions within or on the boundaries of those same dominant systems. In Faulkner's own later classroom simplification of Ike's singular personal, social, and historical situation into the less revealing terms of moral evaluation,[13] Ike would need to resemble the third instead of the second "stage" of moral development in order to respond adequately to such a demand on his wife's part:

> Well, there are some people in any time and age that cannot face and cope with the problems. There seem to be three stages: The first says, This is rotten, I'll have no part of it, I will take death first. The second says, This is rotten, I don't like it, I can't do anything about it, but at least I will not participate in it myself, I will go off into a cave or climb a pillar to sit on. The third says, This stinks and I'm going to do something about it. McCaslin is the second. He says, This is bad, and I will withdraw from it. What we need are people who will say, This is bad and I'm going to do something about it, I'm going to change it. (*Faulkner in the University*, 245–46)

Ike's revery in the woods in the fifth and final section of "The Bear," however, does suggest a certain growing critical awareness, on Ike's part, of these limits to his vision. His symbolic gift of a sack of candy to Sam's grave suggests that his willfully innocent denials of the reality of death in the wilderness should not be taken too literally, that they are not only melancholic resistances—suspensions of mourning—but also partial, tentative gestures in a process of articulating his grief. When he is startled by the snake, he remembers Ash's voice, and "it was fear all right but not fright" as he looked down at the snake: although feeling "again and as always the sharp shocking inrush from when Isaac McCaslin long yet was not" (329), he does not fall from innocence into a panic-stricken fright or hysteria at the blinding thought of his own death. Nor has the generalization implied by the phrase "again and as always" turned repetition of

13. About such ethical simplifications, Richard Brodhead raises the question of "the effect on Faulkner's writing of his great final market, the literary-critical one. It is clear that when the American literary establishment and the academy latched onto him in his last years, Faulkner got good at discussing his work in the way his new admirers were discussing it; and we might wonder whether the pronounced ethical thematics of his late writings are not products of a kind of reincorporation back into his fiction of the literary notions of its last institutional home" (19). Whether this is true of his last works of fiction or not, it does seem to be true of many of his answers to questions at the University of Virginia, as in the passage I am citing from those classroom sessions. The tension between an ethical taxonomy and a critical sense of revisionary possibilities can be felt here between the language of "facing" problems on the one hand and "coping" with them on the other, and of kinds of people on the one hand ("some" who can, some who "cannot face and cope with the problems") and on the other hand "stages" of coping.

that fright into a deadened ironic familiarity with death in general or with
a certain fetishized, repeated experience of shock. Ike has been concerned
from the beginning of "The Bear" to learn, from Sam especially, this distinction between the brave man's fear in the face of his own vulnerability
and limits, and the cornered or cowardly man's fright which a "bear or
deer has got to be scared of . . . same as a brave man has got to be" (207).

For in Faulkner's work it is especially the white man's inarticulate
fright (and its matching ironic defense) that leads him to make "balloon
faces" of what he is frightened of, balloon faces that he can ignore as
different subjects either by bursting and running from them in fright, or
by pretending in irony to master, know, speak for them, or do justice to
them himself. Thus Ike tries here in his fear to articulate as well as he
can, without pretending adequately to name, the snake's "thin sick smell
of rotting cucumbers and something else which had no name, evocative
of all knowledge and an old weariness and of pariah-hood and of death"
(329). He neither runs from the smell in innocent fright as the unthinkable smell of Evil or Death, nor does he name the smell patronizingly as
that of a weary dead pariah (Sam? Old Carothers?) whose story he can
understand and do justice to, himself. The smell reminds him (in his critical
awareness of his limitation and fear) of a gesture and salute (" 'Chief,' he
said: 'Grandfather' "—330) out of another time and an alien tongue by
a man he knows is dead, but for whom he can still find ways thus to articulate his love.

There is a similar but more humorous awareness of limitation, fear,
and love as Ike comes upon Boon's enraged hysteria at his gun and "hoarse
strangled voice" in the story's last scene: like Sam and Ash (and Tennie's
Jim, whose voice will only filter through by way of his granddaughter to
Ike years later in "Delta Autumn"), Boon and his potential counternarrative
have been little listened to in the dominant white discourses of "The Bear"
(331). He has even played, as Jim Bond did in *Absalom,* the double role
of fool and instrument of the curse (in killing Ben). But Ike has also learned,
to some extent, to recognize and love Boon's singular difference.

When the granddaughter of Tennie's Jim speaks to Ike in "Delta
Autumn," he has been thinking or dreaming again of himself and the
wilderness, the white hunter-businessmen and Sam Fathers, and "ample
room for both" (354), only to wake up in the position of paying off Roth
Edmonds' mistress, turning her away from the white planter's door as it
were, without recognizing yet either the "effluvium" of her (racial, though
almost invisible) blackness or her kinship with himself through Tennie's
Jim. When she looks past his movement to give her Edmonds' money,
looking him instead in the face and calling him "Uncle Isaac," he notices

but ignores the "candor" of that look as that of another subject independent of his own purposes and discomfort.[14] Still with a kind of willful innocence, he answers, "Never mind that," thinking that she only borrows from *his* language and family the term of kinship that his own kinsman uses, when it is actually also a name in hers, since he is also part of *her* family (357, 358). Then when she suggests that he spoiled Roth by giving the land to Roth's grandfather McCaslin Edmonds (spoiling him, perhaps, by seeming thus to split between them the innocence and the guilt of their patrimony), whereas she would have made a man of Roth, he still says, "Never mind that too" (360). And when he realizes she is black and his own (and Roth's) kinsman, his willful innocence turns to fright and then to impotent irony: he is first outraged, then says in a grieving voice, "Get out of here! I can do nothing for you! Cant nobody do nothing for you!" (361). But controlling his panic for a moment, he can touch the flesh of her hand and remember "the old strong blood" and Tennie's Jim, as if to recognize in remembrance the possibility of appreciating James Beauchamp's own name and voice better than Ike himself and the rest of them had before, and he can give her General Compson's heirloom hunting horn for the boy, as if to recognize, too, the possibility that she might indeed effect meaningful change in that tradition, if not by making a man of Roth (or of himself), then perhaps by making a better man of her son.

But the limits of his position become here all too uncomfortably clear for Ike. If his relinquishing his patrimony had at the time seemed the only way to signal his recognition of what that patrimony otherwise so ruthlessly ignored, he has since realized that this same relinquishment, at least when repeated with his wife, may have been more a gesture of self-consciousness than a recognition of other subjects with their own historical and social possibilities for agency and resistance. He has realized, for example, that in "saving and freeing his son" from "regret and grief" for "that same land, that same wrong and shame," he has in the same act lost that son, effectively lost his own chance of taking shared responsibility with his wife for giving that son or daughter life and thus lost that child's chance to take his or her own responsibility for revising that patrimony and that tradition.

For now, that this black woman lover of Roth's might figure not as a sentimentalized, innocent victim of that tradition but as an unexpected source of revisionary change from within one of the guiltiest, most troubling aspects of that tradition (an apparent repetition of Old Carothers' incestuous miscegenation), is a possibility that catches Ike and the remaining traces of his tradition by surprise. And Ike reacts to this par-

14. Cf. Benjamin's "aura" (note 7, above).

ticular surprise not with a brave fear but with fright, doing what Freud and Sam Fathers both warn that people do in situations when they feel cornered and frightened: he reacts to the surprise itself and not to this particular threat, by assuming the worst in order at least to repair the trauma and to avoid further surprise.[15] In his fright he sees her only as a balloon face of "repetition and revenge."[16] He desires only to forget her present relation to Roth in a Sutpen-like perfect translation of her into the whitened figure inside the door, who would have no surviving memory of or recognition for anyone left outside: "You are young, handsome, almost white," he tells her, "You could find a black man who would see in you what it was you saw in him, who would ask nothing of you and expect less and get even still less than that, if it's revenge you want. Then you will forget all this, forget it ever happened, that he ever existed" (363). She has to remind him of love, of the possibility that her voice, however frightening at the moment to an old man like Ike, does not necessarily justify Ike's own worst fears about his own and Roth's cursed tradition. She reminds him of the possibility that she might get through to Roth and make a man of him, that the domestic space might not only be a private sanctuary (as it was for James Beauchamp and Tomey's Turl, Lucas and Molly Beauchamp, Rider and Mannie, and as Ike hoped it would be for him), but might also be a space for revisionary change, and that Ike does not have to assume the untranslatable impasse either between the races or between the domestic and the social. This same possibility of repeating those traditions with a critical difference has, after all, informed Faulkner's own ongoing revisions of scenes and relationships like the one at the planter's door, as if to admit the limits of each of his own representations, without, however, giving up on listening for another different voice to speak.

In the next and final, title story of *Go Down, Moses,* Samuel Worsham "Butch" Beauchamp, the black Chicago numbers racketeer and now the convicted killer whose face is "impenetrable," whose eyes "had seen too

15. I take this to be one main reason for Faulkner's inconsistently "go slow" and "Yankee go home" positions in public statements on desegregation in the South. When they are not symptoms of his own fright, these statements may appear more reactionary than they are by being taken out of the context of his career-long concern to understand the workings of reaction and of change. He was concerned not to placate whites or blacks but to stress their involvement and engagement (even when they assume reactionary positions) in the variously repeated and revised symbolic exchanges necessary for radical change in attitudes and relationships between whites and blacks.

16. I borrow this part of Irwin's title to signal again a difference between my reading and his.

much," and whose voice is unrecognizable ("anything under the sun but a southern voice or even a negro voice"), is a somewhat balloon-faced figure that promises in many ways to confirm Ike's worst fears, or rather his most simplistically ironic predictions, of a directly imitative, repetitive revenge in blackface of white wrongs, as Ike imagined that revenge in "Delta Autumn" on the part of anonymous "black men [who] own plantations and ride in jim crow cars to Chicago to live in millionaries' mansions on Lakeshore Drive" (369, 364). But the burden of this story named after a black spiritual and placed at the end of this novel of the same name is to test the possibility of understanding such an apparently ironic historical repetition as significant revision and change, or in other words, to test the possibility that such repetitions might "signify upon" the dominant white society, economy, and religion in terms of which their voices here are heard. The test is whether Butch Beauchamp's story and the grief of his grandmother Mollie Beauchamp[17] can be articulated and understood across boundaries of class, race, gender, and death (here by a white man like Gavin Stevens), or whether Beauchamp's story and Mollie's grief will remain a hopelessly ironic "heap of broken images": that is, whether this grave will remain (as in the opening of "Pantaloon in Black") one grave resembling "any other marked off without order about the barren plot by shards of pottery and broken bottles and old brick and other objects insignificant to sight but actually of a profound meaning and fatal to touch, which no white man could have read" (135). From another angle, the test in reading "Go Down, Moses" will be to appreciate within the momentarily nauseated fright and more habitual, willful irony of a man like Stevens (or Stevens' friend the newspaper editor, or a white woman like Miss Worsham) those revisionary, "signifying" possibilities in Butch and Mollie Beauchamp's stories that Stevens both resists and listens for with a profound ambivalence of fear and love.

17. I take the change in spelling of Molly/Mollie's name since "The Fire and the Hearth" either as an oversight on Faulkner's part or as a variation on the theme of naming that runs throughout the novel: naming conceived as a scene alternately of ineluctable repetition and revenge or of more revisionary repetitions and more reciprocal, symbolic exchange. While these blacks often bore the names of their ancestors' white masters, they were not unduly reverent about the audible or inaudible spelling of those names, as in Lucas Beauchamp's revision of his given "white" name Lucius ("not denying, declining the name itself, because he used three quarters of it; but simply taking the name and changing, altering it, making it no longer the white man's but his own"—281); nor did they decline nicknames, as in the case of Lucas' grandson Butch, a tradition suggestively explored in Toni Morrison's *Song of Solomon* 332–34. For a contrasting view, cf. Matthews, *Play* 273, who associates this inaudible misspelling of Molly's name with Stevens' and the white community's "unfamiliarity [with] and detachment" from Molly's grief. My reading of *Go Down, Moses* in terms of a preoccupation with mourning is obviously indebted to Matthews' important reading of the novel.

"Orphaned of his mother at birth and deserted by his father" (372), Beauchamp was raised until he was nineteen by his grandmother Mollie, the same who reminded her husband Lucas more than once in "The Fire and the Hearth" of their domestic space and their relationship of symbolic exchange as a "dangerous memory" and critical alternative to his otherwise frustrating opportunities for social dignity in the dominant land-based, money-based, and credit-based systems of authority and power: the symbolic fire on their hearth has functioned as an alternative resource for local legends and traditions critically revising those of the "big house." Perhaps because this domestic alternative of Lucas' and Mollie's came to seem to their grandson (as it finally did to Rider) more confining than liberating, Butch Beauchamp turned to his other options, as extremely limited and violently frustrating as they were. Unable because of his race to make his fortune on the land by inheritance or by way of Sutpen's acceptable combination of "courage and shrewdness," Beauchamp is "caught . . . breaking into [Roth Edmonds'] commissary store and . . . ordered . . . off the place and . . . forbidden . . . ever to return" (373). Trying next the money option, as it were (cf. Lucas' visions of hidden gold), and barred from earning that money in a store clerk's job like Flem's, "after a year in and out of jail [in town] for gambling and fighting," he is caught "breaking and entering a store," whereupon he strikes out and is struck down in an attitude of unarticulated, hysterical frustration evocative of Charles Etienne's and Rider's, "his teeth fixed into something like furious laughter through the blood" (372). Eventually he becomes quite successful under another name in the numbers racket in Chicago, where he manages like Flem to capitalize on his own Family's laundered threats of violence, with an apparently barren anonymity in success also similar to Flem's.

But before Beauchamp is electrocuted for killing a policeman, he gives the census taker his real name and the name and address of the woman who raised him, Mollie Beauchamp, and as his occupation, "getting rich too fast" (370), suggesting that his financial success in forcing his way into capital's house and store is not so utterly anonymous as Ike would have feared, that he is not so utterly without a critical, "dangerous memory" of his position once outside the door of power. Like the white men of power whose position inside the door he seems to repeat, he has overcome only by violent denial his actually always marginal position, poised on the margin outside or threshold between these simplifying oppositions — both inside and outside the door, both white and black, both businessman and singular personality, both chaste "Man" and loving "Woman" (especially in his ties to the maternal Mollie).

Once the violence of Beauchamp's success has been legally exposed, Gavin Stevens' first reaction is not to articulate or to appreciate (though

he is variously aware of it) the difficult story of Beauchamp's difficult marginal position. Stevens, who as county attorney *is* "the Law" in Jefferson,
as Mollie says, attempts instead to set Beauchamp, once and for all, decisively and deservedly, back outside the door through which Beauchamp
has forced his way: by Stevens' legal, moral lights, Beauchamp has in
forcing his way by violence thereby forfeited his way (371). With some
emotional violence of his own, Stevens attempts to lay Beauchamp's
(obviously troubling) memory to rest by rationalizing the legal and moral
necessity of his death, as that of a "murderer" and "a bad son of a bad
father," whose dying is "better this way," and whose story Stevens sup-
poses is best kept from Mollie except as the news her grandson is "dead
and buried somewhere in the North" (375–76). Faced with the facts of Beauchamp's death, of Mollie's grief, and of Miss Worsham's solidarity with
that grief, Stevens is ready to admit ironic doubts about these strict limits
to his sympathy, but that irony, typically, tends only to invoke that limit
not yet in order to try to understand but in order to try to ward off what
remains the undifferentiated unknown, articulated only in denial. Thus
Stevens makes a series of concessions to what he types in Mollie and Miss
Worsham as only "some old, timeless, female affinity for blood and grief,"
agreeing to bring the body home in the box provided by the prison, then
in "not just a box," and with flowers (376).

But neither the shared grief of Mollie and Miss Worsham nor its emotional pull on Stevens remains so easily denied when Stevens visits the
Worsham house, where Mollie is staying with her brother Hamp Worsham,
his wife, and with their namesake's (and *Samuel Worsham* Beauchamp's
namesake's) unmarried white heir to the house, who has told Stevens she
"grew up together [with Mollie] as sisters would" (375). When Stevens joins
their "circle about the brick hearth on which the ancient symbol of human
coherence and solidarity smoldered" (380), Miss Worsham cannot get the
others to "hush" their chanting and singing of the black spiritual which
they have adapted to articulate their sense of a wider responsibility for
their loss: " 'He dead,' she said. 'Pharaoh got him.' . . . 'Roth Edmonds
sold my Benjamin.' . . . 'Sold him to Pharaoh and now he dead' " (380).
They adapt this spiritual to their particular accusation and grief just as
the black spiritual as a historical genre has adapted to strategically different,
critical purposes the accommodationist white religion which provided
many of its terms and (sometimes uneasily) sanctioned its expression (see
Genovese). Stevens hears and tries to deny the critical edge to their chanting, with its implication of Edmonds and the (white) law and society in
Beauchamp's death. He tells Mollie no and tries to explain calmly that
she is wrong, but she will not allow him to deny so patronizingly Roth's
part (and his own) in her grandson's story, and his ensuing, desperate sense

of suffocation and nausea suggests the depth of his own unacknowledged involvement in this death, their loss, and their "coherence and solidarity."

His irony has been forced from the beginning, and that forcing signals the very depth of feeling which it tries to deny and obscure—but which it cannot altogether obscure from Faulkner's readers, after he has paid so much attention to how that characteristically Southern, characteristically modernist irony works. Some of the bluff in Stevens' voice is heard as he talks to the newspaper editor even before he learns what trouble it is that Mollie has sensed her grandson is in: "I just hope, for her sake as well as that of the great public whom I represent, that his present trouble is very bad and maybe final too—" (373–74). As he admits to himself a few minutes later, "it seems I didn't mean what I said I hoped" (374). The same "realistic," sardonic bluff carries him briskly past several attempts at interruption and questioning by his editor friend as Stevens sees him again and tells him bluntly and matter-of-factly,

> "We're bringing him home. . . . Miss Worsham and you and me and some others. It will cost—"
> "Wait," the editor said. "What others?" "I don't know yet. It will cost about two hundred. I'm not counting. . . ."
> "Wait," the editor said. "Wait." "And he will come in on Number Four the day after tomorrow and we will meet it. . . . And the hearse out there will be fifteen more, not counting the flowers—"
> "Flowers?" "Flowers," Stevens said. "Call the whole thing two hundred and twenty-five. And it will probably be mostly you and me. All right?"
> "No it aint all right," the editor said. "But it dont look like I can help myself. . . ." (377–78)

The willful irony in this exchange shades into a profoundly humorous appreciation of the unspoken feeling on both sides, voiced only in a parting symbolic exchange of feeble jokes. It is largely unspoken feeling, but it is there to be drawn upon and given new form, as in Mollie's demand for the social means of articulating hers and the community's grief. Thus also Stevens' "set and rapid speech" as he collects money around the square should be appreciated not as a meager attempt to ransom the town's white conscience but as a symbolic exchange, its awkwardness and overt inadequacy making it more valuable than it may seem at first. It more closely resembles Lucas' five-cent gift of candy to Mollie, or Ike's to Sam's grave, than Flem's to Mrs. Armstid. And it suggests a second look at Roth's monthly gift of tobacco and candy to Mollie for the love that is dimly articulated and recognized there even as it is being paid off and denied in his so-called "libation to his luck . . . though actually it was to his ancestors and to the conscience which he would have probably affirmed he did not possess, in the form, the person, of the negro woman who had been the only mother he ever knew" (99–100).

Even when he hears that Mollie wants her grandson's story put in the paper, all of it, and hears the editor say he believes she really does, Stevens still resists, perhaps partly out of his avowed concern for the pain it would cause Mollie to learn the news of her grandson's career, his crime, and his execution, but probably more out of concern for the pain it would and does cause the community and Stevens himself. He is still trying, though feebly and also fearfully, to waive her grief away as a melancholic affinity for the ceremonialized shock of grief "itself" (as if the funeral had completed the process of mourning), and not as a continuing love for the particular boy she raised and lost, for whom she is apparently more ready to begin the arduous process of mourning than Stevens is: *"now that it's all over and done and finished, she doesn't care how he died. She just wanted him home, but she wanted him to come home right. She wanted that casket and those flowers and the hearse and she wanted to ride through town behind it in a car"* (383). Nor does Faulkner himself put Beauchamp's counternarrative in the newspaper or the novel either, except in its disturbingly, suspiciously bare outline. Nevertheless, it is a story that can be better read and appreciated in the surrounding context of the novel's various histories of willful ironies and denials of mourning, fear, and love (like Stevens'), as these histories discover their inescapable connections with stories (like Mollie's) of more courageous and resourceful acts, stories articulating similar mournings, fears, and loves more adequately than in the ironic mode. Faulkner's story here and throughout this novel, as also in *The Hamlet* and *Absalom, Absalom!,* is especially that of the profoundly ambivalent resistance of people like Gavin Stevens (and of the changing discourses of authority, power, and identity in which they speak) to stories like those of Butch and Mollie Beauchamp, stories which they both fear and desire to hear. In Faulkner's work this is a resistance persistently but not infallibly critical of itself, and never completely deaf to criticism in other, surrounding voices. It is a resistance therefore continually revising itself and being itself revised, in all its more or less symbolic exchanges with those other subjects whose voices we both fear and love, notably in the symbolic exchange of humor, and perhaps especially when we mourn specific losses of other voices. Humor was perhaps the keynote of *The Hamlet* because humor marks the surprising *possibility* of such exchanges with radically different voices. Mourning in *Go Down, Moses* marks both the persistent *value* and persistent *difficulty* of such exchanges across racial lines in Faulkner's South and also Faulkner's United States.

Passing the hat in Jefferson for Butch Beauchamp's funeral at the end of *Go Down, Moses* recalls Ike's gift of candy to Sam's grave, also Lucas' gift of candy to Mollie, and especially Roth's regular gift of tobacco and candy to Mollie as "the only mother he ever knew" (100). From earlier works it recalls Flem Snopes's gift of candy to Mrs. Armstid in *The Hamlet* and the gifts of ribbon, beads, and candy ("the nickel's worth of stale jellified glue out of a striped sack"—289) with which Sutpen courted Millie Jones in *Absalom, Absalom!* Although Roth's gift to Mollie is described (in the manner of Roth's defensive cynicism) as a payoff to his ancestors, still, the fact that he "pays" Mollie thus repeatedly (rather than paying her off once and for all), along with the fact that he "pays" his tribute to Mollie (rather than to one of his symbolic forefathers, say, Major de Spain or General Compson), along with the placing of this gift in this series of gifts, suggests something of Faulkner's purposes in testing and retesting the temper of such acts of symbolic exchange.

To read Roth's gift only in the long (modernist) shadow of Sutpen's gifts to Millie as represented by the Compsons would be to recognize in both these gifts only ruthless calculation and the ironic reduction of a gift of candy to a bribe or payment in jellified glue. Such a reading attempts to ignore the ambivalence of fear and love motivating both gifts as uneasy exceptions to calculation or cynicism. Yet the fear and love are real, even when fright and innocence willfully deny that love (as in Sutpen's case) or when irony denies the love along with the fear (as in Roth's case). Faulkner's placing these gifts in a series with other markedly different gifts permits a preference, say, for Lucas' gift to Mollie as a revision of these less overtly reciprocal gifts; but Lucas' gift is not pure of design or compensation itself, and as a revision of those other gifts, it helps to clarify the ambivalence they variously denied.

Sutpen's gifts to Millie already revise his forced attempts to deny his love to the poor-white family he left behind in Tidewater Virginia, to the family of wife and son he left behind in Haiti, to his family in Mississippi, to his hoped-for family with Rosa, and to his friend Wash. Sutpen's denial of that love each time it seems again absolutely incommensurate to his society's demands on him is both a personal and also a social failure, but it never successfully abolishes the ambivalence of fear and love in his gift. Flem's gift, likewise, recognizes ironically the utter inadequacy of his and his economy's token compensations to its victims, but it also makes possible more humorous recognitions—recognitions of the fear and love motivating both such token compensations and the shared judgments of their inadequacy. Roth's gift to Mollie thus also figures both as a payoff and as a gift, proving him not only willfully innocent of his debt to her, nor only cynically resentful of the impossibility of payment, but also uneasily, fearfully trying to find a way to articulate, as in a gift, in grief, or in humor, that love he does still uneasily feel "for the only mother he ever knew."

As Faulkner explored what C. Vann Woodward has called the postwar South's historical sense of defeat and guilt (a sense uncommon in American mythology and history), he must have recognized the social inadequacy of an ironic (modernist) view of history. The focus of such an ironic view is the struggle for power—the repeated struggle to assume the social and familial place of the father, along with that struggle's repeated failures and losses. In Faulkner's revisions of such an ironic view, however, that focus on the struggle for power begins to seem one temptingly reductive, double strategy in the midst of a larger struggle to find ways to articulate a deeper fear and love—the fear and love denied in both the assumption of power and in the guilty or melancholic insistence on its defeat. In Faulkner's work, as in American literature after modernism, as in American society after its several phases of disillusionment and guilt, as in much of the literature and society of America's subaltern groups, including poor white Southerners, women, blacks, other minorities, and other nationalities, the problem becomes (or has been) not so much "facing the facts" again and again of what we have done, as a final judgment on our culture (a judgment shocking at first, then bracing, but eventually dulling in its ironic repetition, and subject to its own mystifications as literary, personal, or political "realism"); the problem becomes instead that of recognizing whom among us we have done it to, why, and how, with what unrecognized ambivalence, how we have avoided and still avoid those recognitions, and how we sometimes might more often find ways of giving those recognitions a more articulate voice. Thus the problem for Roth has become not how to get into the planter's door to pay his eventually self-serving tribute to the white father's power, but how to articulate his (fear-constricted) love for the black family he has incompletely left behind—Lucas, Roth's forsaken black "brother" Henry, and especially his black mother, Mollie. In his next two novels, *Intruder in the Dust* and especially *Requiem for a Nun*, Faulkner would continue to explore this revised version of the problem, now, of articulating a debt and a love not only for a white father but for a black family and especially for a black mother, not a love of himself in his white father's image, but a love of the radically (but recognizably) different in class, race, gender, and person—a love for what he lacks except in his love.

5   Imprisonment, Rape, and Abortion Reconsidered in *Requiem for a Nun*

Iɴ *Go Down, Moses,* especially the two final stories, "Delta Autumn" and "Go Down, Moses," as also in his dedication of the finished novel to Caroline Barr, Faulkner has turned his attention increasingly toward the figure of the black mother, who serves as a focus and difficult interlocutor for his progressively more radical rereadings and rewritings of his society's constitutive, hierarchical distinctions of class, race, and now especially sexuality and gender, which has proven to be for Faulkner the most difficult, most deeply naturalized, ideological set of distinctions of the three. In *Requiem for a Nun* (1951) and finally in *The Reivers* (1962) he returns to material mostly latent since before *Absalom, Absalom!* (1936) and *Light in August* (1932), in order to reconsider the prevailing (modernist, Southern) mood of innocent horror and bitter irony surrounding the loss of Caddy Compson's and especially Temple Drake's (aristocratic, white) female purity in *The Sound and the Fury* (1929) and *Sanctuary* (1931), a loss represented there primarily as the (aristocratic, white) male's horrified or embittered loss of daughter or sister from out of her proper place in *his* psychological, social, and metaphysical systems of thought and action. This modernist representation of that loss has tended in many ways to leave that society's underlying distinctions of sexuality and gender uncritically in place. These distinctions, that is, have been represented under the metaphysical, ahistorical threat of horrifying or ironically inevitable collapse, to the exclusion of other, potentially more searching attempts to attend to those contending social forces and voices continuously engaged in defending, disguising, and also challenging, resisting, and more or less effectively rewriting those same threatened oppositions. Faulkner has explored in *Absalom, Absalom!, The Unvanquished, The Wild Palms, The Hamlet,* and *Go Down, Moses* the motivations, consequences, contradictions, and inadequacies of this Southern, modernist mode and the possibilities of alternative modes of humor, mourning, and love for the task of critically reinscribing questions especially of class and race in more complex psychological, social, and historical contexts. He attempts now to rewrite the collapses, consolidations, and critical displacements of still more deeply entrenched oppositions related to sex and gender. He proceeds by developing still further the models of humor, mourning, and love as formal, cultural, and personal responses to change and difference, and he extends his historical differentiations by tracing again these possibilities of humor, mourning, and love through three broad phases of social and historical change — the change from a "prehistorical" frontier society to a more established (if still semiperipheral) "historical" society, from that "historical" society to "modernity," and from "modernity" to "postmodernity."[1]

The long prose introductions to the three acts of *Requiem for a Nun* serve as extended stage directions for the more intensely focused, somewhat dwarfed dramatic acts that follow: Faulkner has vastly enlarged the notion of stage directions to accommodate not the mere costumes, lighting, and layout of the stage but the larger social contexts and longer historical backgrounds that have become increasingly necessary to (though not monolithically or ironically determining of) Faulkner's and his readers' understanding of those exemplary crises and unexemplary remainders soon to be reenacted within the smaller frame of the dramatic stage.[2] While each of his relatively vast historical stage settings suggests the determining power of these larger backdrops, his historical writing here at the same time works critically against the tendency of much other historical and theoretical writing variously to ratify and naturalize victorious forces in history.[3] That is, each of his stage settings represents not one historical "period" but a transition from one social order (with its own characteristic ways of organizing both its internal and its external boundaries) toward another, differently ordered society, because the costs and weaknesses of

1. The historical configurations discussed here in terms of "prehistorical" frontier societies, "historical societies," "modernity," and "postmodernity" are roughly homologous with the discussion in Chapters 3 and 4 above in terms of precapitalist, land-based, money-based, and credit-based capitalist economies.

2. On the simultaneously inclusive and exclusive functions of framing devices, especially in Faulkner's more modernist mode, see John T. Matthews' "Faulkner's Narrative Frames." Faulkner's increasing use and adaptation of the conventional frames of sketches and short stories in variously problematic relationships to the larger frame of the novel (as in *The Hamlet* and *Go Down, Moses*), as well as his use here of a dramatic frame in an unusually dwarfed relation to its historical introductions, suggest his increasingly critical preoccupation with questions of what such aesthetic and social "frames" regularly work to incorporate and to exclude, in both their smaller and larger forms, both as frames within and as frames around more fluid movements of fear and desire.

3. On this tendency in historical writing, see Benjamin 253–64; on a similar tendency in recent critical writing, especially New Historicist criticism, see Porter, "Are We Being Historical Yet?"

both the older and the newer orders show up more clearly in their renego-
tiations than they normally would in their often invisible ideological consolidations. Furthermore, the three dramatic acts represent crises characteristic of these societies' different ways of organizing boundaries especially
of sexuality and gender, boundaries which are arguably these societies'
least negotiable demarcations. These crises are provoked by three
women—Nancy Mannigoe, Temple Drake, and Cecilia Farmer—representing three historical female cultural roles: that of the sorceress, the hysteric,
and the writer of "*écriture féminine,*" who manages (in the words of
Catherine Clément 9–10) to "pass over into the act, making the transition
to actions, moving to the inscription of the Symbolic in the Real, and hence
producing real structural transformations, [in] the only possible gesture
of departure from sorcery and hysteria."[4] Although Cecilia Farmer is a
figure in the historical introduction to the third act and makes no appearance on the dramatic stage, I hope to show the indirect influence of her
example on Nancy and Temple in their respective roles as sorceress and
hysteric, as both these two in the third act invite each other and are invited
(by Cecilia, as it were, in her inscription of her own name on the window
of the jail where she and her family live, and where Temple and Nancy
later appear on stage together in the final scene) to leave their more conventional dramatic roles as female spectacles before male judges, lawyers,
husbands, governors, jailors, readers, and writers, in order to claim
different roles as speaking and loving subjects, reentering and reconstitut-
ing a critically different, changed realm of active rearticulations of their
desires and loves in the midst of other neglected histories of desire, change,
and difference.[5]

     Act 1's prose introduction, called "The Courthouse (A Name for the
City)," traces a transition Faulkner's readers have seen before, during the
first leg of Thomas Sutpen's family's migration from the frontier society
of the West Virginia mountains toward the plantation society of Tidewater
Virginia: it is the difference between his drunken father's violent social
ejection with the accompaniment of a "harsh laughter" and his ejection
without such an accompaniment, between an ambivalently sympathetic

     4. For my analysis of the figures of the sorceress and hysteric, I am drawing on the
arguments especially of Clément; in the same volume, the third role is alluded to by Clément,
9–10, and elaborated by Cixous, as also in Cixous's essay "The Laugh of the Medusa."
     5. On the most literal biographical level, questions of feminine writing and speaking
are pertinent throughout to Faulkner's repeatedly unsuccessful attempts to encourage Joan
Williams to co-author *Requiem for a Nun* (see Blotner 1302–1463 passim and Williams' *The
Wintering* and "Twenty Will Not Come Again"), as also to one conception he had of *Requiem*
as a vehicle for his friend actress Ruth Ford.

identification with, and love of, the object or victim of such a social ejection or exclusion and an apparent lack of such identification. It is also the difference Lévi-Strauss describes in *Tristes tropiques* between "pre-historic" and "historic" societies' characteristic modes of dealing with the culturally anomalous: either anthropophagically, by "finding a place for anomaly, delinquency, deviancy — a place in the sun at the heart of cultural activity," or anthropoemically, by "vomiting the abnormal ones into protected spaces — hospitals, asylums, prisons."[6] Whether or not this prehistoric alternative ever exists in a pure form (I assume it does not), still, this second, anthropoemic, "historical" mode stands to be threatened by the remembrance of that harsh, ambivalent laughter it attempts institutionally and ideologically to suppress, or by the similarly uncanny outbreak and return of the sorceress, a figure once visible, feared, and revered ("at the heart of cultural activity"), but now normally excluded or imprisoned, not only physically, but culturally and psychologically (especially within the hysteric's unarticulated "remembrance of the sorceress").[7]

As in *The Hamlet*'s bracketing and prefiguration of racial questions that were to be addressed more directly only later in *Go Down, Moses,* so too here in the prose introduction to *Requiem for a Nun*'s first act, the soon to be central issues of sexuality and gender are at first most conspicuous in their absence. Faulkner tells the history of the suppression of the harsh, anxious laughter and fear that are prompted by the fragility and vulnerability of "man's ramshackle confederation against environment" (3), concentrating on the moment of this confederation's transformation by the phallogocentric erection of the courthouse and naming of the city. He stresses precisely the silencing of this society's doubts, debts, costs, and loves — those intersubjective traces of a pre-oedipal contiguity, kinship, and desire that when not silenced will be recoded and devalued as feminine, and naturalized as female.[8] The relative absence of women in this first prose introduction allows Faulkner to stress the historical determinants (rather than any naturalized "biological" determinants) of gender, as it also allows him to stress this first silencing (and silent gendering) in

6. Clément 8, paraphrasing Lévi-Strauss. This distinction might also recall that between the first and second orders of simulation analyzed by Baudrillard — the first (in stucco, for example) openly negating, at the same time that it imitates and competes with, nature as the quintessential cultural anomaly, and the second order (in concrete, for example) suppressing nature from the equation in order to reproduce (and mass-produce) only itself as extensively as possible. Cf. also in Lacanian, Deleuzean, and feminist readings and rewritings of psychoanalysis the important distinctions between pre-oedipal and oedipal configurations of desire.

7. Clément 35, cf. also Cixous, "Laugh of the Medusa."

8. Cf. Chodorow, especially for a more individualized psychological account of a process described here on the different scale of the developmental history of a town.

preparation for Nancy's all the more dramatic breaking of that silence (and dramatic violation of gender codes) in the first dramatic scene of the play. It is the silenced and "disappeared" objects of these phallogocentric codes who will most dramatically disturb (as speaking subjects) those codes' normal functions.

The transformation of a frontier Chickasaw trading post into a town, with its naming and the erection of its courthouse, is set in motion with another characteristically Faulknerian scene of social ejection and exclusion. This scene has not yet become this society's "primal scene," however, since Faulkner here highlights this and other events' unwieldy, stubborn resistance to this society's characteristic historiographic simplifications in terms of innocent horror, bitter irony, and heroic idealization. As Roland Barthes observes, such a primal scene "may exist only insofar as it is framed within the contour of the keyhole" (*Lover's Discourse* 132), whether on a psychohistorical or on a sociohistorical scale, and Faulkner dramatizes the clumsy imposition of that keyhole frame. As in the geography and psychology of a boy's journey from one society to another in *Absalom,* Faulkner will develop here in the history and historiography of a changing town those processes of simplification by which such an unspectacular scene of complex allegiances, fears, and considerable "chance and accident" (4) do become reduced to an originating event in a town's history—the process of making this and other makeshift "beginnings" into "origins" that could not have been otherwise.[9] In particular, he represents a process of silencing and gendering as that process itself becomes mystified and naturalized as a town's legendary and then historical "engendering" of itself, as if out of the silent (silenced) nothing that came before.

Drunken, brawling, and eventually "comatose," "an incidental band of civilian more-or-less militia" get themselves evicted from the settlement one night and unloaded in a nearby swamp, where they stumble upon— or, some say, are stumbled upon by—three or four professional bandits. One of these the militia sergeant recognizes as a deserter from the corps— or, some say, one of the bandits recognizes the sergeant as a deserter from their banditry (5). The divisions and contradictions of such reports emphasize the degree to which these social boundaries and exclusions are still here a matter of mutual and reversible vulnerability and sympathy. Thus militiamen and bandits all return to the settlement as captors and captives, "some said in confederation now seeking more drink, others said the captors brought their prizes back to the settlement in revenge for having been evicted from it" (6). But because it is learned that these captives have a price on their heads in a larger economy and legal system that is con-

9. Cf. Said 6, 316.

siderably more powerful and established than the settlement's own "peripheral economy,"[10] this potentially festive, playful reversal and revenge does effectively raise the stakes, drawing this peripheral economy (of siblings or orphans, as it were) more securely under the influence of the larger (parental, adult) economy, and leading to an imprisonment and breakout that leave behind, "like a smell, an odor, a kind of gargantuan and bizarre playfulness at once humorous and terrifying, as if the settlement had fallen, blundered, into the notice or range of an idle and whimsical giant" (5). The morning-after scene of the breakout, the prison minus its dismantled and removed fourth wall, becomes an "outdoor stage setting" (14) for this (hypostatized, primal) shading of (polymorphous) humor into (rebuked, castrated) terror, pre-oedipal into oedipal, prehistorical into historical, anthropophagic into anthropoemic postures toward the anomalous.

With such explicitly metatheatrical allusions first to the (indoor) "stage" to which this prose history serves as oblique introduction, and then also to the common modern conception of the stage as a room with its fourth wall removed, Faulkner insists on a certain critical reflection on his peculiar choice and use in *Requiem* of a dramatic form, even if (or perhaps especially if) its three long prologues make this a dramatic work in some ways impossible to stage. In another context, A. C. Bradley has suggested that *King Lear* is variously "too huge for the stage," but that its deficiencies as drama may call attention to its other appeals not to the eye and the other senses but to a rarer, more peculiarly poetic imagination (247, 243–79). *Requiem* demands similarly critical reflections on the "fourth-wall illusionism" and related habits of representation on the naturalistic modern stage. "The big modern theater" (as characterized by Eric Bentley) conceals a contradiction, in that it usually "begins by separating audience from actor by the proscenium arch and then proceeds to try to cancel the distance thus established by fourth-wall illusionism"; that is, it attempts to give the audience the illusion that they themselves constitute and thus close off that missing fourth wall (which otherwise makes this a stage), as if thereby to form and recomplete not a stage at all but a real room, since it is rare anyway to see all four walls of a room at once (304, 139). *Requiem*'s self-consciousness about this "fourth-wall illusionism" would thus resemble various strategies of Brecht's "Epic Theater" designed to prevent this same cancellation of a potentially critical, imaginative distance between realistic scenes of theater (as also of history) and modern audiences who are all too ready to observe and reify those scenes uncritically as simply objective and real, and not as artistic, psychological,

10. See Wallerstein.

social, political, and historical constructions; Faulkner is attempting here
to sketch in a similarly self-critical stage, giving a psychological, social,
and historical dimension both to the opening of that theatrical space and
to subsequent attempts to close that opening over again.[11]

By figuring the stage as the site of a frightening jailbreak, the site,
that is, of a frightening breach in the state's incipient power to contain
(and recontain) anomalous social elements, *Requiem* effectively reopens
a marginal space in the public discourse—also a transitional time in the
historical discourse, and the psychic space of a "boundary state" in the
psychological discourse—for an analytic reconsideration not only of
various dominant responses to the terror of that early breach in the infant
state's power, but also for an analysis of underrepresented, underestimated
alternatives to the dominant paths of social, historical, and psychological
response.

In this respect Faulkner's analytic, revisionary returns in *Requiem* to
the beginning "stages" of historical civilization (and of "civilized" codes
of gender and sexuality) strongly resemble Julia Kristeva's own more recent
analytic return, in *Tales of Love,* to the psychohistorical site and disposition of primary narcissism, in order to reconsider there, as in her earlier
Powers of Horror, the infant's primary repression or ab-jection of the
mother and the attendant oedipal investment of the abjected maternal with
its psychological and historical "powers of horror" (as also in *Absalom*'s
attention to persistent structures of innocent horror and that horror's ironic
denial).[12] But Kristeva returns in *Tales of Love* to the scene of primary

11. As Bentley describes the Epic Theater, "Brecht has asked that the fact of disguise,
the dual nature of performance—half actor, half role—be always perceptible. The actor stands
back from the role and looks at it; the audience stands back from the actor and looks at
him; the spectator smokes a cigarette and cannot merge with his neighbor; the stage is not
wholly concealed by another world created by the designer, it is not darkened to suggest
dream and phantasma" (or unobstructed, unchallenged, unreflective "fourth-wall
illusionism"—366). While Faulkner's use of the dramatic stage and of the image of such a
stage for the site of the state's more or less self-conscious emergence out of the wilderness
may be usefully described by analogy with Brecht's use of shock techniques and
Verfremdungseffekt, Faulkner does not quite share Brecht's confidence in the rational critique
and demystification of social relations to be achieved by means of such estrangements. The
critique Faulkner is working out here relies instead on tracing and encouraging potentiali-
ties for resistance in various incompletely colonized, nonsynchronous, intersubjective elements
in this society—a society which extends out into an audience which is estranged but also
uneasily implicated.

12. Cf. Kristeva, *Tales of Love:* "without the maternal 'diversion' toward a Third Party,
the bodily exchange is abjection or devouring; the eventual schizophrene, whether phobic
or borderline, will keep its hot-iron brand against which his only recourse will be hatred.
Any borderline person ends up finding a mother who is 'loving' for her own sake, but he
cannot accept her as loving himself, for she did not love any *other* one" (34).

narcissism in order, too, to analyze and reconsider other, often thus thwarted or diverted possibilities (alternate scripts, subtexts, minor genres, tales) of love, possibilities of love based on a primary identification not with the oedipal father, nor with the father's Phallus, his Name, or the Order of the Symbolic, but with the mother's "*desire for* the Phallus" as an unelaborated Third Party, an imaginary father as "simple virtuality, a potential presence, a form to be cathected," "a coagulation of the mother and her desire," without which "the child and the mother do not yet constitute two" (40–41, my emphasis). In Faulkner's own attempt to reopen this "psychic space" prerequisite to the capacity for love, he also takes both of the two analytic tacks suggested by Kristeva: first, "by starting from Oedipal dramas and their failures — backwards, in other words — one will be able to detect the particulars of primary identification"; but also by attending to "boundary states," including especially "transference love," which will "lead us there directly, locating the Oedipal conflict as ulterior or secondary" (47–48). At the same time as Faulkner surrounds the stage with his own narrative reconstructions of past historical, oedipal failures, he also attempts to forgo that narrative voice to stage Nancy's, Cecilia's, and Temple's dramatic transferences, reinscriptions, and reelaborations of their own desires and loves.

It is precisely to frame and even to curtain off the scene of this frightening social wound that the townspeople hurriedly replace the "ancient monster iron padlock" (3) that has failed them with a wall that would also form part of a lean-to depository for the new town of Jefferson's written records. This first courthouse imposes a double thickness of insulation against such wounds, as it were, backing up a physical violence that tends to provoke emotional reversals and dangerous revenge, with a *written* system of laws and dispossessions designed to forbid, contain, or defuse any such physical or emotional reversals or revenge. Already, before this "transubstantiation into the Yoknapatawpha courthouse," the old lock that finally fails to contain their prisoners has undergone several previous transvaluations tending in this direction from physical force to written law (and its enforcement in institutions and unwritten ideology): it has been "fifteen pounds of useless iron," then a locally symbolic "landmark in the bar of a wilderness ordinary," then it was (tenuously) attached to the leather U.S. mail pouch, though still "not [as] a symbol of security: it was a gesture of salutation [to Washington], of free men to free men, . . . of respect without servility, allegiance without abasement" (8–11). But when the peripheral, frontier settlement does try to use the lock to secure its own prisoners for the sake of their price in that larger U.S. legal economy (and to secure them from certain others whom they might recognize and implicate before those same tribunals — 12), the settlers learn of a frightening (castrating), then heart-hardening difference in scale and power between that larger economy and their own. The morning after the breakout they search for their missing lock around their little settlement's boundaries, "knowing better" now than to expect success. Faulkner turns his characteristically critical attention to the movement from frightened disillusionment into ironic assumptions of unillusion: they search for the lock

> knowing better, knowing that there was no limit to the fantastic and the terrifying and the bizarre, of which the men were capable who already, just to escape from a log jail, had quietly removed one entire wall and stacked it in neat piecemeal at the roadside, and that they nor old Alec neither would ever see his lock again. (16)

Whether or not these bandits' capabilities are as limitless and gargantuan as they seem in the strange morning light of these settlers' surprise, this ancient lock has proven to be no match for men already much more accustomed to dealing with that larger economy of punishments and rewards.

The obvious match for, and (they hope) reassuring limit to, this frightening aspect of the settlement's loss of their "fifteen pounds of useless iron" is the "incalculable weight of federality" that they soon recognize in the "bland, reasonable and impersonal" voice of the U.S. mail rider ("for that moment at least, he was the United States") as he recites the federal laws according to which the lock, by its very attachment to the property of the United States Government, had become either part of that federal property (its theft or loss punishable by law) or a defacement of that federal property (also punishable by law — 20–21). It begins to look as if the settlers, having first attached the lock to the mail pouch, then lost the lock securing the jail, might find themselves even more definitely on the wrong side of this law and of this impersonal man, who, as he recites the relevant laws, "looked at no one. He wasn't even speaking to anyone," this man whom they realize they have known for three years now but have not known after all, "childless and bachelor, incorrigibly kinless and tieless," about whom they decide "everybody knows what's wrong with him. It's ethics. He's a damned moralist" (21–23, 25, 23). To be on the wrong or the right side of such monologic, desexualized impersonality seems a matter of either faceless, blandly punishable opposition, or an equally faceless identification: given these alternatives, they become a town and offer to name their town after him — not after him personally (that would be immoral, since "he was the United States") but in parallel (perhaps sidelong), patriotic, oedipal identification with the regional and also national forefather (Thomas Jefferson) for whom the rider was also named. (The rider notes briefly and intriguingly in passing that he received this name from his mother, but I will return to consider this mother shortly.)[13]

This offer should not be mistaken for a mere ploy to placate the rider: it is overdetermined by the settlers' eagerness not just to escape legal or financial punishment themselves, but also and perhaps especially to escape their newly frightening marginality, to heal the scene of their social wound, to fill this newfound lack, as if with the phallic shape, sound, and systematic power of a courthouse and a (patronymic, official) name: "the courthouse which it had taken them almost thirty years not only to realize that they didn't have, but to discover that they hadn't even needed, missed, lacked; and which, before they had owned it six months, they discovered was nowhere near enough" (26). The force of this eagerness becomes increasingly evident as they labor to build their courthouse, all but Ratcliffe (and perhaps the silently observing Chickasaws) becoming more and more set on denying the motivations and costs of all their labors of civilization.

For all the same reasons that they are willing to pay those costs to cover their lack, they are unwilling to acknowledge any lack that would explain their wanting to pay the cost of covering it. Shaping their needs and desires in the images of the larger culture's signifying (mediating, simplifying, phallogocentric) order of the Symbolic, they simultaneously negate (and alienate) their proper names and faces and the tenuously cooperative nature of their several fears and desires:[14]

> Because somewhere between the dark and the dawn of the first and
> the second day [of their work on the courthouse], something had
> happened to them—the men who had spent that first long hot endless
> July day sweating and raging about the wrecked jail . . . —the same
> men met at the project before sunrise on the next day which was
> already promising to be hot and endless too, but with the rage and
> the fury absent now, quiet, not grave so much as sobered, a little
> amazed, diffident, blinking a little perhaps, looking a little aside from
> one another, a little unfamiliar even to one another in the new
> jonquil-colored light. . . . (27–28)

In this society's version of its as yet ungendered beginnings in castration's "bleeding wound," they look around at their "meagre huddle of crude

---

13. It is perhaps worth noting here, however, the difference between Lacan's account of an oedipal use of (at least) or identification with (at most) the Name of the Father, and, on the other hand, Kristeva's account of a pre-oedipal identification with the mother's *desire for* the father's Phallus or Name (or here, as it were, an identification with the mother's naming of, or speaking of, the father).

14. Cf. MacCannell 86.

cabins" in the "tiny clearing clawed punily . . . into the loin, the groin, the secret parts" of the wilderness, "until at last one spoke for all," speaking in negation of their several marginalities and secret differences, fears, and desires, and at the same time in impersonal identification with their historical future and their name in the larger social orderings and hierarchical fortifications of the Symbolic: " 'By God. Jefferson.' 'Jefferson, Mississippi,' a second added. 'Jefferson, Yoknapatawpha County, Mississippi,' a third corrected; who, which one, didn't matter this time either" (28).

Even this first lean-to courthouse is still too close to what they want to negate, so they hurry to finish it not "in order to own, possess it sooner, but to be able to obliterate, efface, it the sooner, as if they had also known" that morning "that it would not even be a pattern and could not even be called practice" for the larger courthouse they would soon build to replace it (29). This process of nominative, metaphorical, and physical substitution and negation unfolds further in their historical vision (historically efficacious vision) of theirs as "a white man's land; that was its fate, or not even fate but destiny, its high destiny in the roster of the earth" (35), a vision of their historical destiny in which the wilderness, with its wild animals and "wild men" (along with the old white men who would recognize and regret the passing of these "wild men") would all be "obsolescent" obstructions cast silently out of the way of Progress (the women are unmentioned). Calling this their high destiny, they again deny its violence and costs to others as well as themselves, just as they also attempt to deny the abstraction and reduction to common denominators (or integers) that are necessary in this as in any act of addition, summary, or mediation, seeing the new courthouse only as

> bigger than any because it was the sum of all and, being the sum of all, must raise all their hopes and aspirations level with its own aspirant and soaring cupola, so that, sweating and tireless and unflagging, they would look about at one another a little shyly, a little amazed, with something like humility too, as if they were realising, or were for a moment at least capable of believing, that men, all men, including themselves, were a little better, purer maybe even, than they had thought, expected, or even needed to be. (37)

Their mystification of this gap between what they had thought of themselves before and what they are capable of believing now effectively obscures the cost and force of their newly crystallized desire to identify themselves with this higher, bigger, better purity, and to deny their now rather humiliating former ignorance of any such thought, expectation, or need. If, however, that former state was indeed a state of ignorance of (or rather indifference to) these particular thoughts and needs, it also represented an awareness of other, pre-oedipal (or extra-oedipal) contiguities, interdependencies, vulnerabilities, differences, and intersubjective fears and desires, all of which their new (phallogocentric, oedipal) belief in their social purity and historical destiny itself seeks to ignore.

Besides the almost irreducibly unwieldy bulk of psychological and material "chance and accident" (4), almost the only other voice resisting this cultural act of (ideological) forgetting is the slightly more articulate voice of Ratcliffe, the post trader who is the one already most accustomed to negotiating the various gaps and discrepancies between the U.S. government (as represented in the white man's economy of money and credit) and the people most obviously dispossessed by that government and economy, the Chickasaws with whom he trades. The text here glances ahead in Yoknapatawpha's history (and back in Faulkner's career) to this Ratcliffe's great-grandson, V. K. Ratliff, who in *The Hamlet* is the one most used to trading with another, differently dispossessed group, that of rural women: he will trade with them in sewing machines and other uneasily priced odds and ends of new and used goods, tools, news, messages, gossip, tales, and particularly in the odds and ends of humor, this the exemplary trade in which such incommensurabilities are rather foregrounded than denied or disguised as fair profit. It is also noted here in *Requiem* that the difference in Ratcliffe's and his great-grandson Ratliff's spellings of the patronymic family name is due to two intervening generations' illiterate, oral interference in, or material resistance to, this new written economy's pure transmission of their name, a written transmission that is in this case unable wholly to substitute for and to deny the genealogy of those different, speaking subjects whom it attempts to name. Whereas the others involved in founding the town seem determined to think that both courthouses cost "nothing but the labor and—the second year now—most of that was slave" (35), and that the (more significant) rest of that labor was willing labor (labor "a little amazed" but "tireless and unflagging"), still, they cannot help noticing something "esoteric, eccentric, in Ratcliffe's manner, attitude," a note of resistance "like a single chip, infinitesimal, on an otherwise unbroken flood or tide, a single body or substance, alien and unreconciled, a single thin almost unheard voice crying thinly out of the roar of a mob: 'Wait, look here, listen—'" (27).

Ratcliffe speaks thus haltingly not as a primitive or primitivist against these new Symbolic orders of language, history, and civilization, but as one who has himself already been involved in negotiating these translations and transitions. He speaks therefore as one who is suspicious of tendencies around him to deny these accelerated historical changes' costs and motivations, knowing perhaps that these costs and motivations are neither inevitable nor universally the same, but significantly different depending on the forms and directions these various changes take.[15] In Lacanian terms, the Symbolic may well serve as medium for the communication of desire, but not without certain losses in the translation of desires into demands (and gifts), losses which may be more or less mystified or candidly and critically (even if never adequately) addressed as costs incurred in the articulation of desire.[16]

What especially and persistently bothers Ratcliffe is that the others willingly pay Alec Holston fifteen dollars for the lost lock and refuse to accept or even consider the chance to charge the loss to Uncle Sam (who stands to gain most, as it were, from their capitulation to His economy):

> It's like Old Moster and the rest of them up there that run the luck, would look down at us and say, Well, well, it look like them durn peckerwoods down there dont want them fifteen dollars we was going to give them free-gratis-for-nothing. So maybe they dont want nothing from us. So maybe we better do like they seem to want, and let them sweat and swivet and scrabble through the best they can by themselves. (38)

Ratcliffe invokes Old Moster not as a single higher guarantor of the (medieval, early American) "due price" ("Regulation" 442), but as only one in a pantheon of other, unspecified forces controlling "the luck" from somewhere beyond the purview of their new economy. He objects to the idea that the courthouse would be considered a pure gain, measured only by this one economy's standard of value, without any sense of their also quite possibly needing an unaccountable luck; he objects to this idea that this trade might be unlike all other trades in which there are incommensurable gains and losses both, some noticed now, some later, one person's considerable loss often another's insignificant gain (or vice versa), so that a cost must be acknowledged and a value placed on the very act (on every act) of symbolic exchange. This is why Ratcliffe regrets the loss of the fifteen dollars' lagniappe which would have acknowledged and affirmed some of these differences, desires, and incommensurabilities that are being sacrificed for the sake of this exchange. Thus their refusing the money

15. Here Ratcliffe's eccentric voice might be compared to Faulkner's voice among those of other modernists less socially and historically familiar with and thus in many instances less critical of the ironic mode that promised a (falsely) alternative, new keynote, or general equivalent, on which to found the cultural Symbolic of "cosmopolitan" (Western) literary modernism.

16. On the Lacanian implications of symbolic exchange and gifts I am generally indebted to Wilden and MacCannell.

does "no man any good, neither restoration to the ravaged nor emolument to the ravager, leaving in fact the whole race of man, as long as it endured, forever and irrevocably fifteen dollars deficit, fifteen dollars in the red" (32). It is a loss to all parties involved, and a gain only to the exchange system itself, mystified as having nothing whatever to do with its different traders' lucks, fears, or desires.

One other, "almost unheard," potentially critical voice in the mob, or chip on the flood, of this town's phallogocentric history is the before-mentioned statement and almost simultaneous denial by the mail rider Thomas Jefferson Pettigrew that his (and the town's) patriotic name conceals his mother's awareness of certain limits to the nation's and its heroes' destiny and security, a usually unacknowledged vulnerability and "luck" conditioning her (then wholly dependent) infant manchild's eventual success: " 'My ma named me for him, so I would have some of his luck.' 'Luck?' Peabody said. Pettigrew didn't smile. 'That's right. She didn't mean luck. She never had any schooling. She didn't know the word she wanted to say' " (25). It is precisely to deny their own vulnerability to and dependence on this maternal "luck" that the town is so willingly "school-ing" and civilizing itself in the name of its forefather. And it was perhaps to remember the mutual, if different, loves involved in this same "lucky" dependency on this society's denied mother culture that the "motherless son" of one of the settlement's three founders has "married one of Issetibeha's granddaughters and in the thirties emigrated to Oklahoma with his wife's dispossessed people" (7).

Such voices in the mob and chips on the flood of the town's history are extremely few, and liable to inattention, sentimentalization, neutralization, or denial, but they do maintain openings for difference and resistance: Cecilia Farmer's signature will be referred to and developed later in the historical narrative as another chip on another phase of this historical flood, and in the third dramatic act the jailor's kindnesses toward Temple and Nancy, despite his official distances and prejudices, are compared to the actions of that "member of the mob who holds up the whole [lynching] ceremony for seconds or even minutes while he dislodges a family of bugs or lizards from the log he is about to put on the fire" (230). In this case this pre-oedipal connectedness of mutual vulnerability, fear, and desire, although it is here (as often in Faulkner) grotesquely, almost blindingly displaced in the midst of its most murderously violent denial, does survive across and athwart the independent subject's boundaries as determined by the dominant economy.

The possibilities for such unreconciled remainders and resistances to the economy of this historical society are exemplified at the close of the first prologue by a figure that also serves to prepare for Nancy's dramatic breaking of the official courtroom silence (by which her life is to be exchanged for that of Temple's child, as if to equate and cancel the different meanings of both their deaths). The sparrows and pigeons in the courthouse cupola are quiet only

> until the clock strikes again which even after a hundred years, they still seem unable to get used to, bursting in one swirling explosion out of the belfry as though, the hour, instead of merely adding one puny infinitesimal more to the long weary increment since Genesis, had shattered the virgin pristine air with the first loud ding-dong of time and doom. (42)

The pretemporal and apocalyptic religious references here are as appropriate to this stage of their history as was Ratcliffe's earlier invocation of Old Moster: having denied any limitations or oversights in their current historiography (and chronology), which they regard as an economy sufficient in itself to measure and account for time, change, difference, and exchange, they must tend to see any unreconciled, uncounted remainder either as virgin territory (to be idealized or claimed as history's own pretemporal Other) or as an apocalyptic, single end of history itself (as that history has come to be exclusively thought).[17] But instead, the curtain is about to rise neither on this white male history's preconceived, pristine virgin origin nor on its apocalyptic Babylonian whore, but on two of its own dishonored and dispossessed mothers who have not, however, been altogether silenced, with Nancy Mannigoe in the classic female role of sorceress and Temple Drake Stevens in the more modern female role of hysteric.

As the curtain does rise after such a lengthy and historically differentiated prologue to the dramatic action, so Faulkner's representation of this society's continuing historical tensions shifts from a relatively diachronic narrative to the more synchronic possibilities of drama. What follows is a representation not of another clumsy and incomplete social change but of several unevenly developed elements coexisting in the same society and time: social elements existing neither independently nor within a stable hierarchy or superstructure but in critical, potentially transforming relations to one another. One effect of the prologue's diachronic narrative is to have given an unusually insistent historical depth to the courtroom scene revealed here as the curtain rises: this is the very same courthouse that

17. Cf. Cochran xviii, on the teleological element common to Hegelian and Christian historiography.

began as the reconstructed fourth wall and insulating bandage on the deconstructed jail; it is the now familiar site of this society's old bleeding wound and thus the physical site of its engendering and birth out of the "secret parts" of the wilderness. That old bleeding wound has now been reopened and made raw again in another time.

Faulkner's descriptions of the set for scene 1 explain a "symbolism which will be clearer when act 2 opens—the symbolism of the elevated tribunal of justice of which this, a county court, is only the intermediate, not the highest, stage" (43). Well before act 2, however, the social symbolism of this courtroom's intermediate elevation becomes as important to this first scene's characters as to its theater audience and readers: this exemplary institution of this society's "historical" order of written records, impartial and impersonal laws, and decorous silencing and banishment of the anomalous is here strategically confronted and disturbed by one such anomaly in Nancy Mannigoe, the illiterate black "tramp" and now convicted murderer of Temple Stevens' child. She appears as that child's black nurse who has thus betrayed the typical role and trust assigned to her ideologically and economically by her race and gender: to care for people in this predominantly white society in their most vulnerable and dependent stage of life (just as in her previous role as black "tramp" she was expected to cater to white men in their most socially vulnerable moments of sexuality). Before her silencing and banishment by the court to jail and eventually to her death by hanging, she will stand alone and speak as if from another, "pre-historical" order, speaking up in the courtroom from the prisoner's dock, which momentarily serves as her now ritualized, temporary, residual (sorceress's) "place in the sun at the heart of cultural activity" (Clément 8). As in Carlo Ginzburg's study of the heresy trials of the sixteenth-century Italian miller known as Menocchio, here too the prisoner's dock is a rare point of entry for the voice of a marginalized, largely oral, popular culture otherwise lost to "historical" record, a voice not just resisting silence but dramatizing the "reciprocal influence of lower class and dominant culture" (Ginzburg xi–xxvi, 126, xix). Nancy speaks in a way that stresses for all present this court's still "intermediate" status, its invocation of higher authorities only the better to extricate and elevate itself from the sexual and infantile vulnerabilities and violence that Nancy (in her corresponding role as sorceress and betraying, murderous nurse) disturbingly enacts and represents. When the judge attempts implicitly to add God's authority to that of the court as he sentences her to death ("And may God have mercy on your soul"), she dramatizes again how such deferrals to higher authorities both insulate those present and also show their *need* to insulate themselves from a more compromising understanding of, involvement in, perhaps complicity in, the apparent anomaly of her crime.

Instead of silently accepting this institution's power to elevate itself at her expense by opposing its law (as if absolutely, with God's blessings) to her crime, she responds to her sentencing, "(quite loud in the silence, to no one, quite calm, not moving) Yes, Lord" (45). That is, she reminds her audiences of the mystified higher authority to which she can appeal as well as they, by reason of her uncertain authority for what she has done, like their uncertain authority for what they are going to do to her. In the tradition of black spirituals that signified upon an accommodationist white Southern religious tradition,[18] her apostrophe here recalls the similar motivations of this society's own attempts earlier and continuingly to extricate itself from its own "pre-historic," violent circumstances by urgently self-important invocations and impersonations of powerful authorities still hazily distant from its own intermediate codifications of that authority. If such a higher authority is invoked and translated into social codes all the more conveniently for the mystified inscrutability of its power, then the sorceress can invoke her own version of that inscrutable power, effectively making both invocations seem here to be scandalously and unpredictably political and adversarial. She can turn those founding strategies of the dominant culture against the dominant culture, and at the same time adapt them to her own different purposes, although she does so only at the risk of having those purposes go largely misunderstood and usually discounted as insignificant. The court cannot help but hear this outlawed voice disruptively talking back, both preserving its residual place in which to speak and pressing the strategically critical advantage of that residual status; however, the court does its uneasy best to hear in that voice only illicit defiance, the court's own binary opposite, to which it can only respond with its own (now more uneasily) sanctioned violence. This opening scene of ritual judgment having been turned into a scene of contending, imperfectly intermediate judgments that have thereby reopened an old social wound by testing the social bandage, "the curtain starts hurriedly and jerkily down as if the judge, the officers, the court itself were jerking frantically at it to hide this disgraceful business" (45). There is the sound only of an inarticulate woman's voice, rebuked by the bailiff's call for order, then the curtain descends on a moment of darkness, and "then the curtain rises smoothly and normally on" (45). It rises to reveal a scene in a modern living room: the scene of still another set of historical strategies for articulating and rebuking a woman's voice.

The courtroom, after all, as emphasized by this hasty shift of scenes,

18. See Genovese 151–284, and Chapter 3, above.

has become ("in America, the South, between the two great wars" — 46) only the designated strong arm of an otherwise more smoothly organized, more effectively insulated order of modernity. The courtroom has become in the modern world one relatively violent, vulnerable avatar of a now largely displaced "historical" order, displaced along with that other, still older, "pre-historical" order of inscrutable, mystified, but undeniable violence and sorcery that the "historical" system of written laws endeavors both to enlist for its own authority and to suppress and control as criminality and irrational subversion. Both these older orders — "historical" and "pre-historical" — have come to coexist (along with certain latent possibilities of postmodernity) in the uneasy midst of an apparently dominant order of modernity, which is represented less aptly by the courtroom of act 1's first scene than by the "smart, modern, up-to-date" living room of scene 2 (46).

Faulkner signals this scene's modernity especially in terms of money, tragedy, and hysteria. The extensive, powerful modern economies of value, signification, and behavior in which Temple and Gowan Stevens are accustomed to circulate have been disturbed (both in the preceding courtroom scene and in the infanticide which that courtroom scene attempts to contain) by something for which those modern economies apparently offer no adequate means of accounting — and which they offer no means of discounting either, unless by Temple's air and voice, described as "brittle and tense, yet controlled," and full of "repressed, controlled hysteria" (46, 47).[19] Gowan is described as himself "almost a type" of secure placement in these economies by family, colleges, clubs, except that for him these economies' center has not altogether held: he like others of his type has been accustomed to

> performing acceptably jobs they themselves did not ask for, usually concerned with money: cotton futures, or stocks, or bonds. But this

19. Cf. Kristeva on the glib, smooth, almost unbreakable surface of the modern tendency to hysteria: "Resistant to the notion of castration, a woman perhaps accepts it only when confronted with a dying body (her child's in the worst of cases). Moreover, the dramas of individuation demand of her such a violent rejection of the mother, and by the mother, that in the hatred of the loved object a woman immediately finds herself in a known and intolerable country. What analysands are henceforth suffering from is *the abolition of psychic space.* Narcissus in want of light as much as of a spring allowing him to capture his true image, Narcissus drowning in a cascade of false images (from social roles to the *media*), hence deprived of substance or place: these contemporary characters are witnesses to our being unable today to elaborate primary narcissism" (*Tales* 373–74). Faulkner's use of the stage in *Requiem* is one attempt to open up for Nancy, Cecilia, Temple, even for Gowan, in the midst of this modern hysteria, an apparently closed-off, drowned-out, critically reflective "psychic space" that would make it possible to articulate change, difference, and love.

face is a little different, a little more than that. Something has
happened to it—tragedy—something, against which it has had no
warning, and to cope with which (as it discovered) no equipment, yet
which it has accepted and is trying, really and sincerely and selflessly
(perhaps for the first time in its life) to do its best with according to
its code. (47)

By the end of the scene this sincere effort according to Gowan's code seems
to have failed, collapsing into his own barely controlled, "crazy" laughter,
bordering "just on hysteria" (61, 60). Something tragic has happened,
without here any higher realm of order, authority, or vision either to give
that tragedy meaning or to be confirmed in spite of the tragedy, but as
a characteristic inhabitant of modernity Gowan still misses some such
higher or deeper realm, and the absence of that realm still shapes the
apparent deficiency of his code. In contrast to the "historical" order dramatized in the preceding scene, these modern economies are characterized
by their inability even formally to account for or to cope with an authority
or threat (even mystified as an inscrutable authority or outlawed threat)
coming apparently from beyond their borders or from outside their systems
of value and exchange. Something has shaken the web, but there is absolutely no accounting for it: beyond these borders and outside these systems
seems to lie only an unrepresentable, unthinkable madness or a blankly
incomprehensible death, realms signaled in these economies only in the
frustrated intensities of a self-conscious, self-protective irony or, here,
especially by a controlled hysteria. Perhaps articulate, perhaps significant,
but unmeaning, unconnecting, frantic movements of desire move through
an extensive but shallow and confining closed circuit.

Temple refuses to cry when she returns home after the trial, though
Gowan's uncle Gavin Stevens expects her, even prompts her to cry with
the offer of his handkerchief: she rejects this one expected feminine expression of grief, presumably aware of its extreme inadequacy except as designated cultural catharsis, and fearful of thereby losing control of her own
more particularly potent, unarticulated hysteria. She speaks instead, more
or less rapidly, tensely, harshly, speaking of her vindication and triumph
in the legal system, of possible threats and bribes by Stevens as Nancy's
lawyer, of "some excuse" she assumes Nancy has for what she did, but
her speech becomes most frustratedly intense in the vicinity of what she
will not discuss with Stevens: any involvement, understanding, or complicity of hers in what has happened. Her controlled hysteria, the systematic
distractedness of her speech, fails her only at the thought that Nancy might
have somehow successfully resisted (at whatever cost) this economy of
threats and bribes, might not have betrayed to Stevens and the law what-

ever relationships she had with Temple. Temple stops at this thought "in a sort of amazement, despair" (55), unable to believe or understand why Nancy and herself perhaps after all "dont stink" in the way she has come to think that every human being does, thinking that everyone has his or her price in this economy: more specifically, she is unable to understand "what reason they would have for not stinking" (56, 57), so desperately and determinedly has she internalized this economy in the place of loves and griefs she cannot yet address. But only to think this anachronistic possibility of opposition and resistance is to begin to improve on her controlled hysteria.

Both she and Gowan attempt the verbal violence of calling Nancy a "nigger dope-fiend" and "dope-fiend nigger whore" (50, 53), but that third-person, verbal violence feels as unsatisfying to them as the official violence and revenge granted them by the court, as Gowan admits: "I wish to God that what I wanted was only revenge. An eye for an eye—were ever words emptier? Only, you have got to have lost the eye to know it" (59). Their verbal and legal violence buys them a power over Nancy that feels empty, largely leaving aside as it does their proven, felt vulnerability to her verbal, legal, and physical violence against them, however powerfully forbidden, repaid, or denied in their more "historical" and "modern" economies. Economies based on general equivalents such as money, the law, the name of a city, aphorisms, or even on much more flexible and subtle (more characteristically modern) mediations such as a common ideology or system of language, facilitate social exchange only at a certain cost; there are certain losses and gains in each translation which may be more or less candidly renegotiated, accepted, denied, or mystified.

Gowan and Gavin discuss in economic terms an exchange Gowan has made by which he has thought to purchase "immunity" from responsibility for Temple's loss of her chastity in the events of *Sanctuary* eight years before: he has since married her and abstained from drink, as if to cancel her dishonor and his own, but now this bargain seems as cheaply irrelevant to his grief over the loss of their child as it is also irrelevant to his admission that Temple was not just "kidnapped into a Memphis whorehouse" because of his own failure as her drunken gentleman escort, but actually in some yet unexplained sense participated in her abduction and "loved it" there, as she has apparently not "loved it" with Gowan (62–63). Gavin compares Gowan's abstinence as a response to the loss of his "man's self-respect in the chastity of his wife," along with the legal demand that Nancy pay with her life for the child's death, to a suicide reminiscent of Quentin's, killing oneself in order to "stop having to be forever unable to forget: nothing; to plunge into nothing and sink and drown forever and forever" (64). That is, this economy, again, with an apparently hysterical irrelevance, unsuccessfully, blindly holds at bay psychic material which it fears simply cannot be thought, notably the idea that the chastity which for him is her supremely necessary value may be of a lesser concern to her than some independent feminine sexuality and subjectivity and even love that he cannot or will not understand.

The exceptional value of a woman (as also of children) in Gowan's modern economy, if we compare that economy with that of language as an exchange of words, depends at once on this potentially independent feminine subjectivity and voice and at the same time on the control of that potentially independent voice: as Clément explains, again with reference to Lévi-Strauss, while the economy of language "entropies," or "perfects itself to the detriment of the information that it carries and progressively separates itself from the wealth of the original meaning," "the exchange of women [and children], on the other hand" (as the other "axis of exchange that makes men's cultural law"), "has kept its original value [or at least a residual, resistant value], for women are both sign and value, sign and producer of sign. . . . [since] it happens that women talk, that they step out of their function as sign" (28). What for Gowan has seemed the site of her kidnapping and imprisonment seems now perhaps more ambiguous, perhaps no more confining for her than the apparently empty terms of their subsequent, largely compensatory marriage in a more perfectly entropied economy. Like Nancy's voice in the courtroom, this unseemly realm of criminality and illicit sexuality hints at possibilities of other axes of exchange, implying not just negative, anachronistic values, but alternative ones; it hints, that is, at possibilities of inversion and also transvaluation of values that have been largely and silently associated with the feminine.

The third and last scene of this first act completes the articulation between Faulkner's nonsynchronous historical explorations and Temple's more specific situation as a modern hysteric about to undergo an extended analysis and transference onstage. It is to be an analysis waged as a struggle and negotiation between herself and her predominantly masculine spectators, and as an attempt to explore and articulate her own implication in, and potential empowerment from, the disruptive act and voice of her feminine forebear, the sorceress as embodied in Nancy. When Temple alludes to the "philosophers and other gynecologists" who already pretend to know what women will do, and whose knowledge is readily codified and disseminated even in aphorisms (67), she signals her oppressive awareness of the range and depth of predominantly masculine spectators, authorities, and more or less organized bodies of knowledge arrayed against the chances of her taking any actively alternative role in her own analysis. This amounts also to an incipient awareness of the odds against

a feminist reading of her character, inasmuch as "hysteria is feminism lack-
ing a social network in the outer world," as Dianne Hunter has suggested,
and inasmuch as hysteria, "as a visible mode of expression, . . . seems
to invite spectacular treatment" (113, 113n). This scene, however, sets out
not only the odds against her rewriting her own analysis in the unavoidable (but contradictory, overextended, nonsynchronous, and therefore
adaptable) terms and contexts of alien assumptions and traditions; it suggests as well her determination to confront and to risk struggling against
those odds for the sake of articulating her own peculiarly different purposes
and perspectives and loves in (a less spectacular) language and in her changing relationships with certain other people, especially Nancy and the surviving child they have raised between them.[20] At the same time, this scene
also outlines the odds against (as well as for) Temple's and Nancy's coming

20. This scene makes almost no mention of Gowan, and I take Temple's marriage with
Gowan as rather a secondary consideration in her motivation to undergo the trials of her
"analysis" in the course of this play. The emotional achievement of her analysis is much
less the salvaging of her marriage with Gowan than her mourning of her daughter and her
reunion with Nancy and her surviving child, even though a move in Gowan's direction is
made in the last lines and gestures of the play. I am tempted to read this last-minute feint
toward a more conventionally romantic, heterosexual ending in much the same skeptical
spirit as Shirley Nelson Garner reads the ending of Woolf's *Night and Day,* that is, as a
betrayal of the emotional center of the work in the two women characters' developing relationship with each other. Compare also Janet Adelman's " 'This Is and Is Not Cressid': The
Characterization of Cressida," which would suggest that Temple is not being simplified or
split as Cressida or Cordelia is, but is in some ways being reintegrated with her alienated
selves in Nancy and in "their" surviving child. This seems especially true if we compare the
development of Temple in *Requiem* with that of Judith Sutpen of *Absalom* (silently ambiguous
almost to the end), Caddy Compson of *The Sound and the Fury* (fragmented and silent
throughout), or the Temple Drake of *Sanctuary* (not only silent but almost unthinkably contradictory in her innocence and corruption). But a reading of *The Reivers* would suggest
that perhaps this is too limited a view of the possibilities even for heterosexual, marital love
(faintly) suggested by Faulkner's ending in *Requiem,* possibilities developed out of the experience of more clearly marginalized loves. Cf. Kristeva's prediction in another context that
"there will be new codes of love in those regions where a new map of the *particular* without
property is being drawn, where new, eternally temporary idealizations (yet indisputable in
the present instant) captivate us. This is being talked about on psychoanalytic couches, sought
after in those marginal communities that dissent from official morality—children, women,
same-sex, and finally heterosexual couples (the most shocking because the most unexpected)"
(*Tales*). To extrapolate further from Kristeva's argument, the potential for love in Bucky's
case would depend not only on Temple's struggle with her own "abjection" as a hysterical
mother, but also on Gowan's similar analysis and treatment as a borderline father incapable
of loving or being loved: "There has been too much stress on the crisis in paternity as cause
of psychotic discontent. Beyond the often fierce but artificial and incredible tyranny of the
Law and the Superego, the crisis in the paternal function that led to a deficiency of psychic
space is in fact an erosion of the loving father. It is for want of paternal love that Narcissi,
burdened with emptiness, are suffering; eager to be others, or women, they want to be loved"
(*Tales* 378).

alive as other, speaking, loving subjects whom their writing, reading, and watching spectators can learn in their turn to respect and love.

Temple has returned from California, she tells Gavin, "Because apparently I know something I haven't told yet, or maybe you know something I haven't told yet" (69). As in Freud's ambiguity about analysis either as a discovery or as a working through of the primal scene (Lukacher 136–67), she is warily unsure of whose knowledge this untold "something" already is and whose it will become as it is told, but she does have some interest herself in telling it. She invents a "coincidence" to cast her own relationship to this unknown in the peculiar ambiguity of the uncanny: like Nancy's sorcery, it is utterly strange and unfamiliar (out of the outlawed or higher, judgmental blue, as it were) and at the same time intimately familiar and implicating, an unexpected question her son drops "right in my lap, right out of the mouths of—how is it?—babes and sucklings" (68). Gavin correctly deduces her intimate interest in the untold motivations for Nancy's act from Temple's return before her execution date as also from her regular attendance at Nancy's trial; he believes no more than she does her (symptomatic) attempt to deny that interest by explaining her regular trial attendance in terms of the dominant legal and marital economy—"herself watching the accomplishment of her revenge; the tigress over the body of her slain cub" (71). He knows only that her grief is more complex and profound than that economy of revenge could have possibly satisfied, just as he also knows that her legalistic talk about falsifying affidavits to overturn that legal verdict (hysterical talk, "patient, only a little too rapid, like the smoking"—72) is also somehow insufficient to her interest in saving Nancy, which has something to do not just with "Mrs. Gowan Stevens" in her conventional, hysterical role as bereaved mother, outraged employer, and faithful wife to the family's legal and nominal head, but much more with "Temple Drake" in her own infamous past connection to Nancy's underworld of murderers and whores (74–76).[21] He

21. The choice between Temple's two names is perhaps an exemplary instance of more general differences between my reading of *Requiem* and that of Noel Polk—also between mine and those like Vickery's which Polk is here arguing against—in their New Critical oppositions of "civilization" and ironic "realism" on the one hand to idealism and moral anarchy on the other: "In this way Temple's married name is *not,* as many commentators have suggested, a denial of her genuinely sinful, evil past. It is indeed quite the reverse: it is for her a recognition of, and an attempt to bring under control, to 'civilize,' that anarchic, destructive part of her—the Temple Drake part—which produced that past" (95). Polk sees Gavin as needlessly, cruelly prying into a "truth" and a "past" Temple would be better to leave alone now that she has largely brought it under civilized control; Nancy's act should be declared and pardoned as insane. I see Gavin less in the role of male victimizer than in the more ambiguous role of Temple's analyst, medium of the Symbolic order and object of her transference: she risks such analysis for the sake of possibly rewriting her own *differently* civilized version of her truth, her past, and her name.

knows this is where "the truth" lies that they need in order to supplement the insufficiency and "injustice" of the legal verdict, but he does not know whether to call it truth, love, pity, "Or courage. Or simple honor[,] honesty, or a simple desire for the right to sleep at night" (77).

Laying out the ground rules for their analysis of the truth of her past, she insists on eliminating both the first and the last of these descriptions of their goal in analysis, at least in the "simple" way he wants to understand them: she is not after the truth on his terms, inasmuch as his terms would usually position herself and her past as the silent object and spectacle of a truth which is either naturalized as an anonymously objective truth, or religiously sanctified as a redemptive or judgmental higher truth, a truth which in either case is told for its own sake,

> Just to get it told, breathed aloud, into words, sound. Just to be heard by, told to, someone, anyone, any stranger none of whose business it is, can possibly be, simply because he is capable of hearing, comprehending it. Why blink your own rhetoric? Why dont you go on and tell me it's for the good of my soul—if I have one? (78)

When Gavin equates this redemptive or judgmental function with the right to sleep at night, she reminds him again that (in her modern hysteria) she has already become accustomed to sleeplessness: she wants neither a more secure accommodation to the present nor a simple exorcism of her confessed and repented past (the truth as a static horror, as in *Sanctuary*), but a renegotiation of the unsatisfactory articulation of that past in her (hysterical) present.

Thus it is not for the sake of that "simple" truth that she will retell her story, but for the sake of "something else, then," which she asks him to admit and then herself identifies as the child sleeping on the sofa onstage. Here, too, she indicates the importance of the child and at the same time must insist on resisting his interpretation of that importance: insofar as the child is Gavin's "plant" to insure her full confession and repentance of any past or present deviance from her conventional role as wife and mother (herself ideally as childlike and innocent as her charge), she knows that she might as well keep quiet and let the law take its smooth and efficient course, with whatever injustice toward Nancy and sleeplessness of her own (79–80). Similarly, she must insist to Gavin that Temple Drake (as the spectacle he understands her past as) is dead, and that she will not tell "everything" in the way that he demands, as if the simple facts will either speak for themselves or will be given their shape, meaning, and judgment only by another's voice (his, the Governor's, God's, the Symbolic's).

That is, she resists analysis, even refuses it, asking him to leave, but only in order to claim an equal voice in that analysis, and to begin the

hazardous transference which recognizes his continuing part in the orders
of language, knowledge, and authority that have variously robbed her of
that equal voice before. She does suggest agreement with Gavin that "The
past is never dead. It's not even past" (80), and after several silent gestures
toward the child (83–84), she reinitiates the analysis and agrees again to
its enabling fiction of telling everything. The child in this respect functions not just as Gavin's plant, drawing her into the spotlight and surveil-
lance by the Symbolic in her role as obedient cultural midwife; her relationship with the child, like her relationship with Nancy and with her own
past as Temple Drake, may function instead as a dimension, disposition,
and stage of her life that has not yet been given a voice sufficient to its
importance to her (especially as the site of her unmourned love for Red).
And the disturbing injunction to "tell everything" (precipitated by Nancy's
disturbing act of desperation and thus related to that act as an internal
to an external disturbance of this dominant white culture) may be the very
discontinuity Temple needs to be able to interrupt her (functional, but
sleepless) hysteria, as Mrs. Gowan Stevens, long enough to begin working
through her own and Nancy's guilts and tragedies toward some better
understanding and articulation of their pasts, their relationships to each
other, to men, and to their remaining child. She can agree to the enabling
fiction of telling everything, even when that seems to mean repeating the
incriminating horror of her past before one of those ironically judgmental
authorities most likely to understand it as such an incriminating horror,
but she takes the risk of this transference only thereby herself to attempt
to deconstruct (in his presence and in his language) these silently but pervasively oppressive versions of her own past and of his authority, to repeat
not the dead letter but the potentially lively rewriting of her past (what
I have called a revisionary repetition).

As the audience learns mostly later, Temple needs and wants to find
some other option in her relationship with the child than the ones she has
felt she had—either to raise the child in sleepless, hysterical respectability,
in an oedipalized family and society where the overriding and undermining
issues are this child's questionable paternity, Temple's questionably complete loyalty to her loveless marriage and questionably complete reforma-
tion of her guilty past, or on the other hand desperately to flee that child,
family, and respectability into an apparently compulsive repetition of that
still loveless, still guilty past. She needs and wants to find in her past a
thwarted, renewable possibility of love—a love for her dead child, for her
soon-to-be-dead friend Nancy, for their surviving child, and perhaps even
for Gowan (especially in his own recognizable grief for their child).

Compared with the title of act 1, "The Courthouse (A Name for the
City)," act 2's title, "The Golden Dome (Beginning Was the Word),"

suggests its preoccupation with a later stage of the law's development from the institutionalized force of a "historic" society to the more pervasively systematized and mythologized (dehistoricized, universalized) ideological power of a modern state, both in its conspicuous visual symbols like the statehouse dome and in its less conspicuous wordings and structurings of language. The bulk of this second act's prologue does represent the history of Jackson, Mississippi's capital, but not as a conflict of historical forces, not even (as in act 1) as a victory of particular historical forces over a devalued, prehistoric insecurity and vulnerability. Instead, this more modern historiography (here in parodied form) reduces both the prehistorical and the historical past to the one blurred and flattened plane of a guidebook mythology,[22] in which both pasts are strictly subordinate parts of the one master narrative of the horizonless, unopposed system of the inevitable present. This representation of the self-construction of the modern state and language dramatizes what Temple is up against in risking to that system's authorities and language the story and analysis of her own past, but it also dramatizes the already proven possibility that Nancy, in her supposedly anachronistic (effectively nonsynchronous, residual) prehistoric role as sorceress, can disturb that modern system's actually incomplete assimilation and control of certain archaic forces as well as other unsettling traces of "historical" uses of legalized force; it dramatizes, too, the possibility that Temple's risky confession/analysis may allow her to articulate her own dissident, critical voice in spite of, and in the midst of, her own modern hysteria.

In the prologue to act 1 this society in its "historical" stage was trying hard to expel, confine, and cover its own uncertain tracks out of a prehistoric wilderness, whose different demands that society remembered all too well. As it confirms and consolidates its modernity in the prologue to act 2, this society now rewrites history as myth, recreating both its strange, archaic past and its conflictual, historical past in its own modern image, which "in the beginning was already decreed" (87). Faulkner calls repeated attention to just how curious such retrospective distortions of time and agency are, by means of odd syntactical maneuvers such as his conspicuous omission of the preposition in his allusive subtitle (stressing its chicken-and-egg-type paradox: "Beginning Was the Word"), or his description of reptilian heads that "curved the heavy leather-flapped air" (87), or his description of the Ice Age earth as "dragging upward beneath the polar cap that furious equatorial womb" (87). As in a myth, active and passive forces have become interchangeably equal partners in the same tableau, pageant, or parade of tributary pasts. The undifferentiated "father-mother-

22. See McHaney on Faulkner's ample use of a WPA guidebook on Mississippi as a source for this prologue.

one womb" is as easily accommodated into this pageant as is the "luck" that the name Jackson partly promised its founders and that they (now) easily admit they needed then; they are here remarkably unlike the mail rider and the founders of Jefferson who were so quick to reject this same idea of the mail rider's mother about the talismanic effect of Thomas Jefferson's name. Thus also the profit and loss denied by the founders of Jefferson are here comfortably acknowledged because they have since been securely systematized in "a new time, a new age, millennium's beginning [in] one vast single net of commerce [that] webbed and veined the mid-continent's fluvial embracement" (91), thanks to men whose "mouths were full of law and order, all men's mouths . . . round with the sound of money, [in] one unanimous golden affirmation [that] ululated the nation's boundless immeasurable forenoon: profit plus regimen equals security" (92). This is of course a retrospective, mythic, New South, chamber of commerce version of the American "forenoon" in its "Golden Age." Its own dispossessions are made to seem as undeviating, as inevitable, and thus as natural as any other of the indistinguishable wave after wave of dispossessions preceding it here. Each new wave of dispossessions comes in the name of a more regularized profit, with the promise of a new security from those very dispossessions and profiteerings by which each has thrived.

However, now that the modern world is in place (is everywhere), as symbolized by the statehouse's preeminent, silently governing golden dome, the once tumultuous waves of history seem only a rhythmic ebb and flow, in a system without outside or even a past or future except those created in its own image. The golden dome functions here like the epistemic structuring principle of thought that supposedly cannot, therefore, itself be thought (Derrida, "Structure"), or like the modern ironist's position undeniably in the world but, in the systematization of his irony, supposedly not of the world; the dome is "incapable of being either looked full or evaded, peremptory, irrefragable, and reassuring" (97): reassuring because any outside or alternative seems so unthinkable. The prologue ends with a listing of "chronic" and "acute" (both implicitly symptomatic) "diversions" from the dullness and confinement (in a "freedom" of hysterical movement) of such a supposed end of history. The chronic diversions listed include various sports, music, and fashion competitions and festivals, this culture's ritualizations of residual conflicts and celebrations. The acute diversions, religion and politics, are more directly residual traces of the prehistoric and historic orders that have preceded this one: they may be acute, but still usually amount only to localized diversions. Temple's and Nancy's stories as they are retold under this golden dome in the dramatic section of act 2 will attempt to be more than such diversions.

In act 2, scene 1, Temple, Gavin, and the Governor (and Gowan, listening silently and in hiding) begin to explore the strange, silent territories of Temple's past and of her relation to Nancy: that these territories are unfamiliar, all parties to this analysis and narration agree, but the peculiar status and function of that otherness are very much at issue. Scene 1 demonstrates in the case of this particular biographical history the inadequacy of that modernist historiography introduced on a large scale in this act's prologue. Scene 2 will bring Nancy's act to bear nonsynchronously and forcefully on the inadequacies and contradictions of that modernism.

After much difficulty beginning her story before the present audience, Temple both summarizes that difficulty and begins her story in earnest when she admits that she hired Nancy "to have someone to talk to," because she "couldn't find anybody except a nigger dope-fiend whore that could speak her language," someone who "made her debut into the public life of her native city while lying in the gutter with a white man trying to kick her teeth or at least her voice back down her throat" (105). She here frames "the rest" of her story as an explanation of why she needed Nancy to talk to (105) and, by implication, why she eventually needed the tragedy of Nancy's act (and the reevaluation of that tragedy) in order to break out of the endless circulations of her hysteria into a meaningful voice of her own.

Sitting not in the intermediate but the "still higher, the last, the ultimate seat of judgment" (98), the Governor, like the symbolic golden dome, speaks modernity's supremely supple, unthreatened, monopolizing language, confident that the articulation of Temple's story into the words and sounds (and judgments) of that language will take care of any disturbance she might be experiencing in her feminine, irrational confusion. At one point he urges her to think of the difficulty in getting to the bottom of the story she's telling not in terms of a barrel into which she is driving a hen (herself, as it were, being driven into the dark dead end or blockage or double bind their language and system of judgments offer her for the loss of her child's and Nancy's lives): "Don't call it a barrel. Call it a tunnel. That's a thoroughfare, because the other end is open too. Go through it" (122). Good advice, except that the Governor does not take these losses' real disturbances seriously, any more seriously than Freud sometimes took his own hysterical female patients' accounts of sexual abuse by fathers or representatives of fathers. We learn later the Governor has no serious plans to save Nancy's life, but he believes in the "talking cure"—without, however, believing in any real necessity to disturb the way we talk.

Gavin plays the bad cop to the Governor's good one, part of that same well-oiled, virtually digitalized economy of mutually dependent oppositions, but Gavin speaks the harsher style characteristic of his rather different role in a (somewhat anachronistic, but here supportive) adversarial legal system, along with his recent fictional role as half lawyer, half detective (in *Intruder in the Dust,* 1948, and *Knight's Gambit,* 1949). His frequent function as would-be midwife to Temple's story here is to translate, or to interrupt and correct, or if necessary to preempt and commandeer her story in its hysterical tendency to stray from the way he expects and wants it told. Gavin here (resembling Mr. Compson in *The Sound and the Fury* and *Absalom, Absalom!*) might be said to speak Faulkner's modernist mind on sex and gender as these positions attempt and fail to do Temple's story the much more difficult justice it demands. As Temple puts it, the "main obstacle" in telling her story is that "I'm trying to tell you about one Temple Drake, and our Uncle Gavin is showing you another one" (135). But she does have to find her way around his (and her own) modernist way of telling.

In brief, he attempts first to cast Temple Drake as the innocent victim of a frightful evil hypostatized and heaped on Popeye, "a psychopath, . . . a little black thing with an Italian name, like a neat and only slightly deformed cockroach: a hybrid, sexually incapable" (121), who "should have been crushed somehow under a vast and mindless boot, like a spider" (126). With these shades of racism and fascist anti-Semitism (modernity's more systematized versions of anthropoemic postures toward the anomalous), Gavin attempts rather desperately to project evil on an absolutely other (under) world, as Temple remembers his (supposedly) doing eight years before, telling her "how there is a corruption even in just looking at evil, even by accident; that you can't haggle, traffic, with putrefaction—you cant, you dont dare—(she stops, tense, motionless)" (112). This scenario of the primal scene as an irremediable horror is of course no help to Temple once she is even accidentally corrupted, however cathartic it may be for Gavin as third-person spectator. Temple departs from this scenario when she admits at several places and in several ways that "Temple Drake liked evil" (117), or what he is casting as evil. And when she begins to speak of falling in love with someone within this underworld and of the importance to her of her later talking with Nancy about their shared experience there (further blurring Gavin's boundaries of innocence and evil), Gavin takes over again and takes another more typically modernist tack at telling her story.

The innocent victim inevitably crosses over into the realm of evil by attempting (as she must) and failing (as she must) to "haggle" with "evil." She is as unable as any Faulkner character is to do as she remembers one (presumably vastly simpler) Hemingway character recommending, "just to refuse to accept it, no matter who remembered, bragged" (133). According to Stevens, she tries to reform by "manumitting" her inevitable but unpredictable payment for her past (140), and by striking "not a bargain, but an armistice with God" by which He would spare her child if she made no such further claims, "since He—if there was one—would at least play fair, would be at least a gentleman" (141–42). Speaking here the modern languages of money, law, and sport, Stevens suggests that she has done all she can to prepare for the inevitable "avalanche" when she missteps, thereby proving herself the ironic "better man, [because] you outfaced even catastrophe, outlasted it, compelled it to move first; you did not even defy it" (144); by holding it off she proved herself the better man again even in the moment of catastrophe because all that it "could deprive you of, you yourself had already written off six years ago as being, inherently of and because of its own fragile self, worthless" (145). Avoid all loss by liquidating into this economy's own abstracted terms all potentially (eventually) worthless investments in particular persons or things: in this way Gavin describes Temple's attempted defection from her marriage not as an attraction in any way to Red's brother but as a simple calculation of the excessive overhead (in repentance and addictive gratitude) of her propriety and marriage compared with what she can gain by selling out of her marriage and returning to evil. It is a thoroughly modern arrangement, "a new and safe method of kidnapping: that is, pick an adult victim capable of signing her own checks" and "not forc[e] but actually persuad[e] her to come along under her own power" (145). As Gavin tells it, the accepted certainty of catastrophe in Temple's kidnapping makes "even rape become tender" (146); she can be persuaded so easily in cost-benefit terms because there is assumed to be particular love in neither relationship. But Gavin has largely omitted from these calculations the issue of Temple's love for her child and for Nancy, an omission (as becomes clear in scene 2) which Nancy finally did not allow Temple herself to make. While the hysteric typically "does *not* write, does *not* produce, does nothing—nothing other than make things circulate without inscribing them," the sorceress is different in that she "transforms, she acts" (Clément 37, 36). Clément's description of the hysteric resembles Lentricchia's of the modernist, who sees "no road through to action" (56). For Temple, as modernist hysteric, neither role in which she has been cast by Gavin and by the dominant modernist economy—neither the role of innocent victim of horror and evil nor that of ironic self-castrator, the victim of rape who "asked for it"—is adequate to actively articulate her desire. So her desire endlessly circulates, or switches restlessly between this digitalized economy's double binds of unsatisfying alternatives. Nancy acts, but with uncertain connection yet to any voice.

Act 2's second scene dramatizes the dialogue and events leading up to Nancy's murder of Temple's child, framed and staged as a flashback, as if Temple is remembering and reporting it but without the mediation of retrospective narrative, as if without the "obstacle" of Gavin's narrative terms but also not yet in a specifically different voice and terms of her own. It is the scene instead of Nancy's critically nonsynchronous intervention in Temple's own near reification of her past. Nancy has listened in hiding offstage to Temple's speech with Pete (perhaps she has also listened to Temple's analysis and transference with Gavin, the Governor, and Gowan) and comes onstage to intervene, trying first to explain the contradictions of Temple's hysteria, then trying to get Temple to voice those contradictions clearly herself. Failing at both these efforts, Nancy desperately abandons that contradictory language (of the modernist hysteric) ("I've hushed" — 162, 165) to act (as sorceress) in the only way she can find to inscribe a value and love which the dominant language and economy have left almost completely out of account. She acts in order to demonstrate irrefutably to Temple that Temple herself must also act, is in fact already acting, even in her hysterical vacillation, with consequences which the terms of that hysteria quite insistently overlook. Having heard Temple refuse a second chance to burn the incriminating letters (in order to keep the option of changing her mind, or circulating — 154), Nancy will not let Temple pretend she is either the innocently surprised victim or the ironically heroic, martyred victim of this kidnapping. Nancy emphatically points out how Temple's thinking is trapped between the alternatives of being either the faithful wife or the unfaithful whore, whether Temple is talking about her relationship with Pete or about sending her older child to his grandparents to protect that child from his father's impugning of his paternity. In both cases Nancy shows how Temple's alternatives revolve around the husband and father, whereas Nancy is "talking about two little children" (159). Nancy reminds Temple of at least one time when Temple "fought back" for that older child, although Temple's sense of her alternatives otherwise tended to omit this other dimension of her desire and this possibility of resistance to the phallogocentric structure of her family and society: as Nancy tells her, "now you have quit" (160). Nancy tries to get Temple to admit that she can expect neither to leave the six-month-old nor to take her along, that these alternatives are a double bind with regard to Temple's love for the child: love loses either way (161). Nancy tries to get Temple at least to voice this exclusion, "to say it out in words yourself, so I can hear them" (164), but Temple's difficulty with the words ("Yes! Children or no children!" — 164) is heard only in the exclamatory tone with which she both pronounces the words and tries to cut off the dialogue.[23]

23. The suppression of Temple's feelings for her child under the pressure of her two male-centered alternatives — chaste wife or unreformed prostitute — suggests an adult female

The grain of Temple's voice, however, is as insufficient as other symptoms of her hysteria are to break the grip of that hysteria's governing terms. Until Nancy acts, the note of difference and potential resistance in Temple's voice is as inarticulate and ineffective as the strangeness of Nancy's voice noted in stage directions at two points during this scene: "When Nancy speaks, . . . we dont realise until afterward what it signifies" (165). The scene ends with the scream and darkness with which Temple first greeted the murder (as an unqualified horror); but reconstructing the events and dialogue that led up to that horror has been a crucial step in beginning "afterward" to understand what Nancy's words and actions did "signify" and in beginning thus to be able to mourn the loss of their child. Nancy's speeches and Nancy's act have made the governing terms of Temple's modernist hysteria more available to potential consciousness and inarticulate criticism for what those terms otherwise neglect, invisibly and resolutely; perhaps those governing terms are becoming for Temple here less absolutely than the golden dome "incapable of being either looked full or evaded" (97).

Scene 3 puts Gowan in the Governor's chair, unnoticed yet by Temple, setting her up for the sort of dramatic irony she has long been determined in her hysteria to avoid, but which she manages here to overcome. Previously, she has accepted and adopted all too eagerly, frantically, indebtedly, her society's limited, damning view of her (best-hidden) past, "something," as she says later, which she "spent eight years trying to expiate so that my husband wouldn't have to know about it" (181). In terms of her transference with Gavin and the Governor, Gowan is the most immediate obstacle to her overcoming her hysterical entrapment in his inadequate terms for her past and for her continuing desires: in her sordid past, she is either that other, evil underworld's immaculate, innocent victim, or, if she could have loved anything or anyone in that world, she is evil herself; more lately, she is either her husband's chaste wife or that role's dialectical opposite, a prostitute (never mind about her love for a child of uncertain paternity who fits into neither of this patriarchal economy's con-

version of the dilemma facing the male child as described by Chodorow and others: the male child learns to define himself in the rejection of his relationship with his mother, and learns either then or later to substitute exogamous partners for his forbidden mother. So too, under the terms of the predominantly masculine economy organizing the exchange of women, Temple acts out in an exaggerated (symptomatic) form the rejection of the mother in herself and the particular (vs. commodified) woman and lover in herself—as if that rejection is required in order for her to enter into that same system of exchange. "The hysteric is trying to *signify* the original eros by every means: the odors she wards off, the headaches which are metaphors for her aching sex, . . . all the possible forms of anesthesia" (Clément 39). I am including the more general strategy of irony among these possible forms of anesthesia.

ceptions of her role). Her transferences with Gavin and the Governor have suggested how vastly systemic the background of Gowan's authority as husband and father is, but throughout these transferences Gowan himself has been the occluded first obstacle to her articulation of her love for Red, for Nancy, and for her children. Her preoccupation with whether he knows or does not know about her hidden past has prevented her from articulating a different way to know that past, including now the loss of one child and the uncertain paternity of the other. Thus the importance of working through this dramatic irony in the transference of her analytic "confession."

In her longest speech of the play, Temple finds the means, as it were, to overcome that crucial dramatic irony about her own personal past, by considering the site of her white society's hidden past in the county jail, where Nancy was taken after the murder and before which the child's funeral procession passed, as all others in the town do. Temple remarks how that white society regards imprisonment in the jail as "ghastly" for "some white person you know" but "does not even think about" easing the stay or hurrying the escape of the more regular black prisoners, about whom "all of a sudden you find out with a kind of terror, that . . . they have escaped having to escape" (169). Being imprisoned and overlooked by this society, doing most of its manual work, and witnessing its funerals, they have found in this imprisonment, this work, and even in grief not a ghastly "alarm or anguish" but a certain "confederacy" and "peace" with those nether realms of work and suffering, their hands as shaped to prison bars as to the handles of "plows and axes and hoes," so that their hands can "see" and find those handles in the dark,[24] just as someone like Nancy can see in the dark to find the white baby's "trouble and discomfort . . . and see to remedy it. You see. If I could just cry" (170). Temple's apparent non sequitur here suggests her own (and her society's) tendency in "alarm or anguish" to escape and avoid suffering and work, here particularly that of mourning, and her need to learn these blacks' and especially Nancy's different perspective on the loss of her child (as on her funeral), or to learn enough of that different perspective at least to begin to cry.

Temple is risking here the sentimentalization of black suffering, for the sake of a possible alternative to her own white society's hysterical need to escape suffering rather than to find ways to articulate it, but she does go on to remember the story of at least one black man (the story of Rider, in "Pantaloon in Black") who was just as hysterically incapable of mourning as she is. That is, many members of this marginalized race may be

24. Compare Hegel's account of the Master's disturbing dependence on the Slave's contact with the material world. Here—less than in Hegel or than in another ironic work like *Absalom, Absalom!*—that contact seems less an undermining, dialectical dependence than a potentially nondialectical, unexpected extra alternative.

able to invest their works and loves in unexpected places and undervalued persons, and they may be more accustomed to coping with suffering than those occupying more privileged positions in the dominant economy, but their closer, less systematically mediated contact with the particular objects of their loves and losses may well come at an extra cost in more difficult translatability into other objects of desire, or at least into other terms for any particular lost object. Temple wants to be able to acknowledge her love and loss and thus be able to cry, but she also wants to be able to articulate her struggle and "fight back" within the economy that so pervasively devalues those loves and losses. She remembers not only Nancy in the jail but also especially the residual force of Nancy's verbal resistance in the courthouse, "disrupting and confounding and dispersing and flinging back two thousand years" of legal tradition by reminding the court of another authority on which she has based her own actions and her own judgment of those actions (172). Nancy has thereby reintroduced a dangerously "pre-historic," anthropophagic, black-spiritual countermemory of an unaccountable, higher authority to which this court may still pay perfunctory tribute, but which the court has actually assimilated to its own more regularized legal authority. (They explain to her that her plea has "nothing to do with truth but only with law, and this time she said it right, Not Guilty, and so then the jury could tell her she lied"—172).

Temple recovers quickly from her discovery of the dramatic irony of Gowan's presence because she is no longer thinking so exclusively in the spectacular terms of her predominantly masculine audience: she does not expect Gowan's reluctant apology to make either him or her innocent again or to make theirs a "natural and normal home" in which the paternity issue will never arise again (179). But Nancy has bet her life on Temple's being able to fight back, not just to prove the father wrong but to make that issue irrelevant to her love for the child. Nor does Temple any longer expect the Governor to save Nancy: "Of course he wouldn't save her. If he did that, it would be over" (180). From her own standpoint, it would be over because Temple would never have recognized the need to continue resisting this system of values out of her love for her children. She reflects that her male child would have been surrendered to his father or to the state, as if his connection with herself and with the feminine is dead with the female child. As for the Governor, he can recognize that Nancy has made a "purchase" with her "poor crazed lost and worthless life," but the terms of his speech indicate he is unprepared to question the economy that has made her life so "worthless" that her purchase costs her her very life (181). For him (as for much of the community that witnessed the death of Joe Christmas in *Light in August*), her "crazed" life and death are a tragic spectacle outside the pale of his understanding or authority, unfortunate but perhaps inevitable, one of the extremely tragic but ironically accepted (finally unaccounted and incidental) prices of his society's very existence.

Temple, too, considers "wildly" (hysterically) that hers and Nancy's suffering has been "just suffering. Not for anything: just suffering" (181), but the scene and act close with her adoption of Nancy's anachronistically religious terms to affirm an alternative value in something her society's dominant economy tends to see (and try to escape, through pretended innocence or cynical irony) as "just suffering," but which Nancy and Temple here agree may instead be suffering "To save my soul—if I have a soul. If there is a God to save it—a God who wants it—" (182). She is not decided on these questions, but they are radically different questions, affording her a new standpoint of resistance. Nancy's and the child's deaths may prove to be a tragedy not in tragedy's anthropoemic position, outside the society's exclusive boundaries and reinforcing those boundaries as the society defines itself against such anomalies, but a tragedy instead in tragedy's anthropophagic position, focusing at the society's very center that society's otherwise pervasive and neglected sufferings and costs, those oppressions that are otherwise "incapable of being either looked full or evaded." They are also therefore oppressions (of blacks, children, and especially women) that are incapable of being resisted without tragedies like Nancy's and Temple's and the analysis they inspire.

Act 3's title, "The Jail (Nor Even Yet Quite Relinquish—)," suggests its double movement in history: it continues and elaborates act 2's panoramic portrait of modernity, but does so without betraying, forgetting, or mythologizing modernity's different pasts, notably in the old jail, which will play a crucial role in both the prologue and the dramatic scene that follows. Also, modernity figures here much less exclusively as the one governing perspective on those pasts, less the one (panoptical) perspective itself "incapable of being either looked full or evaded"; instead, this prologue obliquely and critically displaces that still immensely powerful, still central perspective in favor of other perspectives especially from the jail. Starting as if from Temple's reevaluation (in act 2, scene 3) of the before unnoticed "confederacy" with work and suffering achieved by the blacks who are in and out of this jail, and from her related notion that those hands lying restfully between the bars can "see" in a different way from that of the rest of her society, this prologue manages to make modernity not the one unconscious subject, but both the conscious (more dialogized) subject and also object of a much more critical historiographic consciousness, managing thus to decenter that one monolithically modernistic perspective by dint of this crucial addition of a characteristically postmodern sense of nonsynchronous, nondialectical, uneven social development.

Faulkner's prologue quite clearly differentiates three distinct historical phases of dispossessions contributing toward the consolidation of modernity's power, even while he also stresses (this new stress itself a function of the fourth phase) the imperfections and oversights of this progressive consolidation: the "overlapping" in the midst of this "unbroken— ay, overlapping—continuity," and the forgotten histories, the countermemories to be rediscovered "not in the church registers and the courthouse records" in the new center of the town, but scrawled, drawn, and imaged on successive layers of the inside and outside walls of the jail, recording that more material history from a vantage point located no longer at the anomalous, anthropophagic center (as the maternal "dam" from whose "dug" the "unweaned" courthouse was torn), nor even opposite the courthouse an arm's length outside its anthropoemic boundary, nor quite assimilated into the modern order, but "diagonal" to the rest of the town, left behind in a "backwater" one block from the town's new center, facing "not even on a side-street but on an alley" (182, 183), its "record and history indisputable in authenticity yet a little oblique, elliptic or perhaps just ellipsoid" (214).[25]

The first wave of (maternal, anthropophagic, pre-oedipal, prehistorical) dispossessions, that of old Mohataha, her people, and her wilderness (in the "groin" of which this jail was born), have been imaged on the jail's walls (effaced now in the dust of the roads) in the imitative prints of the pioneers and long hunters,

> who made the same light rapid soundless toed-in almost heelless
> prints as the red men they dispossessed and who in fact dispossessed
> the red men for that reason: not because of the grooved barrel but
> because they could enter the red man's milieu and make the same
> footprints that he made. (187–88)

Faulkner signals the distinct historical change (toward an anthropoemic, oedipalized, historical order) as the traces of these soft prints in the road are printed over in turn by the hard-heeled brogans of the husbandman, "who dispossessed the forest man *for the obverse reason:* because with his saw and axe he simply removed, obliterated the milieu in which alone the forest man could exist" (188, my emphasis). And immediately next

25. Cf. again Ginzburg's retrieval of Menocchio's marginalized, oral, popular, and specific voice from the unnecessarily elaborated (fascinated) records of his heresy trial.

come the forerunners of modernity's more systematic economy, "the land speculators and the traders in slaves and whiskey who followed the husbandmen, and the politicians who followed the land speculators" (188), imprinting the "heavy leather heel engaged not in the traffic of endurance and hardihood and survival, but in money," the thoroughness of modernity even replacing the moccasins on the few remaining Chickasaws' feet with "Eastern factory-made . . . shoes sold them on credit out of Ratcliffe's and Compson's general store" (189).

This installation of modernity is accomplished for the Chickasaws in one generation's memory; it overtakes others at different points and at different, ever accelerating speeds. For example, in a brief revision here of Sutpen's story in *Absalom, Absalom!*, "the town knew now," after the fact, that it was not Sutpen, or any moral deficiency of his or his slaves or hounds that had harnessed the architect to Sutpen's destiny. Though the town tried to project the rapacity of that destiny on him, it was instead the entire town's destiny, "the long invincible arm of Progress" (193), gradually understood in its own self-justifying, ironically retrospective, all-encompassing terms, not morally but systematically, in terms of the ever-branching system of railroads and "a commodity . . . an economy: Cotton: a king: omnipotent and omnipresent: a destiny of which (obvious now) the plow and the axe had been merely the tools; not plow and axe which had effaced the wilderness, but Cotton" (195).

But at every turn the flood of this history leaves bits of its flotsam in the backwater of the obliquely observing jail: drunken Indians, highwaymen, and especially now Cecilia Farmer. The metaphor continued from act 1 of apparently random bubbles and chips on the flood functions both as a leftover reminder of that flood's past movements and indecisions and also as an infinitesimal indication of possible new changes in its continuing movement. At first the story of Cecilia Farmer's dated signature on the jail's windowpane and of her and her unknown soldier's brief "looking at one another for that moment across the fury and pell mell of battle" functions as one "significantless" incident dwarfed and overwhelmed in the larger disaster of Jefferson's and (almost a year later, with its own emphasized nonsynchronous quality) the South's defeat and reconstruction. But the "weightlessness" of such a minute chip on the flood is "its own impunity" (199), and the jail's oblique record survives just as the old "unvanquished" ladies' spirits and memories also survive into a time of other wars and other tremendous changes when the monument these ladies raise has become an easy target for jokes.

This same apparently insignificant humor, however, is one of the first few signs of resistance under the modern dome of "the county's hollow inverted air," which has soon become "one resonant boom and ululance of radio: and thus no more Yoknapatawpha's air nor even Mason and Dixon's air, but America's" (210), and which becomes soon thereafter the air of "one world . . . one universe, one cosmos," filled still with the "one boom" (212–13). In a nightmare crescendo of the Signifying Order's inescapable power (we are reminded of Faulkner's own dislike of radio), this "one boom" fills the "vast hollow sphere of his air" with the distracting murmur of everything he (or she) needs to say—"his fears and terrors and disclaimers and repudiations and his aspirations and dreams and his baseless hopes, bouncing back at him in radar waves from the constellations" (213). The old jail—and humor—endure to remark the imminent disappearance of a dingy old man on his back kitchen steps, "(to disappear from the surface of the earth along with the rest of the town on the day when all America, after cutting down all the trees and levelling the hills and mountains with bulldozers, would have to move underground to make room for, get out of the way of, the motorcars)" (213).

Only the jail and humor and a few old men and women, along with the servants whom these last sometimes bailed out of the jail and a few others associated with the jail (the New Negro, cattle thieves, murderers, the jailor's family), endure to remember other neglected pasts but also to suggest other, potentially different movements in the present, "until suddenly you, a stranger, an outlander" (the reader) enters the narrative (217). Here Faulkner's project in recording the jail's long and strange history aligns itself with Cecilia's signature on the jail window, challenging her reader and his to hear and appreciate the uncanny strangeness of the perspective from the jail in this woman's voice and name, "significantless" as they may seem (that word itself resisting her glib devaluation by the Signifier).[26] He would have his reader notice that "something curious was happening or had happened here" and in places like it just off the main highway system—for example, that those who remember Cecilia Farmer's story are not "dying off as they should as time passed," but "actually increasing in number" (217).

It is in many respects a story like the one told to Quentin Compson in *Absalom, Absalom!*, descended orally from old women like Rosa Coldfield, the "great aunt: the spinsters, maiden and childless out of a time when there were too many women because too many of the young men were maimed or dead" (220). But here the story is not a modernist waste-land story, to be written out to its all-encompassing, ironic dead end and marked paid: the story here does lead toward a legacy of farmland

26. Compare the triple negative of this determinedly nondialectical, oxymoronic description of her watching: "not even waiting: meditant, *not* even *unim*patient: just patienceless, in the sense that blindness and zenith are colorless" (220, my emphasis).

"which had been rendered into a desert (assuming that it was still there at all to be returned to) by the iron and fire of civilisation" (221–22), but the story opens out onto the possibility of Cecilia Farmer and her new soldier-husband attempting to reclaim and "begin a life" there again. They do not begin all over again in the same cycle, starting again with the wilderness and the frontier, but start out of the ruins of this civilization, as Farmer herself has started from the backwater jail and her new soldier-husband from his army's defeat in the war. She has drawn him back from the (repetitive, already assimilated, mythologized) automatic temptation of the West, the idea of "no longer having to remain undefeated" (223): the idea, that is, of starting over as if without any past defeats, in another (compulsively repetitive, American) innocence.[27] This is to be a start not before but after, or diagonally aside from, irony.

As the outlander leaves the jail to "get back onto a highway you know, back into the United States" (and as the reader leaves this prologue and Cecilia Farmer's story for Nancy's and Temple's), he hears the unassimilable strangeness and radical difference of Cecilia Farmer's voice, "as though out of the delicate antenna-skeins of radio . . . across the vast instantaneous intervention, from the long long time ago: '*Listen, stranger; this was myself: this was I*'" (225). The lingering promise of such an unassimilated subject's and moment's articulate resistance to the "one boom" of modernity's vast skein, after the modernist experience with the reductive dialectics of enlightenment, civilization, signification, and other systematizations, is fraught with all the anxious ambiguity of the rest of the promises of postmodernity and "woman's writing." Along with the possibility that she would found somewhere a resistant "matriarchy" of farmers, "bequeathing to them in their matronymic the heritage of that invincible inviolable ineptitude" for the work of modern civilization as we know it, is the more paranoid possibility that has occurred to the outlander-reader as "he" (or she) prepares to leave, returning to civilization with the doubly uncanny voice of the primarily repressed:[28] the possibility that this articulated, legible trace of a maternal, anthropophagic order is an engulfing, devouring, castrating threat ("no symbol there of connubial matriarchy, but fatal instead with all insatiate and deathless sterility"), a radical chal-

27. Compare with Nancy's later (233) not being fooled by hope, i.e., by the usual (particularly American) deferral of resistance in a projection of hope onto the next generation's (Bucky's) innocence, without the necessary critical sense of (and resistance against) the odds already firmly ranged against that innocence, odds allowing him that innocence only to lead him later into his elders' ironic cynicism and repeated deferrals of resistance and action in hope.

28. These are the "Powers of Horror" posed by the return of the ab-jected maternal and feminine as explored in Kristeva's book of that title, and the site of a common modern diversion from the path of primary identification with maternal desire and the capacity for love.

lenge to everything familiar and familial and seen therefore in that familiar system's mirror image:

> Lilith's lost and insatiable face drawing the substance—the will and hope and dream and imagination—of all men (you too: yourself and the host too) into that one bright fragile net and snare; . . . drawn to watch in patient and thronging turn the very weaving of the strangling golden strands. (224)

The outlander-reader considers such temptingly familiar, if contradictory, mythological identifications of Cecilia Farmer's voice as that of a "demon-nun and angel-witch; empress, siren, Erinys: Mistinguett, too, . . . for you to choose among," but as he leaves, her specific voice and name resist all these equivalents: " *Listen, stranger; this was myself: this was I* " (225). It is a kind of warning to the reader who now returns to the dramatic stage not to judge too hastily the murdering (demon)-nun of Faulkner's title.

The curtain rises on act 3's one dramatic scene—the now self-consciously dramatic scene of the jail with one wall removed—to reopen still further both Temple's emotional wound and this community's archaic old social wound. Faulkner's book has probed several layers of symptomatic reactions to and attempts to close that old, still bleeding wound, until the object of his (itself symptomatic) spectacular, archeological inspection has become a subject speaking from out of that blood and suffering in the "woman's writing" of Cecilia Farmer, in ways that challenge the specular situation of this final scene. The stage for Temple's analysis has traced its way back to this society's painful beginnings in the jail with its fourth wall removed. As if in the train of the prologue's and Cecilia Farmer's direct address of their readers, this scene features Nancy's enigmatic but equally direct, repeated challenge to Temple (and to the uncomfortably implicated audience) not to look to Nancy to tell her "what" to believe in (Nancy does not know), but to act on Nancy's example to the extent of articulating her own different response to the suffering of her past and the continuing suffering of "tomorrow and tomorrow and tomorrow" (236, 243). Temple must not cover over or otherwise flee that suffering but speak from her experience of it, in her continuing mourning of her female child and of her female friend Nancy, and in her continuing, potentially loving relation with her male child and with her husband.

Some of the difficulty Faulkner, his modern audience, and also Temple herself may experience in listening and responding to such "woman's writing" is suggested by Temple's opening dialogue with the jailor, who is described in stage directions (here and then again later) as "almost gentle, almost articulate" in his feeling for hers and Nancy's suffering (229, 244). In spite of the outspoken racism of his and the town's opinions of Nancy and of Stevens for "defending a nigger murderer," and in spite of his concern about the unseemly reflection on the town if "some stranger[,] say, some durn Yankee tourist" were to see Stevens on the sidewalk outside Nancy's cell, singing along with her—in spite of these allegiances to the system in which he acts and thinks his assigned part, he can still admit to having come to enjoy her singing and that of the other prisoners, enough to have to correct himself in speaking of "Na—the prisoner," and enough to refer to the jail (at least in humor, "almost articulate") as a "singing school," for which he has thought of having the Marshal "comb the nigger dives and joints not for drunks and gamblers, but basses and baritones" (226–29). Gavin Stevens' joining in with Nancy's hymn singing marks an advance from his near suffocation by Molly's singing in "Go Down, Moses," and here not only the jailor and his wife but other passing "folks" have begun stopping to "listen to [the prisoners' singing] instead of going to regular church" (228), as if these voices may be articulating alternative, nonsynchronous values of which "regular church" preserves only a token trace. Temple recognizes the jailor through his inarticulateness as (typically) "innately, inherently gentle and compassionate and kind" (230); her own similar problem is to articulate her feeling (her love) for Nancy not as a (judgmental) offer to forgive Nancy but as her own plea that Nancy forgive her, first reversing the judgment in order to get somehow beyond that judgment: "How can I say that? Tell me. How can I?" (230). That is, she must resist the judgment that would divide them from each other (scapegoating Nancy for Temple's and her society's complicity in this tragedy) in order to learn instead to hear and speak and love from out of the suffering she and Nancy share.

Alice Jardine writes of "the valorization of the feminine, woman, and her obligatory, that is, historical connotations, as somehow intrinsic to new and necessary modes of thinking, writing, speaking" (*Gynesis* 25). Nancy here likewise explains to Temple (and Stevens) that she (Nancy) has had to break the habit of "hoping"—for example, hoping that the Mayor or Governor would willingly overrule such systematically "historical connotations" of the abjected feminine, the black, and the criminal; as sorceress she has acted out the extremes of these historical connotations (as "nigger dope-fiend whore" and murderously suffocating nurse-mother) in the interest of a more radical "salvation" from such judgments and their demeaning effects on herself, Temple, Bucky, and the other child Temple neglected and Nancy murdered. Such a radical break is difficult for her to articulate without reinstating what she is trying to resist. She can tell Temple, "just believe," but she cannot or will not answer Temple's repeated question, "believe what?" (234, 241, 243). Or perhaps Nancy cannot do so except by thus challenging Temple to admit that she already knows what she has to do (for example, "fighting back" for Bucky), she needs only the courage to articulate into different words and deeds that countermemory and counterknowledge born from her own love and suffering (by addressing the different, more strategic question of "how?"). Nancy's resistance here to the nominalization and perhaps neutralization of her belief (her "just believe") closely resembles what Jardine describes as the postmodern and feminist "transformation of woman and the femi-nine into *verbs* at the interior of those narratives that are today experiencing a crisis in legitimation" (*Gynesis* 25, my emphasis).[29]

Insofar as Nancy does characterize her belief in religious terms, it is marked by the warily ambiguous quality of resistance of black American religion more generally, as studied especially by Genovese. Her provocative readings of dominant "regular church" ideas offer a good example of what Carlo Ginzburg has called for in the history of ideas; since "only knowledge of the historical and social variability of the person of the reader [of his-torically current ideas] will really lay the foundations for a history of ideas that is also qualitatively different" (xxii). Nancy startles Temple by speak-ing of her own judgment and execution as "getting low for Jesus" (234), and she defends her use of the language of prostitution on the grounds that, whatever Jesus might say, what he *is* is a man (and this is the way she knows to get something she wants from men, starting from her "histori-cal connotations"). Her suffering, then, is not a surrender but an act that both implicates and indebts Jesus as an alternative force and ally who may be useful but is neither impeccably pure of motive nor unquestionably infal-lible. "Your pay for the suffering," she explains, may be the ability to "believe" or "trust" in this alternative source of strength, and Temple recog-nizes in the ambiguous second-person pronoun here the suggestion of soli-darity, the idea that the suffering and the pay are not "just each one's for his own," but instead that Nancy's and others' suffering (along with Temple's own) may contribute to Temple's ability to believe and "fight" (236, 237). Nancy compares herself and other people to mules who can work for God "and do it good, only he's still got to be careful," because this God is clearly not omnipotent or invulnerable, and these mules are warily, unpredictably, and dangerously independent in their dealings with him (238).

Thus Temple also hears in what Nancy is saying the possibility that

29. Jardine continues later, "The object produced by this process is neither a person nor a thing, but a horizon, that toward which the process is tending: a *gynema*. This *gynema* is a reading effect, a woman-in-effect that is never stable and has no identity" (25).

Nancy's suffering and the "salvation" it buys in Nancy's own and Temple's ability to "work" may have something to do not only with earning forgiveness in heaven from the six-month-old she murdered (as Stevens suggests) but also with other less spectacular tragedies which may be either overshadowed or brought to light by that murder—Temple remembers here the six-month-old foetus Nancy was carrying and lost when one of its possible, anonymous fathers kicked her in the stomach. That is, Nancy's murder of Temple's child, which might be understood as a symptomatically coincidental and spectacular, compulsive repetition of a trauma in Nancy's own past, might also be understood, as Temple begins to understand it here, as a (revisionary) attempt to "fight back" for, to actively mourn, and to "believe" in some unknown kind of reunion with, that child who "never had a father and never was even born" (241). She would articulate and activate that mourning precisely by challenging Temple to "fight back" for another child Nancy has come to love—Bucky—who has almost been surrendered, as it were, to this same "buzz-saw" order of systematically anonymous fathers, on similar suspicions of illegitimacy.[30] Temple may come to understand Nancy's murder, that is, as an unpredictable, dangerous attempt to break an even more dangerously insidious cycle that has already claimed Nancy's own unborn child, and that seems to threaten to claim both of Temple's children if Nancy does not act, drastically, perhaps even mistakenly ("I dont know. But I believes"). It is a challenge to Temple to mourn her own lost child as Nancy has mourned hers, by "believing" in the work and suffering they have shared and "fighting back" for the child she still has left and perhaps thus for the inscription of new and different relationships among child, father, mother, and mother's co-worker and friend. Although Temple tries to shy from the challenge as she parts from Nancy, tempted by powerfully ideological, repetitive options of hope and irony, still, it is clearly up to Temple to articulate in the unspectacular "tomorrow and tomorrow and tomorrow" what is "almost gentle, almost articulate" (almost loving) in the racist, patriarchal jailor's (and Faulkner's) ambivalently hard and "no hard feelings, Nancy" (244, 236, 242).

In the context of Faulkner's career, the tragedies at the center of

---

30. Cf. Jardine, paraphrasing and feminizing Lyotard's reflections on related, larger issues of legitimation: "Over the past century, those master (European) narratives—history, philosophy, religion—which have determined our sense of legitimacy in the West have undergone a series of crises in legitimation. It is widely recognized that legitimacy is part of that judicial domain which, historically, has determined the right to govern, the succession of kings, the link between father and son, the necessary paternal fiction, the ability to decide who is the father—in patriarchal culture. The crises experienced by the major Western narratives have not, therefore, been gender-neutral. They are crises in the narratives invented by men" (*Gynesis* 24).

Requiem for a Nun may also be understood thus as revisionary repetitions of other tragedies in these tragedies' more modernist background, notably those involving imprisonment, rape, and abortion. The "imprisonment" of Temple in the Memphis underworld in *Sanctuary* seemed a shocking affront to, then an ironic (mirror) reflection on, the ingrown, closed society of Temple's upper-class, white, patriarchal father and brothers (or compare Addie's imprisonment in *As I Lay Dying*). Here in *Requiem* that tragedy of imprisonment, both in the Memphis underworld and also then in the Jefferson jail, becomes a starting point for voices of neither shocked silence nor ironic realization but of a new strength and resistance in mourning, voices rearticulating the experience of that suffering into different, less confining, potentially more loving psychological and social relationships.

Similarly, the corncob rape of Temple in *Sanctuary* seemed a shocking affront to, then an ironic reflection on, Temple's own "innocence" and that of her father's society in their legitimized but murderous violence against the (equally innocent) Lee Goodwin and his "common-law wife": here, however, that horror-script rape has been quietly omitted from the story.[31] In Temple's determination to escape the confinement of her hometown by doing "the one thing which she knew they would forbid her to do if they had the chance" (118), her one ironic regret was not the rape and certainly not the sex (and love) with Red, but that her kidnapper did *not* "have sex for his weakness, but just murder" (and thus that she became his blackmailable witness and alibi—121). Eight years later, the prostitution that has replaced that rape in representing the sexual underworld is part of a much more generalized prostitution and commodification of sexual and nonsexual love which does not, however, preclude the mourning and rearticulation in strangely different voices of those loves thus systematically and reductively betrayed.

And of course Nancy's murder of Temple's child may also be understood thus as a revisionary repetition of the attempted abortion in *Light in August,* of Wash Jones's infanticide in *Absalom, Absalom!,* and of the abortion in *The Wild Palms.* What seems in the first case a horrified attempt to return to innocence becomes in *Absalom* a calmly ironic acceptance of a hypostatized reality. In *Wild Palms* Wilbourne learns (from his own suffering and as if from the humor of "The Old Man") to regret the abortion and the oversimplified alternatives in terms of which he and Charlotte were thinking, but the novel ends before he can articulate the

31. Compare the omission of Sarty's shocked, innocent perspective in Faulkner's revision of "Barn Burning" in *The Hamlet.* The rape now seems in some ways a melodramatic focus for a horror not of Popeye in particular but of Temple's loss (in almost any circumstances) of her virginity.

work of mourning he has decided to undertake. Here in *Requiem*, however, an infanticide that seems in many ways another ironic refusal of any possibility of change is gradually and painfully reconceived. First it is reconceived against a vast backdrop that does confirm the tremendously systematic odds against the possibility of effective resistance by Nancy, Temple, or their children. But then it is also reconceived in the context of alternative, unexpected sources of courage and resistance found in the very work they have done and suffering they have experienced in their own devalued and underestimated positions in this society, effecting what Alice Jardine has called "a micropolitics of affirmative, nondialectical resistance" ("In the Name of the Modern"). In recasting an abortion again as an infanticide, Faulkner bypasses the reductive terms of the supposedly biological issue of live baby vs. not-yet-fully-alive foetus, in order to raise instead the more clearly and broadly social issue of the necessity of radical breaks in certain habits of thought and practice surrounding sexual and gender issues in particular, but extending as well to issues of race and class. They are breaks which have been implicit from the beginning of Faulkner's career-long probing of such old and variously tragic, still bleeding social wounds, wounds he reopens in order to rediscover, beneath the layers of hardened but not dead, still itching scar tissue, other tenderer, still fearful, but persistent possibilities of love.

Postscript: *The Reivers'* Postmodernist Repetitions

IN *The Reivers* (1962), Faulkner gives these revisionary repetitions one last twist near the end of his career, turning back again to his Memphis whorehouse material in a less dramatic, more humorous mode than in *Requiem for a Nun*. It is material he has treated with increasingly critical versions of first innocent horror and disgust at a social scandal, then ironic, cynical acceptance and reification of a more systematic social malaise, and then dramatic analyses of a psychological, social, and historical wound in order to rediscover and articulate alternatives to this dialectic in voices and possibilities of humor, mourning, and love. However, by this time in Faulkner's career and in the history of the West, the modernist vacillation between innocent horror and ironic cynicism, and the modernist, ironic tendency (preoccupied with that vacillation) to reduce its many and various excluded or subordinated others to one Other of disillusionment, knowledge, reality, history, chaos, or nothingness, have been somewhat dissipated and differentiated (though not superseded) as a result of historical (and aesthetic) repetition—as a result, that is, of both the failures of compulsive repetitions and the persistence of revisionary repetitions of this modernism.

Faulkner's last tale is told not by an idiot Other whose sound and fury signify either a horrifying or a predictable nothing, but by an old man to a grandson and namesake, recreating and reimagining not the intense shock or the confirming lesson of his own initiation into experience so much as that experience's speed, variety, interest, humor, and desirable surprise. This is to say not that *The Reivers* does not repeat the Faulknerian primal social scene, but that such scenes arrive so frequently and unpredictably as to preclude either intensity or preparedness. Miss Reba bars eleven-year-old Lucius Priest's entry into her Memphis "boarding house" (and into the current cultural Symbolic of sexuality, gender, money, credit, power, and language) for only a moment: then "at once I smelled something . . . like a smell I had waited all my life to smell" (99); soon Lucius is watching the "rich instantaneous glint of gold out of the middle

of whatever Minnie said" (116); then he is listening despite himself to Otis'
explanation of Everbe's beginnings in prostitution (at about Lucius' age)
with Otis charging admission to a peephole (equipped with a box for folks
about Lucius' size). Here Lucius is always already involved, as suggested
by the (innocent) violence with which he tries to "destroy" in Otis both
"the demon child who debased her privacy and the witch who debauched
her innocence . . . more: not just those two, but all who had participated
in her debasement" (157).

Lucius' awareness here of the reductive strategy of his violent innocence is already leading toward a more ironic sense of his and Everbe's
and others' systematic victimization by larger economies (and "Laws") of
class, race, and gender:

> hating all of us for being the poor frail victims of being alive, having
> to be alive—hating Everbe for being the vulnerable helpless lodestar
> victim; and Boon for being the vulnerable and helpless victimised;
> and Uncle Parsham and Lycurgus for being where they had to,
> couldn't help but watch white people behaving exactly as white
> people bragged that only Negroes behaved. . . . (174)

Victims all, says irony, except that this ironic clarity, along with its implicit
nostalgia for a restoration of innocence and for returning home, lasts only
momentarily, "when sudden and quiet and plain inside me something said
Why dont you?" and Lucius (his bluff called) feels again his own undeniable, living, loving, interested involvement with these irreducibly different,
unpredictably resourceful other subjects: "Everbe was loose again" (175).
With a woman's "no sense of shame at the idea of being knocked out"
(111), Everbe doesn't quit resisting victimization even when she has had
to break her promise to stop being a victim by profession. Miss Reba, too,
articulately if incompletely resists victimization by the Law, as do Boon
and especially Ned, who at times plays Uncle Remus and at other times
risks an outright challenge of the Law's authority, as when he reminds the
Constable, "There's somewhere the Law stops and just people starts" (243).

The Reivers is like the horse race about which Ned explains to Lucius
that "it had too many different things all mixed up in it"—for example,
too many different subjects with too many different objects of desire—
too many, that is, for either innocence or irony to work, except as a boy's
remembered, momentary gestures at perspective and comprehension. In
the midst of changing configurations of both power and resistance, Ned
knows "we cant take none of them extra things out. So the next best we
can do is, to put a few extry ones into it on our own account" (232). Instead
of modernist explorations of the repression and denial of the more or less

singular Other, or the dramatic representation of those explorations and discoveries, this novel enacts a more postmodern participation in the proliferation and circulation of imperfectly accountable, quite plural humors and loves. The "others" here variously feared, mourned, laughed at, laughed with, and loved, live not only somewhere out beyond or far beneath the dominant currencies of sexuality, gender, money, credit, power, and language, but also within that variously imperfect Symbolic's sinuous movements — even its movements of violence and defense — as those same movements flare, falter, twist, and change under the changing influences of repetition, revision, and love.

Works Cited

Index

Works Cited

Abraham, Nicolas, and Maria Torok. *The Wolf Man's Magic Word*. Trans. Nicholas Rand. Theory and History of Literature 37. Minneapolis: Univ. of Minnesota Press, 1986.

Adelman, Janet. " 'This Is and Is Not Cressid': The Characterization of Cressida." In *The (M)other Tongue: Essays in Feminist Psychoanalytic Interpretation*, ed. Shirley Nelson Garner, Claire Kahane, and Madelon Spengnether, 119–41. Ithaca: Cornell Univ. Press, 1985.

Barthes, Roland. *Image, Music, Text*. Trans. Stephen Heath. New York: Hill and Wang, 1977.

Barthes, Roland. *A Lover's Discourse: Fragments*. Trans. Richard Howard. New York: Hill and Wang, 1978.

Baudrillard, Jean. *For a Critique of the Political Economy of the Sign*. Trans. Charles Levin. St. Louis: Telos, 1981.

Baudrillard, Jean. *Simulations*. Trans. Paul Foss, Paul Patton, and Philip Beitchman. New York: Semiotext(e) Foreign Agents Series, 1983.

Beck, Warren. *Man in Motion: Faulkner's Trilogy*. Madison: Univ. of Wisconsin Press, 1961.

Benjamin, Walter. *Illuminations*. Ed. Hannah Arendt. New York: Schocken, 1969.

Bentley, Eric. *In Search of Theater*. New York: Vintage, 1954.

Bloch, Ernst. "Nonsynchronism and the Obligation to Its Dialectics." *New German Critique* 11 (Spring 1977): 22–38.

Blotner, Joseph. *Faulkner: A Biography*. 2 vols. New York: Random House, 1974.

Bordo, Susan. "Anorexia Nervosa: Psychopathology as the Crystallization of Culture." *Philosophical Forum* 17.2 (Winter 1985–86): 73–104.

Bradley, A. C. *Shakespearean Tragedy: Lectures on Hamlet, Othello, King Lear, Macbeth*. London: Macmillan, 1952.

Breitwieser, Mitchell R. *Cotton Mather and Benjamin Franklin: The Price of Representative Personality*. New York: Cambridge Univ. Press, 1984.

Breitwieser, Mitchell R. "Early American Antigone." In *Theorizing American Literature: Hegel, the Sign, and History*, ed. Bainard Cowan and Joseph G. Kronick. Baton Rouge: Louisiana State Univ. Press, forthcoming.

Brodhead, Richard H., ed. *Faulkner: New Perspectives*. Twentieth Century Views. Englewood Cliffs: Prentice-Hall, 1983.

Brodhead, Richard H. "Introduction: Faulkner and the Logic of Remaking." In Brodhead, *Faulkner: New Perspectives* 1–19.

Brooks, Cleanth. "On *Absalom, Absalom!*" In *The Novels of William Faulkner*, ed. R. G. Collins and Kenneth McRobbie, 159–83. Winnipeg: Univ. of Manitoba Press, 1973.

Brooks, Cleanth. *William Faulkner: Toward Yoknapatawpha and Beyond.* New Haven: Yale Univ. Press, 1978.

Brooks, Cleanth. *William Faulkner: The Yoknapatawpha Country.* New Haven: Yale Univ. Press, 1963.

Brown, Calvin S. *A Glossary of Faulkner's South.* New Haven: Yale Univ. Press, 1976.

Certeau, Michel de. *Heterologies: Discourse on the Other.* Trans. Brian Massumi. Theory and History of Literature 17. Minneapolis: Univ. of Minnesota Press, 1986.

Chase, Richard. *The American Novel and Its Tradition.* Baltimore: Johns Hopkins Univ. Press, 1983.

Chodorow, Nancy. *The Reproduction of Mothering: Psychoanalysis and the Sociology of Gender.* Berkeley: Univ. of California Press, 1978.

Cixous, Hélène. "The Laugh of the Medusa." Trans. Keith Cohen and Paula Cohen. *Signs* 1.4 (1976): 875–93. Rpt. in *New French Feminisms,* ed. Elaine Marks and Isabelle Courtivron, 245–64. Amherst: Univ. of Massachusetts Press.

Cixous, Hélène, and Catherine Clément. *The Newly Born Woman.* Trans. Betsy Wing. Theory and History of Literature 24. Minneapolis: Univ. of Minnesota Press, 1986.

Clément, Catherine. "The Guilty One." In Cixous and Clément, *The Newly Born Woman* 3–59.

Cochran, Terry. "Foreword: History and Exile." In *Questing Fictions: Latin America's Family Romance,* by Djelal Kadir. Theory and History of Literature 32. Minneapolis: Univ. of Minnesota Press, 1986.

Cooke, Michael G. *Afro-American Literature in the Twentieth Century: The Achievement of Intimacy.* New Haven: Yale Univ. Press, 1984.

Deleuze, Gilles. *Différence et répétition.* Paris: Presses Universitaires de France, 1968.

Deleuze, Gilles. *Nietzsche and Philosophy.* Trans. Hugh Tomlinson. New York: Columbia Univ. Press, 1983.

Deleuze, Gilles, and Felix Guattari. *Anti-Oedipus: Capitalism and Schizophrenia.* Trans. Robert Hurley, Mark Seem, and Helen R. Lane. Minneapolis: Univ. of Minnesota Press, 1983.

Deleuze, Gilles, and Felix Guattari. *Kafka: Toward a Minor Literature.* Trans. Dana Polan. Theory and History of Literature 30. Minneapolis: Univ. of Minnesota Press, 1986.

De Man, Paul. *Blindness and Insight: Essays in the Rhetoric of Contemporary Criticism.* 2d ed., rev. Theory and History of Literature 7. Minneapolis: Univ. of Minnesota Press, 1983.

Derrida, Jacques. "Economimesis." Trans. R. Klein. *Diacritics* 11 (1981): 3–25.

Derrida, Jacques. "*Fors:* The Anglish Words of Nicolas Abraham and Maria Torok." Trans. Barbara Johnson. Introduction to Abraham and Torok, *The Wolf Man's Magic Word* xi–xlviii.

Derrida, Jacques. "From Restricted to General Economy: A Hegelianism without

Reserve." *Writing and Difference*. Trans. Alan Bass. Chicago: Univ. of Chicago Press, 1978.

Derrida, Jacques. "Structure, Sign, and Play in the Human Sciences." In *The Structuralist Controversy: The Languages of Criticism and the Sciences of Man*, ed. Richard Macksey and Eugenio Donato, 247–72. Baltimore: Johns Hopkins Univ. Press, 1972.

Douglass, Frederick. *Narrative of the Life of Frederick Douglass, An American Slave*. 1845. Garden City, N.Y.: Anchor-Doubleday, 1973.

Durkheim, Emile. *Suicide: A Study in Sociology*. Trans. John A. Spaulding and George Simpson. New York: Free Press, 1951.

Faulkner, William. *Absalom, Absalom! The Corrected Text*. New York: Random House, 1986.

Faulkner, William. "Barn Burning." *Collected Stories of William Faulkner*. 1950. New York: Vintage-Random House, 1977.

Faulkner, William. *Faulkner in the University: Class Conferences at the University of Virginia, 1957–58*. Ed. Frederick L. Gwynn and Joseph L. Blotner. 1959. New York: Vintage-Random House, 1965.

Faulkner, William. *Go Down, Moses*. New York: Vintage-Random House, 1942.

Faulkner, William. *The Hamlet*. New York: Random House, 1964.

Faulkner, William. "An Introduction to *The Sound and the Fury*: Another Version." Ed. James B. Meriwether. *Mississippi Quarterly* 26 (1973): 410–15. Rpt. in Brodhead, *Faulkner: New Perspectives* 23–28.

Faulkner, William. *Lion in the Garden: Interviews with William Faulkner, 1926–62*. Ed. James B. Meriwether and Michael Millgate. New York: Random House, 1968. Rpt. Lincoln: Univ. of Nebraska Press, 1980.

Faulkner, William. *The Mansion*. New York: Vintage-Random House, 1964.

Faulkner, William. *Pylon: The Corrected Text*. New York: Vintage, 1987.

Faulkner, William. *The Reivers*. 1962. New York: Vintage-Random House, 1966.

Faulkner, William. *Requiem for a Nun*. New York: Vintage-Random House, 1951.

Faulkner, William. *Selected Letters of William Faulkner*. Ed. Joseph Blotner. New York: Vintage-Random House, 1978.

Faulkner, William. *Sherwood Anderson and Other Famous Creoles: A Gallery of Contemporary New Orleans*. 1926. Facs. rpt. *Texas Quarterly* 9 (1966): 41–96.

Faulkner, William. *Uncollected Stories of William Faulkner*. Ed. Joseph Blotner. New York: Vintage-Random House, 1981.

Faulkner, William. *The Unvanquished*. 1938. New York: Vintage-Random House, 1966.

Faulkner, William. *The Wild Palms*. 1939. New York: Vintage-Random House, 1966.

Feidelson, Charles, Jr. *Symbolism and American Literature*. Chicago: Univ. of Chicago Press, 1953.

Freud, Sigmund. "Beyond the Pleasure Principle." *The Standard Edition* 18: 7–64.

Freud, Sigmund. "Inhibitions, Symptoms, and Anxiety." *The Standard Edition* 20: 77–175.

Freud, Sigmund. "Mourning and Melancholia." *The Standard Edition* 14: 239–60.

Freud, Sigmund. *The Standard Edition of the Complete Works of Sigmund Freud.* Ed. James Strachey et al. 24 vols. London: Hogarth Press and the Institute of Psychoanalysis, 1953–73.

Gates, H. L., Jr. "The 'Blackness of Blackness': A Critique of the Sign and Signifying Monkey." *Critical Inquiry* 9: 685–723.

Genovese, Eugene D. *Roll, Jordan, Roll: The World the Slaves Made.* New York: Pantheon-Random House, 1972.

Ginzburg, Carlo. *The Cheese and the Worms: The Cosmos of a Sixteenth-Century Miller.* Trans. John and Anne Tedeschi. Baltimore: Johns Hopkins Univ. Press, 1980.

Girard, René. "Perilous Balance: A Comic Hypothesis." *Modern Language Notes* 87 (1972): 811–26.

Greenblatt, Stephen. *Renaissance Self-Fashioning: From More to Shakespeare.* Chicago: Univ. of Chicago Press, 1980.

Guattari, Felix. "Becoming a Woman." *Molecular Revolution: Psychiatry and Politics,* trans. Rosemary Sheed, 233–35. New York: Penguin, 1984.

Harvey, Robert M. "The Theme of Paternity in the Ethical Thought of Jean-Paul Sartre." Diss., Univ. of California, Berkeley, 1988.

Hemingway, Ernest. *A Farewell to Arms.* New York: Scribners, 1929.

Horkheimer, Max, and Theodor W. Adorno. *Dialectic of Enlightenment.* Trans. John Cumming. New York: Continuum-Seabury, 1972.

"Horse Trading." *Foxfire 4: Fiddle Making, Springhouses, Horse Trading, Sassafras Tea, Berry Buckets, Gardening, and Further Affairs of Plain Living,* ed. Eliot Wigginton, 215–51. Garden City: Anchor-Doubleday, 1977.

Howe, Irving. "Faulkner and the Negroes." *William Faulkner: A Critical Study,* 116–34. 3d ed. Chicago: Univ. of Chicago Press, 1975. Rpt. in Brodhead, *Faulkner: New Perspectives* 47–63.

Hunter, Dianne. "Hysteria, Psychoanalysis, and Feminism: The Case of Anna O." *Feminist Studies* 9 (1983): 465–88. Rpt. in *The (M)other Tongue: Essays in Feminist Psychoanalytic Interpretation,* ed. Shirley Nelson Garner, Claire Kahane, and Madelon Sprengnether, 89–115. Ithaca: Cornell Univ. Press, 1985.

Huyssen, Andreas. *After the Great Divide: Modernism, Mass Culture, Postmodernism.* Bloomington: Indiana Univ. Press, 1986.

Irwin, John T. *Doubling and Incest/Repetition and Revenge: A Speculative Reading of Faulkner.* Baltimore: Johns Hopkins Univ. Press, 1975.

Jardine, Alice A. *Gynesis: Configurations of Woman and Modernity.* Ithaca: Cornell Univ. Press, 1985.

Jardine, Alice A. "In the Name of the Modern: Feminist Questions d'après *Gynesis.*" Feb. 27, 1987. French Department, University of California, Berkeley.

Jay, Gregory S. "Values and Deconstructions: Derrida, Saussure, Marx." *Cultural Critique* 8 (1987–88): 153–96.

Jehlen, Myra. *Class and Character in Faulkner's South.* Secaucus, N.J.: Citadel, 1976.

Kartiganer, Donald M. *The Fragile Thread: The Meaning of Form in Faulkner's Novels.* Amherst: Univ. of Massachusetts Press, 1979.

Kenner, Hugh. "Faulkner and the Avant-garde." In *Faulkner, Modernism, and*

Film, ed. Evans Harrington and Ann J. Abadie, 182–96. Jackson: Univ. Press of Mississippi, 1979. Faulkner and Yoknapatawpha 1978. Rpt. in Brodhead, *Faulkner: New Perspectives* 62–73.

Kierkegaard, Søren. *The Concept of Irony: With Constant Reference to Socrates.* Trans. Lee M. Capel. Bloomington: Indiana Univ. Press, 1965.

Kierkegaard, Søren. *Repetition.* Fear and Trembling *and* Repetition. Trans. Howard V. Hong and Edna H. Hong. Princeton: Princeton Univ. Press, 1983.

King, Richard H. *A Southern Renaissance: The Cultural Awakening of the American South, 1930–1955.* New York: Oxford Univ. Press, 1980.

Kristeva, Julia. *Powers of Horror: An Essay on Abjection.* Trans. Leon S. Roudiez. New York: Columbia Univ. Press, 1982.

Kristeva, Julia. *Tales of Love.* New York: Columbia Univ. Press, 1987.

Lentricchia, Frank. *After the New Criticism.* Chicago: Univ. of Chicago Press, 1980.

Lévi-Strauss, Claude. *The Savage Mind.* Chicago: Univ. of Chicago Press, 1966.

Lévi-Strauss, Claude. "The Structural Study of Myth." *Journal of American Folklore* 78 (1955): 428–44. Rpt. in *The Structuralists: From Marx to Lévi-Strauss,* ed. Richard T. De George and Fernande M. De George, 169–94. Garden City: Anchor-Doubleday, 1972.

Lévi-Strauss, Claude. *Tristes Tropiques.* Trans. John and Doreen Weightman. New York: Atheneum, 1978.

Lord, Alfred B. *The Singer of Tales.* Harvard Studies in Comparative Literature 24, 99–123. 1960. Rpt. New York: Atheneum, 1965.

Lukacher, Ned. *Primal Scenes: Literature, Philosophy, Psychoanalysis.* Baltimore: Johns Hopkins Univ. Press, 1986.

Lyotard, Jean-François. *The Postmodern Condition: A Report on Knowledge.* Trans. Geoff Bennington and Brian Massumi. Theory and History of Literature 10. Minneapolis: Univ. of Minnesota Press, 1984.

Lyotard, Jean-François, and Jean-Loup Thébaud. *Just Gaming.* Trans. Wlad Godzich. Theory and History of Literature 20. Minneapolis: Univ. of Minnesota Press, 1985.

MacCannell, Juliet Flower. *Figuring Lacan: Criticism and the Cultural Unconscious.* Lincoln: Univ. of Nebraska Press, 1986.

Marcuse, Herbert. "The Affirmative Character of Culture." *Negations: Essays in Critical Theory,* 88–133. Boston: Beacon, 1968.

Marx, Karl. Review of *On the Jewish Question,* by Bruno Bauer. *The Early Texts,* ed. David McLellan. New York: Oxford, 1971. Rpt. in *Karl Marx: Selected Writings,* ed. David McLellan, 39–62. New York: Oxford Univ. Press, 1977.

Matthews, John T. "Faulkner's Narrative Frames." In *Faulkner and the Craft of Fiction,* ed. Doreen Fowler and Ann J. Abadie. Faulkner and Yoknapatawpha 1987. Jackson: Univ. Press of Mississippi, 1989.

Matthews, John T. *The Play of Faulkner's Language.* Ithaca: Cornell Univ. Press, 1982.

Maupassant, Guy de. *The Complete Short Stories of Guy de Maupassant.* Garden City: Hanover, 1955.

McHaney, Thomas L. "Faulkner Borrows from the Mississippi Guide." *Mississippi Quarterly* 19 (1966): 116–20.

Melville, Herman. *Moby-Dick: or The Whale*. Vol. 6 of *The Writings of Herman Melville: The Northwestern-Newberry Edition*, ed. Harrison Hayford, Hershel Parker, G. Thomas Tanselle. Evanston: Northwestern Univ. Press and Newberry Library, 1988.

Millgate, Michael. *The Achievement of William Faulkner*. New York: Random House, 1966.

Minter, David. *William Faulkner: His Life and Work*. Baltimore: Johns Hopkins Univ. Press, 1980.

Morris, Wesley. *Friday's Footprints: Structuralism and the Articulated Text*. Columbus: Ohio State Univ. Press, 1979.

Morrison, Toni. *Song of Solomon*. New York: Knopf, 1977.

O'Brien, Michael. *The Idea of the American South: 1920–1941*. Baltimore: Johns Hopkins Univ. Press, 1979.

Parker, Andrew. "Between Dialectics and Deconstruction: Derrida and the Reading of Marx." In *After Strange Texts: The Role of Theory in the Study of Literature*, ed. Gregory S. Jay and David L. Miller, 146–68. Tuscaloosa: Univ. of Alabama Press, 1985.

Parker, Robert Dale. *Faulkner and the Novelistic Imagination*. Urbana: Univ. of Illinois Press, 1985.

Polk, Noel. *Faulkner's* Requiem for a Nun: *A Critical Study*. Bloomington: Indiana Univ. Press, 1981.

Porter, Carolyn. "Are We Being Historical Yet?" *South Atlantic Quarterly* 87.4 (Fall 1988): 743–86.

Porter, Carolyn. *Seeing and Being: The Plight of the Participant Observer in Emerson, James, Adams, and Faulkner*. Middleton: Wesleyan Univ. Press, 1981.

"Regulation of Prices and Wages in New England." In *American Colonial Documents to 1776*, ed. Merrill Jensen, 441–42. Vol. 9 of *English Historical Documents*. London: Eyre and Spottiswoode, 1955.

Renza, Louis A. *"A White Heron" and the Question of Minor Literature*. The Wisconsin Project on American Writers. Madison: Univ. of Wisconsin Press, 1984.

Rogin, Michael Paul. *Fathers and Children: Andrew Jackson and the Subjugation of the American Indian*. New York: Vintage, 1976.

Rosaldo, Renato. "Grief and a Headhunter's Rage: On the Cultural Force of Emotions." In *Text, Play, and Story: The Construction and Reconstruction of Self and Society*, ed. Edward M. Bruner, 178–95. Washington, D.C.: American Ethnological Society, 1984.

Said, Edward W. *Beginnings: Intention and Method*. 1975. New York: Columbia Univ. Press, 1985.

Sartre, Jean-Paul. *Search for a Method*. Trans. Hazel E. Barnes. 1963. New York: Vintage-Random House, 1968.

Saussure, Ferdinand de. *Course in General Linguistics*. Ed. Charles Bally et al. Trans. Wade Baskin. New York: McGraw-Hill, 1966.

Scherer, Olga. "A Polyphonic Insert: Charles's Letter to Judith." In *Intertextuality in Faulkner*, ed. Michel Gresset and Noel Polk, 168–77. Jackson: Univ. Press of Mississippi, 1985.

Schmitz, Neil. *Of Huck and Alice: Humorous Writing in American Literature.* Minneapolis: Univ. of Minnesota Press, 1983.

Schmitz, Neil. "Tall Tale, Tall Talk: Pursuing the Lie in Jacksonian Literature." *American Literature* 48 (1976): 471–91.

Schneiderman, Stuart. *Jacques Lacan: The Death of an Intellectual Hero.* Cambridge: Harvard Univ. Press, 1983.

Schor, Naomi. "*Eugénie Grandet:* Mirrors and Melancholia." *Breaking the Chain: Women, Theory, and French Realist Fiction,* 90–107. New York: Columbia Univ. Press, 1985. Rpt. in *The (M)other Tongue: Essays in Feminist Psychoanalytic Interpretation,* ed. Shirley Nelson Garner, Claire Kahane, and Madelon Sprengnether, 217–37. Ithaca: Cornell Univ. Press, 1985.

Shapiro, Jeremy J. "The Slime of History: Embeddedness in Nature and Critical Theory." In *On Critical Theory,* ed. John O'Neill, 145–63. New York: Seabury, 1976.

Slatoff, Walter. *Quest for Failure: A Study of William Faulkner.* Ithaca: Cornell Univ. Press, 1960.

Slotkin, Richard. *Regeneration through Violence: The Mythology of the American Frontier, 1600–1860.* Middletown: Wesleyan Univ. Press, 1973.

Smith, Albert C. " 'Southern Violence' Reconsidered: Arson as Protest in Black-Belt Georgia, 1865–1910." *Journal of Southern History* 51 (1985): 527–64.

Stevens, Wallace. *The Necessary Angel: Essays on Reality and the Imagination.* London: Faber, 1951.

Stonum, Gary Lee. "Faulkner's Last Phase." *Faulkner's Career: An Internal Literary History,* 153–94. Ithaca: Cornell Univ. Press, 1979. Rpt. in Brodhead, *Faulkner: New Perspectives* 195–207.

Sundquist, Eric J. *Faulkner: The House Divided.* Baltimore: Johns Hopkins Univ. Press, 1983.

Sundquist, Eric J. "Faulkner, Race, and the Forms of American Fiction." In *Faulkner and Race,* ed. Doreen Fowler and Ann J. Abadie. Faulkner and Yoknapatawpha 1986. Jackson: Univ. Press of Mississippi, 1987.

Taussig, Michael T. *The Devil and Commodity Fetishism in South America.* Chapel Hill: Univ. of North Carolina Press, 1980.

Unger, Roberto Mangabeira. "Postscript." *Knowledge and Politics,* 337–41. New York: Free Press-Macmillan, 1984.

Vickery, Olga W. *The Novels of William Faulkner.* Baton Rouge: Louisiana State Univ. Press, 1959.

Wallerstein, Immanuel. *The Modern World System.* New York: Academic Press, 1974.

Wilden, Anthony. *System and Structure: Essays in Communication and Exchange.* 2d ed. New York: Tavistock, 1980.

Williams, Joan. "Twenty Will Not Come Again." *Atlantic Monthly,* May 1980, 58–65.

Williams, Joan. *The Wintering.* New York: Harcourt Brace, 1971.

Willis, Susan. "Aesthetics of the Rural Slum: Contradictions and Dependency in 'The Bear.' " *Social Text* 2 (1979): 82–103. Rpt. in Brodhead, *Faulkner: New Perspectives* 174–94.

Woodward, C. Vann. *The Burden of Southern History*. Rev. ed. Baton Rouge:
    Louisiana State Univ. Press, 1968.
Wyatt, David M. *Prodigal Sons: A Study in Authorship and Authority*, 72–76,
    77–80, 94–100. Baltimore: Johns Hopkins Univ. Press, 1980. Rpt. as "Faulk-
    ner and the Burdens of the Past" in Brodhead, *Faulkner: New Perspectives*
    92–116.
Yeats, W. B. *The Collected Poems of W. B. Yeats*. Definitive ed. New York: Mac-
    millan, 1956.

Index